LIVING
THE DREAM

Also by Michael Seidman

From Printout to Published

LIVING
THE DREAM

An Outline for a Life in Fiction

MICHAEL SEIDMAN

Carroll & Graf Publishers, Inc.
New York

Excerpts from "Paladin of the Lost Hour" and "Soft Monkey" by Harlan Ellison, from the Author's collection ANGRY CANDY, are copyright © 1985, 1986, and 1987 by The Kilimanjaro Corporation. Used by arrangement with, and permission of, the Author and the Author's agent, Richard Curtis Associates, Inc., New York. All rights reserved.

First Carroll & Graf edition 1992

Carroll & Graf Publishers, Inc.
260 Fifth Avenue
New York, NY 10001

Library of Congress Cataloging-in-Publication Data is available.

ISBN: 0-88184-871-9

Manufactured in the United States of America

For David H. Bradley, though he insists
that I give up my day job

and

For Ed Gorman who brought two and one together

Acknowledgments

While literally hundreds of people have contributed to the development and writing of this book, I would be seriously remiss if I did not thank Kevin R. McDonald of Apple Computer, Inc. whose continued support and contributions were invaluable in the process.

Contents

CONTENTS ●●●

Introduction

"I've always wanted to write, but . . ."

"I have this idea for a story, but . . ."

"I can do better than that, but . . ."

There's a commercial running on television in New York right now, enticing us to play the state-run Lotto game. It's a nice commercial: we see several people who tell us what they'd do if they won three million dollars. One young woman says, "I'd become a bestselling author, even if I had to buy every copy of my book."

I fantasize about winning the game, too. But my dream consists of taking the money, moving to the Mountain Time Zone, and writing.

She wants to be an *author*, I want to be a *writer*. There are millions of people who want to author books or stories or articles. Fortunately for those of us competing for an editor's attention, most of them don't want to do the work necessary to make the dream a reality. They don't want to *write*.

And it is work. Publishing—books, magazines, newspapers—is a bottom-line-oriented business and those in the industry expect their suppliers—you—to be the same way. It's only in the Dire Straits hit of some years ago that you get money for nothing. You'll be expected to be professional—to deliver clean copy, as promised, in the proper format and at the agreed-upon price. Do that regularly, and with material that helps your publisher make a profit, and the dream comes true.

Doing it, though, takes much more than desire. It takes drive—a virtually single-minded ambition. It takes research—into the markets, into the subject matter, into the traditions of a category. It takes ability. You do have to put the words together in a way that engages the reader's interest, and holds it until the period on the last sentence. It takes patience. The overnight success is the stuff of legend. It takes a lot of self-trust. You can't be swayed by every comment you hear. And it takes a strong ego. Writing is probably one of the most egocentric occupations someone can undertake.

Living the dream takes all that and more. It also takes the ability to be alone with your thoughts, isolated for stretches at a time, to disappear within yourself, even in a crowd; to block all distractions and commit yourself to the work at hand.

You can do something about all but one of those requirements. Unfortunately, the final ingredient is beyond your control, because timing and luck also play a role in making things happen. But I think you will agree that we make our own luck. We create what we expect, as L. Ron Hubbard used to say.

More than anything, you have to stop dreaming and start living . . . and writing.

Michael Seidman
New York, New York
January 1992

Chapter 1

....

IT'S ABOUT TIME

When we talk about writing, and tack on a "but," we're usually leading into "I don't have the time right now."

Well, right now is the only time you do have. Yesterday is gone and no matter what the cast of *Annie* would have us believe, tomorrow is just a fantasy. You will never, ever have any more time than you do right at this moment. If you're going to make writing a career, you have to start giving yourself the time right now.

Think for a minute about all the time you waste every day, and no fair calling it relaxation. What did you do while you were eating your sandwich at lunch today? If the answer is "read this book," you get a pass. This time. I wrote the first draft of the introduction—as well as most of the chapters—on a yellow pad between bites. If you took a pad and pencil and organized some notes, you made the right use of your time. If you spent the hour watching the girls go by and didn't come away with at least a mental outline of a story to rival Irwin Shaw's "The Girls in Their Summer Dresses," you lost a step in the race to get your work to an editor before someone else does. It is that simple.

One of the most frequently offered suggestions for time management is list making. Think about what you have to accomplish each day, write the tasks down in order of importance, though avoiding *prioritizing* them, and then make a schedule, assigning time for each. Now, put the time you're going to write at the top.

That's right—at the top, first thing. If you put it anywhere lower, you're going to find everything else squeezing it out of your schedule. Of course, if watching Oprah is more important . . .

When are you going to tell the world to go away, sit down, and do your work? That depends on you. Some people can write at six in the morning; others don't even start to breathe on their own until midnight. It may take some trial and error, but you'll find your peak time, and once you do, stick to it—day in and day out, that's your writing time. Tell your family, tell your friends—and most important, *tell yourself*. It'll only take a week or so, and it will become habit. Just as a runner misses the high when he doesn't jog for a day or two, your mind will let you know that you've got to get back to work.

Okay, you have your list, but you kept changing the time assigned to writing. Oh, sure, you cut the fat, but between going to work, getting the kids off to school, making dinner, walking the dog, and grabbing meals, there just wasn't any time left to write, right?

Wrong! Very few of us have the leeway, when we start out, to spend eight hours a day writing. That doesn't mean that there's *no* time, though. Get up an hour earlier at the start of your day, or go to bed an hour later. Your body will accommodate you.

If you finish a page a day (and some days will be far more productive; only occasionally will you do less), you'll have your novel finished in less than a year. You should be able to get the first draft of a story done in a week or so. An article might take a few days.

There's no guarantee, at least at first, that spending more time writing is going to increase your productivity. There may be more words, but the name of the game is quality, not quantity. Just as a runner doesn't start off with a marathon, new writers have to pace themselves. Ideally, you'll write for an hour in the morning, and perhaps another half hour at night. Keep in mind that whatever time you're working, for however long, it is time that is going to be spent at the desk. Once you sit down, you don't get up until the five-o'clock whistle blows. You don't take phone calls, you don't go to the window to see if it's started raining, you don't suddenly remember that you didn't defrost the chicken.

There is one factor that is difficult to control. Unfortunately, our families don't always understand what is driving us, or support our efforts. And who can blame them, really? Most often, they figure you're taking time from them, and all they see are the balls of discarded paper; all they hear are the groans of dismay when the work isn't going well or when the rejection letter comes, or if no response arrives at all, which is far worse.

When I started out, fitting my writing in between editing sessions on someone else's work, my wife indulged my habit. Then my markets dried up, the magazine I was contributing to went out of business. I kept writing for a while, but didn't sell anything. I became frustrated. This wasn't worth it, I thought. Who am I kidding? I asked myself. Why am I doing this? I began to confuse issues: what was more important, writing or selling? Could they be separated? One thing I was sure of: If I didn't write, I wouldn't sell. I was living proof of that, because I stopped writing. It was easy enough to blame everyone else: my boss for keeping me so busy I didn't have the time; the editors because they didn't buy (what wasn't right for them); everyone was at fault except for me.

Lisa indulged me for a while. Then, one day, she asked me if we could sell the typewriter. We needed money (some things never change), and it wasn't doing anything. She'd look at the old I.B.M. Selectric, look at me, look in her wallet . . . and I'd bury my face in something else. Finally (I'm a slow learner, but I do learn) I sat down and started putting one word after another on sheets of blank paper. Sometimes they made sense. Sometimes there was a journal entry, something I called "To What End?" I didn't know; I did know that I was writing again. I looked at old notes. Lisa left me alone.

Except to encourage, to see to it that our two daughters, because the family was growing, left me alone when I sat down to write. She encouraged me to barter my services in exchange for a computer (a Kaypro 10, which became obsolete three weeks after I got it but that served its purpose until I was able to become a Machead) because we thought it might make writing easier though it does bring other problems to the process. And while we could have used the money, getting the computer was more important at that moment. Lisa didn't let me say, *"I have this idea, but . . ."*; she insisted that I get my butt down and start putting those ideas on paper. She taught me again a lesson I had forgotten: that there were other markets, other approaches. That if the writing was good it would sell, finally.

We make our own luck. Lisa even let me skip doing the dishes so that I could get started that much earlier. And I know that if I had had that kind of encouragement and support when I was younger, when I was growing up and first started to dream, all of this wouldn't have taken so long. But it finally happened, and checks arrived, and the words have become fruitful and multiplied.

It becomes easier when the checks start coming in and the members of our family can start seeing the results of our labors. It's also amazing how much easier it becomes to give up a little sleep once we've increased the odds of getting paid for the effort.

It also helps to keep in mind that most of the writers whose books you see have nine-to-five jobs. It is only the rare few who are self-supporting, full-time writers. They're the ones who made it, who paid their dues, who gave up a couple of years of sleep in order to get to that point.

They did what you have to do: Wake up and stop dreaming.

Chapter 2

GETTING
STARTED
Part 1

You awake? Good. Then let's get started. No, not writing, not yet. There are a lot of things you have to do first.

It's become painfully obvious to me over the years that too many writers are working in a vacuum. That isolation is so deep that I'm certain they won't see this book, just as they don't have any awareness at all of any of the traditions or requirements or sources of information that are allowing you to get a good start out of the blocks. And I don't know how to reach them.

Every now and then, when one of their manuscripts comes across my desk and I'm feeling expansive, I'll send the writer a letter, recommending books they might read, magazines they must subscribe to, places they can go (no snide remarks, please; I'm being a kinder, gentler editor) so that they don't keep making the same mistakes. Those occasions are becoming less frequent as the number of misguided submissions mounts. Still, hope springs eternal . . .

You probably know what it is you want to write, and we'll discuss that at greater length, later. But that isn't enough. Nine out of ten new businesses started in this country fail. And of all the elements that contribute to that figure, the one that most experts acknowledge as having the biggest impact is the lack of research, the lack of understanding of what the public wants, needs, and is willing to spend money on acquiring.

The second is underfunding.

Writing as a way of life is a business; research is your first obligation to yourself. As for the underfunding, don't give up your day job.

Markets for your writing are volatile. Magazines appear and disappear, book publishers merge or submerge, their lists changing from season to season as readers' tastes change. Right now, as an example, that staple of the paperback racks, the men's action/adventure novel, is undergoing radical change. Maybe the editors sent too many mercenaries into action in the world's hot spots. Maybe too many Delta teams and Rambo clones tried to free too many prisoners of war. Maybe we read about too many drug dealers and punks in the daily papers. Whatever the reason, sales in the category have gone flat—and if that's the type of book you're writing, you should know about it before you begin.

Espionage fiction is experiencing a similar shaking out right now. The simultaneous appearance of both Tom Clancy and *glasnost,* coupled with the crumbling of the Berlin Wall and collapse of the Soviet sphere of influence in Eastern Europe began the process of that old standby, the C.I.A.-K.G.B. confrontation, no longer having the same profitable marketability. Add the collapse of the Soviet Union and the fall of the Evil Empire, and the market has been turned topsy-turvy. While well-established writers in the category may be able to milk it for some time longer, there's a vacuum out there, and you might very well have the idea to fill it.

How are you, excluded from the power lunches and high-level machinations of the editorial board meetings, (you should only know what really goes on! On second thought. . . .), supposed to know what it is we think we're looking for at any given moment? There are several things you should do.

Visit a few big bookstores regularly. A few, because no one store, not even branches of the major chains like B. Dalton, Waldenbooks, or Crown or the so-called Superstores, like Powell's Books in Portland or The Tattered Cover in Denver, can carry everything. Study all the titles, all the new releases, as well as the shelves displaying the books in your chosen category. Keep an eye on the logos as well as the titles. See who is publishing what. Many publishers are identified with particular genres—sometimes exclusively. Others, while known for dominance in one area or another, have much more broadly based publishing programs and should not be ignored.

The drawback here is that the new releases you see today were acquired for publication anywhere from one to two years previously. Right now, early in 1992, I've just completed my tentative schedule through the end of the year and have begun slotting some titles for the first half of '93. You're interested in selling a book that won't see print for a year or more—*if it is bought today.* So, just because you see lots of "X" on the racks, you can't assume that there's going to be the same need when your manuscript is finally read by some bleary-eyed editor. A publisher may be overinventoried, the category may have begun choking to death on sheer quantity, or the publisher may have decided to shift emphasis because of sales figures or other indicators.

To keep things in perspective, then, get friendly with the bookstore's manager or owner or clerk—whoever is most available to you. Speaking with him on a regular basis will give you lots of insights into what is going on. After all, people love to speak about themselves and what they do. It won't be long before the manager will tell you that sales of one thing or another are up or down or that the publishers are showing lots of true-crime titles for next season or that suddenly the store can't stock enough books about rock musicians. That's exactly the same information the publishers' reps are getting and sending back to the home office.

As the relationship develops, you may be given the opportunity to see the catalogues the reps are leaving with the store, the sample covers, and other materials used to sell the books to your friend. Look at how the publisher is treating certain titles, what is getting the most attention and what is mentioned in passing. Then look at the shelves, look for the publishers' titles, and see if you can discern a change. Are they cutting back on horror fiction, perhaps dropping the genre altogether? Is that important to you?

I'm not going to tell you how to develop a relationship with someone, but I would suggest that subtlety goes a long way. Don't interrogate the manager; don't make the person feel as if you're using him. Do let him know why you're so interested, thank him—and remember to buy a book or two every now and then.

There's a wonderful extra to this relationship. Think about the day when you go into the store and tell your friend about the sale of your book. Not only do you have immediate sales support, there's also the very good possibility that the store will sponsor an autograph party for you or give your book a special display. Publishers and booksellers have learned the value of promoting local authors—many stores even have "local author" tags on their shelves and racks calling attention to the fact, and publishers are more than happy to supply them—and you're almost the store's pet writer by now. So, your publisher is happy, the store personnel are happy, and, while you probably aren't any closer to the bestseller list, you're happy, too!

Another good thing may evolve through this friendship. If it has progressed nicely, the manager might be willing to read your manuscript and, if he likes it, offer to pass it to one or another of the reps to send to an editor. I receive a couple a month this way. And editors do tend to treat those manuscripts not only with alacrity, but with kid gloves. None of us wants to upset a sales rep or an account.

How important can this relationship be? Let me put it this way: Some years ago I took a part-time job at New York's Mysterious Bookshop, working on Saturdays, so that I could see what was going on from that side and, too, so that I could speak with the customers and find out what these knowledgeable readers wanted in their mystery fiction. If it's important enough for an editor, it is important to you, too.

While the bookseller knows *his* market, his customers, you have to get to know the nation (if not the world) and the specific needs of dozens of publishers. That's why you subscribe to *Writer's Digest* or *The Writer*. If you are anything at all like me, you turn to the market reports first, and then go on to read all the extra stuff. You also see to it that you have copies of their various market guides— *Writer's Market* or *The Writer's Handbook*—depending on the directions you want to take in your career. You want your own copy, so that you can write in the names of new editors as they move from publisher to publisher.

Keep in mind that the kind of lead time necessary to prepare those market listings often means that they've become dated, especially when you are dealing with book markets. A writer's magazine once listed my expressed need for cozy mysteries. By the time it appeared, though, the word had been out on the street for months, and I wasn't looking for that category quite as actively. How did this market need become known?

Virtually every area of genre fiction has a peer organization: Mystery Writers of America, Science Fiction Writers of America, Romance Writers of America, Horror Writers of America, Western Writers of America, and the Private

Eye Writers of America are the major ones, and there are other, smaller, special-interest groups within those categories. While these are national organizations, some of them have regional chapters; getting in touch with headquarters will bring you the information you need. While the requirements for active membership vary, though all include publication, they all welcome associate members, and the fees are worth every penny because one of the benefits is the organization's newsletter.

Gossip, news, tips, and *current* market reports, often no more than a month old, are regular features. They also offer articles on trends, editorial moves, and other invaluable information for any writer, and especially for someone hoping to make a mark in a category.

The organizations all sponsor conferences, meetings, and award ceremonies, and if you can get to one of those events, it can turn into a very successful mining expedition. The local chapters often have their own newsletters and run meetings and conferences, too. Unlike the more general workshops for writers, most of the people you will meet are professionals, which means only that they've sold their writing. And they are usually friendly and helpful . . . and probably the very writers you've been reading and inspired by. Just sitting in a hospitality suite or bar, listening to the conversations—and being invited to join in —can do more for your flagging spirits than anything I've ever discovered. Anything legal, anyway! It's also nice to learn that these writers have all gone through the same rites of passage you're experiencing.

Another great feature of some of the meetings is that time is set aside not only for the usual—and usually boring —editors' panel, but for the members to make appointments with the editors and agents who are present. These meetings allow you ten or fifteen minutes to sit down, discuss your work with the people who are going to buy it, and to find out what it is they are looking for *right now*. While editorial appointments are sometimes part of the more general conferences, at these meetings the editor goes in assuming that you are already part of the network. It helps. A little.

Don't expect anyone to read your work on the spot; in fact, don't even ask them about the possibility. Mention that you have sample chapters with you (bring four or five sets, just in case) and wait for the response. Some will rise to the bait; others, like me, will give you a business card and ask you to mail the material. You can do that immediately; be sure to give the background of the submission in your cover letter.

There's little that can be of as much benefit as these conferences. With the exception of the Mystery Writers of America, which insists on holding its annual Edgar Award dinner in New York City, the organizations do what they can to move around the country, making it possible for writers to attend without having to take a bank loan. If you can possibly attend, even if only every couple of years, you will be well rewarded.

And while we're on the subject of genre fiction, don't forget to look for the so-called "fanzines" and "prozines" that appear regularly and which almost always contain up-to-date information about what is going on, as well as reviews, articles, and essays that will keep you in touch with your markets—both the publishers and the readers. There are literally dozens of these journals, ranging in look and style from the slicks like *The Armchair Detective, Mystery Scene, Locus,* and *Romantic Times* to mimeographed and stapled sheets that are published whenever someone has the time and money to do a new issue. Addresses for some of the major magazines, as well as the organizations, are at the end of this chapter.

Kathy Ptacek, most well known as a horror writer, publishes a market newsletter that is chatty, idiosyncratic, and enormously useful. *The Gila Queen's Guide to the Markets,* or more information about it, can be obtained from Kathy at P.O. Box 97, Newton, NJ 07860.

There is one last magazine that is a must, and that's *PW* —*Publishers Weekly*. It is read by editors, booksellers, wholesalers, librarians—anyone and everyone involved with books. Including smart writers. Reviews—sadly unsigned—news about book publishing as an industry, production, international book fairs, bookselling . . . you name it, it's here. It is unquestionably the most important publication on your reading list. It is, however, expensive, so you might want to share a subscription with a couple of friends or within your workshop. If all else fails, your friend at the bookstore may let you browse through his copy or your library will have a copy, either in general circulation or behind the desk.

Joining a writers group and/or attending conferences can be another source of information, but a lot depends on the makeup of the group and the scheduled speakers. Some groups are essentially support organizations, which is an important function, but for another time; others, with selling writers as members, can put you in touch with editors and agents.

The value of a conference depends on who the speakers are. If your exclusive interest is in y.a. (young adult) fiction, and none of the lecturers or workshop leaders have that background or expertise, and if the topic is not on the schedule, you will want to think twice before attending. While editors try to give as much help as possible, they are often specialists, and cannot do more than encourage you in areas they don't know. I find it terribly frustrating, for instance, when someone approaches me with questions about selling their poetry—or, worse, requests to read it. I'm not only not qualified to answer specific questions, I don't think I'm in a position to judge the quality or marketability of the work. While the problem isn't quite as severe in mainstream fiction—most of us can field the majority of questions, or fake it decently—you're still better off making certain the editors are people who might reasonably be expected to help you.

There's one last publication to which you will want to have access, and that's *LMP, Literary Market Place*. This is an annual publication that might very well be described as the industry yellow pages. Publishers—and key personnel —are listed, as well as agents (with some information about them, but not much), a multitude of other writers' organizations and societies, newspapers, magazines, and virtually every other supplier of services to the industry is almost certain to have an entry. *LMP* is usually available at the public library. Make sure to use it in conjunction with your other resources.

At this point you may not have all the information available to you, but you certainly have enough to get started with confidence. As you continue to work, other guides and aids will come your way, and it only makes sense to use them. You can never know too much about what you're doing, but it takes only one hole in your knowledge to bring you to a dead stop.

And since you're not going to stop . . .

■ ■ ■

Magazines and Organizations

Mystery Writers of America
60 East 42nd Street (Suite 1166)
New York, New York 10165

Science Fiction and FantasyWriters of America
5 Winding Brook Drive #1B
Guilderland, NY 12084

Romance Writers of America
13700 Veterans Memorial Drive (Suite B15)
Houston, Texas 77014

Western Writers of America
P.O. Box 823
Sheridan, Wyoming 82801

Horror Writers of America
P.O. Box 1077
Eden, North Carolina 27288

Private Eye Writers of America
1750 4th Street (#602)
Cayahoga Falls, Ohio 44201

Sisters in Crime
6040-A Six Forks Road (Suite 163)
Raleigh, North Carolina 27609

MYSTERY SCENE
P.O. Box 669
Cedar Rapids, Iowa 52406-0669

THE ARMCHAIR DETECTIVE
129 West 56th Street
New York, New York 10019

LOCUS
P.O. Box 13305
Oakland, California 94661

ROMANTIC TIMES
55 Bergen Street
Brooklyn Heights, New York 11201

PUBLISHERS WEEKLY
R. R. Bowker
249 West 17th Street
New York, New York 10011

Chapter 3

GETTING STARTED
Part 2

Okay, so now you know as much as possible about the market for the category or genre you've chosen. Have you given any thought as to why you've decided to write mysteries as opposed to, say, horror? Sometimes, it matters.

I received a letter some years back, when I was the editorial director of a house with a strong romance fiction list, from a young (I assumed) man, a sophomore at Yale. He told me that he'd decided to write a romance over his summer break and would I please give him some plots. Really! No, stop laughing, this is the truth. I'm not making it up. And once I stopped gasping, I realized, yet again, that too many writers choose a category because they think it is simple, and that all they have to do is put some meat on a basic skeleton, and they're home free with cash in their pockets. Nothing could be further from the truth.

As you've learned by researching the markets, each publisher defines categories according to its own needs, and those definitions are nothing if not subject to change without notice. You have to know the formula, but you also have to know which terms in it are variable. It may not always be possible to define those terms, but if you know the category, you can sense them in your gut. In writing, familiarity doesn't always breed contempt, it often gives birth to direction and creativity.

It all goes back to the old maxim: Write what you know. I always add, "Write what you like" to the statement, because you may know something, but if you don't really like it, love it, that lack will show up in your storytelling. There's no way in the world that that Yale student will be able to write a romance. (I don't even know if he can live one, but there's no reason to get personal.)

The thing you have to understand with every fiber of your being is that you can't decide to write a particular type of book simply because your investigations revealed that there seems to be a market for it. At least once at every conference I attend, someone comes up to me and asks if I'm interested in seeing their completed manuscript, describing a particular category. If I say no, they ask what I'd like to see. I respond. And they say, "Okay, I can do that." More often than not, they can't.

There are some writers who can. I've worked with a number of mystery writers who also have successful careers authoring traditional westerns, and there are others who move with equal ease between horror and mystery, science fiction and western . . . but these writers are exceptions to a rule. They are also writers who grew up reading and loving the various categories in which they work. They understand and, more important, appreciate the conventions and traditions that govern the genre and know what the readers want and are willing to accept because, first and foremost, they are also readers themselves.

Editors usually specialize in certain areas and they know exactly what is necessary to fulfill the market needs. And they know when you don't. If it isn't the right stuff for you, don't expect it to be right for anyone else. It takes commitment, it takes really loving it, reading it, knowing it.

By now the more perceptive among you have noticed that there's something of a focus here: I'm emphasizing category fiction because that is where most books sales take place. All of the mass market paperback houses, and many of the hardcover publishers, base their entire publishing program around category slots. Most of the people who buy books regularly buy category fiction . . . and usually in paperback. One of the reasons more category books don't get on the bestseller list is that there are too many books. There are too many because everyone is doing them, diluting the readership. But they are creating and sustaining—at least for a few years—a market for your work. Faced with the choice of too many books but continuing markets versus fewer markets (thus tougher competition—as if it could get any tougher) but the chance of better sales, which would you vote for? For someone who wants to write, the choice is clear.

And clear, too, is the fact that too many writers rush into a genre without understanding it at all. Or, they confuse them, cross-pollinate them, or otherwise blur the lines. Personally, I love the idea: My 1987 story, "The Dream That Follows Darkness," began as a horror story, written after I heard Charles Grant speak at the Oklahoma Writers Federation conference. Inspired, and knowing that he was looking for material, I went home and got to work. When it was done, however, what I had written was not really a horror story. It was more of a contemporary romance (in the broadest sense of the category), with a reincarnation subplot that stretched all the way back to King David, was published in *The Twilight Zone* magazine, and was selected as one of the three best western short stories of the year, nominated for the Spur Award by the Western Writers of America. But if I ever decide to do the novel that's lurking in that story, I'm in deep trouble. I don't have the foggiest idea right now of how to market it to a publisher or, as a publisher, of how to sell it to the public. And until one plot or another takes control, I won't have the answer. My best guess is that it is a fantasy with Native American mythos as a background. But which of my many options present the most lucrative market? The easiest one to sell to? Wheels within wheels . . .

Writer's Digest and *The Writer* both publish extensive lists of how-to books—by top names in the fields—that offer an excellent guide to everything you have to know. For now, here's a shorthand tour which will, if nothing else, let you know how editors view the categories. It is not all-inclusive, we're only going after the basics of the mainstay genres, and as you'll see, many have offshoots that are often seen as categories of their own. What you will get from what follows is some sense of what we're thinking about on my side of the desk. If you know your category, because it is what you're reading and working in, you may not need to read any further. But if you're still casting about for direction, or if you realize that knowledge for its own sake has certain advantages, you'll stay with me.

Once upon a time, I took a course called Epic and Romance Literature. The romances they were talking about were the stories of the knights and damsels in distress, the search for the Grail, and battles against fantastical creatures. They took place on landscapes most people would never see, countryside created from hyperbole. The French called these stories *romans*. All category fiction evolved from those tales told in the royal courts and courtyards, in marketplaces and town squares. The line of descent is easy enough to follow. Consider the structure of any piece of category fiction: We have a hero (or heroine), at any rate, a central character who has to surmount and conquer overwhelming odds. This person's quest—for love, for justice, for peace—takes place somewhere exotic, if not fantastical, someplace we will never visit: the mean streets of the private investigator, the surface of an as yet undiscovered planet, the plains of Wild Bill Hickok, some grotesque hell or the never-never land of an historical romance.

In the course of the hero(ine)'s search, he will do battle with dragons, demons, or other monstrosities, real or imagined. The battle rages back and forth over the course of the story, death (or worse) awaits on every turn of the page. The quest, whatever it may be, expressed or expressly understood, drives all the action. Our storytellers are presenting us with a *roman*. Which, as we all know, is also the French word for novel.

Sometimes, late at night, when someone is feeling either pedantic or argumentative, the discussion turns to our roots as writers, and at those times we hear (yet again) that everything derives from the Bible, or from a collective subconscious, or, as Otto Penzler, the founder of Mysterious Press, likes to point out, from the tales of the Brothers Grimm. Who's to argue? What difference does it make? Blind Homer was the Tom Clancy—and probably the Joan Collins, too—of his day. The point is that you are working in a time-honored tradition. There are morals (a la Aesop) in these stories, no matter how immoral they may appear. There's a point, there's entertainment, there's an explication of how we live.

That's important to keep in mind when someone looks down a patrician nose at you and calls you a hack. And they will. They will because your novel sells more easily than some heavy-handed exploration of some self-indulgent, psychiatrist-dependent, *angst*-ridden writer's constant questioning of his place in the scheme of things. All of humanity's myths began as stories told around a campfire in an attempt to explain the world around the tribe. And as far as we've supposedly come from those days when a mortgage consisted of banging a bear over the head and taking over his cave, we haven't learned that much. The questions still exist, complicated rather than simplified by what we now know about ourselves. Just as a little bit of sugar helps the medicine go down, and as you can catch more flies with honey than with vinegar, making the lesson easily understood, enjoyable, putting it in the language of the people you are trying to reach, helps you.

I mention this now particularly because of something I've been seeing happen among romance writers. Without question, it's their turn in the barrel. They're an easy target because the so-called bodice rippers, with their garish, nursing-mother covers, are so obvious. Johnny Carson and Andy Rooney make mock of them. And so do lots of writers who should know better, mystery writers and science fiction writers, for instance who, until recently, were subjected to the same abuse. Called hacks, consigned to some literary purgatory known as "pulp," damned by the self-proclaimed community of literary snobs as practitioners of "popular fiction," they fought long and hard for respect . . . but don't offer it to their fellows who write romances. And those writers, women mostly, but some men as well, are beginning to grouse, loudly.

They don't like being looked down upon, and who can blame them? But they have something in their favor: their bank accounts, their control of the racks, the demand for their work. They are living the dream and doing it profitably. No matter what genre you decide to exploit, no matter what direction your writing takes, never think so much of yourself that you feel you can mock someone else, nor so little that you think the sound and fury of the idiots signifies something.

You may be told that you are prostituting yourself and your art, no matter what category of popular fiction you specialize in. Remind your critic that Shakespeare's plays are as formulaic as any example of contemporary formula writing they would care to cite. Point out that Charles Dickens wrote against deadline, finishing sections of novels in time to get them into the next issue of the pulp he was contributing to. The reason we read them today, the reason anything becomes a "classic," is because of the timelessness of the message and the writers' control of their language.

One day a couple of years ago, I was working on a story and the radio was supplying some white noise in the background. The announcer, in speaking of the upcoming Mostly Mozart festival at New York's Lincoln Center, asked whether we would be listening to the works of The Beatles two hundred years from now. I think the answer is yes, just as I think it is entirely reasonable to assume that our grandchildren might be reading Raymond Chandler (if our grandchildren are reading at all; a frightening thought given the reading levels in the country today) before they read whoever the current darling of the establishment may be as you read these words.

Okay, a quick reality check. The first categories we're going to consider are the obvious ones; almost without question your favorite reading—and your first writing choice—is either mystery/suspense, science fiction/fantasy, horror, romance, or western. In addition to their common ancestry, they all share one other trait. What is it?

Time's up. I mentioned the role of the prehistoric storyteller, the shamanistic root of the tales we tell to explain the world around us. Popular fiction, which is just another rubric for what we produce (in his book *The Art of Fiction*, the late John Gardner called it "drugstore fiction," for obvious reasons), not only explains, it reassures, it provides happy endings.

Educators tell us about the children who grew up fearing The Bomb. My daughters worry more about pollution and the destruction of the earth that it portends. Other generations had other fears. Whatever it is that frightens us, though, we all want to know that it will be fine in the end.

There's also no denying the witness of the news media: abused women and children (and the occasional male, but liberation still doesn't allow them to admit to it openly. They have to go out and beat tom-toms in the woods and scream at the moon. Whatever works), a desperate—and often life-threatening—fascination with cults, a lack of respect for human life that allows people to murder without remorse; all these, and an unending list of other examples, merge with stories of natural or unnatural disaster.

And while there are positive stories galore, it is the ugly that remain uppermost in our minds.

Pop fiction writers look at the question, "Is that all there is?" and say, "No." Mystery writers offer their readers justice, even if not the rule of law, as the evildoer meets a deserved reward. Unless he's an exciting enough character to go on in future books. Those who create worlds that still may be in science fiction take their readers somewhere around the corner from Betelgeuse, and show them a better world. Through the nightmares of horror writers, fans get to do battle with fears made manifest by cloaking them as vampires or "old ones," or whatever the imagination has dredged up from its Jungian depths, and then defeating them. The western brings to the reader a time of honor and personal strength, of conquest of a harsh, savage, and unforgiving land, and with it the ability of someone to win, through perseverance. And the romance, mirroring the trials and tribulations, albeit exaggerated, of every love affair, and setting the story in some time or place which is not ours, can take the reader from "Once upon a time" to "and they lived happily ever after."

They are exactly the same story. They do the same things for their readers. No matter which category you choose, in addition to its own requirements, you have an obligation to your reader to offer that bright spot, that reassurance. Don't think for a minute that readers don't notice. Back in the late seventies, I edited a novel by Dave Klein titled *Blind Side*. It was a brilliant and evocative story of a serial murderer and the sports writer who tracks him. But, at the end, almost everyone we had come to care about was dead, including the hero's wife. While the novel was widely praised, and sold several hundreds of thousands of copies, a lot of readers informed me that they'd never read another novel by that author, because he didn't offer any hope at the end.

With that warning, then, let's begin that survey of the categories. I don't know where you want to start, but I'm going to begin with the western.

Chapter 4

GENRIFICATION:
A tour of popular fiction

The Western

After kicking some dirt into Bart's grave on Boot Hill, Tim
tipped his hat to the schoolmarm and mounted his horse,
Paint. The stallion reared and wheeled, forelegs pawing
the setting sun. Then, they galloped off toward the west,
leaving behind the memory of . . .

The myths of the wild West, kept alive today in the
traditional (or category) western, began to be collected in
the late nineteenth century by eastern writers filling a
need. The Civil War had ended and the West was being
opened, often by rootless men suffering from an earlier

epidemic of poststress syndrome. There were the Indian Wars to be fought here, gold to be found, a land to be tamed and conquered. When newspaper readers in the urban East couldn't get enough of the stories of what was going on, enterprising reporters began to write pamphlets about what they were witnessing. And if enough wasn't happening, the writers made it up. Since that worked, some men who never got any closer to the West than the east bank of the Hudson River got into the game. Researching your markets is not a new concept.

Today, the western has a small but loyal following, and every indication is that some younger readers are coming into the fold. In that, it is very much like another peculiarly American art form: jazz. Both evolved because of a particular set of conditions, both were wildly popular, and both eventually found a level that allows them to exist, to exert some small influence, and to find new fans. For now, then, these novels are a minor part of any publishing program, with a strong regional appeal—and a very solid following in Germany, Scandinavia, and, it appears, the newly freed countries of Eastern Europe. The good news is that the stories are no longer the simplistic tales of the pulp era. Characters are becoming more fully developed and well rounded. History plays more of a role. And the bad guys are sociologically correct according to today's mores.

The readers have also gotten more sophisticated. While the basic storyline of a confrontation (cavalry vs. Indians; sheepherder vs. cattle baron; sheriff vs. rustler; railroad vs. everyone) remains a must, the writer has to be careful in terms of description. You can't have a man using a repeating rifle if that weapon hasn't gotten to the territory yet, nor can he be battling Comanches up in Minnesota. The readers now know what a cattle drive was like, what a herd of stampeding buffalo might have looked and sounded like, what a Lakota warrior wore into battle. If you're using elements like those, make certain that you know what you're talking about. A rule, really, any time you set pen to paper.

There's a question we ask in our editorial meetings when we're discussing western submissions: "Can you smell the horse droppings?" We phrase it differently, but you get the idea. All too often, writers are submitting novels which are westerns only because of their locale and the fact that the author has labeled it that way. What they've sent, actually, is a novel in western dress, with no feel of the period (or our expectations of what the period felt like) or the situations that were driving events. Editors have become sensitive to this, and the good ones make certain that the book has the right feel.

While we do try to keep things accurate, we haven't yet gone overboard. By that I mean that we don't blue pencil the shootout on the dirt street in front of the saloon, even though we've become aware of the fact that it's only been recorded as happening once. We don't complain if your cowboy doesn't use the butt of his revolver as a hammer when he's fixing the fence . . . even though that was one of the most popular uses for a side arm. And if your gun-man is a quick-draw artist, fine, even if he isn't part of Buffalo Bill Cody's Wild West Show. Certain traditions deserve to live on, even if a number of writers are beginning to rethink this aspect of the category, trying to paint realistic pictures of how the shootout at the O.K. Corral probably went down. Another major "revision" is in the depiction of the Battle of Little Big Horn and the events leading up to it and, by extension, Indian/white relations generally.

The category western, whether you are looking for the ever more rare hardcover or mass-market publication, is usually between 50,000 and 70,000 words; each house has its own guidelines. While the old joke was that the hero only kissed his horse, never the woman, that's changed, as has the role of the female. We've finally recognized that the women who helped settle the West were necessarily strong and shared most of the work. Some authors are experimenting with female leads, but that is still in the formative stage. Eventually, I'm certain, there'll be a breakthrough to parallel the onslaught of female private investigators we're seeing now in the mystery field. One strong piece of evidence is the search by western editors for female writers; another is the apparent growth of popularity of the category among women readers. One theory is that this spurt is being fueled by the western romances.

The usual locale is between the Mississippi and the Pacific, though the story can begin in the east, and from Canada down into Mexico. Most stories are post-Civil War, but the period of the mountain men, which began much earlier, became very popular during the late eighties, and appears to still be going strong.

Another very nice thing—in terms of giving you more room in which to work—is the acceptance of western novels that focus on the various Indian nations, a trend that began long before the anachronistic *Dances with Wolves* and which has been better handled by writers versed in the category.

As always, reading what's available, seeing what the competition is doing, not only offers a feel for what is acceptable, it shows you areas that might need your special talent and insight.

Unlike most of the other categories, the western isn't bedeviled by a slew of subgenres. Like the heroes, the western is pretty straightforward, and variations on the theme have not cropped up on the shelves. However . . .

Because traditional westerns were asexual for so long, a number of so-called "adult western" series were created by publishers looking to expand their market. Most of these are done on a work-for-hire, flat fee, no (or minimal) royalty basis. The action of the story is regularly interrupted by a liaison between the hero or heroine and the love interest of the moment. Not surprisingly, purists complained long and loud about this development and the less well-written series have had their obits appear in the *Tombstone Gazette*.

The good thing about this variant is the learning experience it offers a new writer. Just like the pulp magazines of an earlier generation, they provide writers with a place to learn their craft. The pay may not be all that you could hope for (then again, it never will be), but contracting for a couple of these will give you the opportunity to discover whether you can get to the end of a novel, to practice all the writing tricks that you'll need to become successful, to hone your skills. (This is the case with all work-for-hire writing.)

When Larry McMurtry's *Lonesome Dove* was published, the feeling in the western writers' community was that it would spur a new market for the traditional western. Unfortunately, the bestsellerdom, the Pulitzer Prize, and the Spur Award it gathered—as well as the very popular TV movie—has had no noticeable effect on the category. The book was published as fiction, not as a western, and the hundreds of thousands of people who read it did not move on to the western racks at their bookstores to look for more. (Of course, it is entirely possible that their local bookstores didn't have western racks.)

McMurtry's book, and such others as John Byrne Cooke's *The Snowblind Moon* and Greg Matthews's *Heart of the Country,* are westerns by any definition of the genre, but they have also appealed to the general—mainstream fiction—market. Longer, more complex stories, they are more intricately woven tapestries. Which is not to say that the traditional western is, by definition, simplistic. *Shane,* always at the top of any list of best western novels, is filled with the undercurrents that mark all good works of fiction.

There is a resurgence of interest in a class of novel that might be called novels of the frontier, big books in the tradition of *Northwest Passage* and *The Big Sky.* They are westerns, but because they look "big," because the review media pays attention to them, the general reader discovers them, too. And denies that he reads westerns. If you can find a major theme, then, and can think in terms of writing more than 100,000 words; if you are prepared to research and bring every one of your novelist's skills to bear on the project, this unrecognized subgenre of the western might be right for you. Just don't deny that you're writing a western.

There have been several truly successful western writers: Ernest Haycox, Zane Grey, and Louis L'Amour come immediately to mind. When L'Amour died a few years ago, word went out that the booksellers were looking for someone new to replace him. As of now, no one has been crowned king. (And I question how seriously the booksellers are looking, but that's another problem.) The point is, there's room for you.

▪ ▪ ▪

The Mystery

The mystery is what the mystery is.

In the Talmudic tradition there's something called *pilpul,* which might best be defined as hairsplitting. Determining the definition of the mystery often calls for an exercise in pilpul. The individual tastes of a writer, reader, editor, or bookseller go a long way in deciding how your submission will be treated. It may not be fair, but it's life as we live it. In fact, there are so many questions that lots of people in the field have taken to calling themselves *crime,* rather than *mystery,* writers.

The best definition I've ever heard says that a mystery novel is one in which there is a crime—or the threat of one—and the story hinges on bringing the criminal to justice or preventing him from acting. Crucial to it all is that the crime must be a crime worth solving, which explains why most stories deal with murder or place a woman and/or child in jeopardy. While many of the women crime writers (and women generally) deplore that aspect of the fiction, the truth is that most people react more strongly to a threat against women than one against men. We still perceive them as being weaker. No matter what the crime, however, the approach allows for the inclusion of everything from *Butch Cassidy and the Sundance Kid* to the works of Robert Ludlum, Sidney Sheldon, and even Harold

Robbins and Arthur Hailey, since so many of their novels are concerned with a criminal activity of some kind, though not necessarily the types of crime we generally associate with the genre.

For a strict constructionist, a mystery is a novel in which the puzzle, the whodunit, is paramount. That leaves espionage, thrillers, and suspense in limbo. Some years ago, I attended a mystery weekend at Mohonk Mountain House in New York. You know the kind of thing: a crime takes place in front of the guests who then have the rest of the weekend to figure out who did what to whom by questioning the actors. As they had been for a few years, the script was created by Donald E. Westlake, a well-known and respected mystery writer who specializes these days in the "caper" style of storytelling. During some free time at lunch, I asked the guests what they thought of Don's novels. Most of them hadn't read any; they didn't even know he was a novelist. They were puzzle people, pure and simple. While that is an extreme example of the state of mind, it did prove instructive as I worked on the development of a mystery line.

It is not only the writers who have taken to defining themselves more broadly; critics—as opposed to book reviewers—speak in terms of *criminous* fiction. The word allows for consideration of all the varied forms we've created in an attempt to find justice in the world. Although you'll never find a book in the library or the bookstore under a sign reading CRIMINOUS FICTION, the label is one which appears often enough these days that it is important to keep in mind. If you don't know how to identify your work, calling it criminous may help. (It may also leave the editor very confused, especially if she is narrowly focused when considering the category. How's that for a confidence builder?)

I'm sorry if all this sounds not only terribly confusing but also a bit like a tempest in a teapot cozy, but consider this: When Bouchercon, the annual mystery fan convention, was held in New York City back in 1984, the organizers got in touch with Alfred Knopf, John le Carré's publisher, and asked them to take an ad in the convention journal supporting his most recent release. "Why?" the p.r. person asked. "He doesn't write mysteries." Which will come as a surprise to anyone who shops in mystery specialty shops on a regular basis.

If you look at the spine of a paperback book, you'll see a slug under the publisher's logo. That is supposed to help everyone involved in the process know where the book should go on the shelves, how it should be counted when the publisher tries to ascertain how certain categories are selling, and just to let everyone know what the book is. We have a wide range of choices when we're dealing with crime fiction: Mystery, Suspense, Thriller, Espionage, and Adventure are all possibilities, and there's no guarantee that what you're looking for will be properly labeled.

All of which is beside the point, isn't it? You know what you're interested in writing, what you want to read, and how you want to have your work considered. So, forget the philosophical musings, the confusion, and let's get back to one of the primary principles of writing: K.I.S.S.— Keep It Simple, Stupid. With as little mystery as possible about it, here are the basics of the mystery genre. And we'll all ignore the fact that if you ask ten different people who claim to read mysteries to describe the books they buy, you'll receive eleven different answers. After all, that's the pleasure of pilpul.

The most common form in the genre is the amateur detective, a Miss Marple or that Fletcher woman on *Murder, She Wrote*. The story is pure puzzle, the outcome positive, and the reader, who is in competition with the detective to reach the solution first, comes away knowing that justice not only exists, but that he can make it happen, which takes us back to the things that make category fiction work. It doesn't matter that things don't happen this way in the real world . . . except to cops.

Major Bruce Shaw, the recently retired Chief of Detectives in Oklahoma City, is more than a little perturbed with the depiction of police in crime fiction, and not only when amateurs are beating the cops to the criminal. One of the things that has become almost a standard in mystery fiction is the denigration of police officers; they are shown as corrupt, incompetent, bullying, and a thesaurus of other negatives. It is not a universal failing, but appears often enough to worry Shaw, who recognizes the power of fiction to form public opinion. (In other instances it might be called propaganda.) Just something to keep in mind when you're creating law enforcement personnel for your stories.

One of the complaints writers of hardboiled crime fiction have about the so-called traditional form is that it has nothing to do with crime as it really happens, and that there is nothing "real" about the characters or settings. That isn't quite true, of course. The cozy mystery is very much a class-oriented social satire: the busybody detector who knows more about the cast than anyone else, and the portrait drawn of the characters and their lifestyles is a very pointed commentary that bears on reality. It may be beside the point, because it is the puzzle that counts, but it underlies the story in the better examples of the fiction. The criminals, however, are far more clever than your run-of-the-mill, real-life perp.

What you are called upon to offer the reader is every clue, fairly presented, as well as a small pantry of red herrings. The reader must be able to solve the crime, based on the information your detective has uncovered. The game is in being able to get to the end and have the reader dead certain that he's solved the case . . . and then prove him wrong. You know how it works: the heroine calls everyone together in the library, reveals everything that has been discovered, and then names the killer. Only it isn't the person everyone thinks it is, because . . . The reader turns back quickly to the page where that information was first uncovered and wonders how he missed it. The rule, and it must be honored, is that the reader and detective learn everything at the same time. We never know any more than the protagonist. It is in how each makes use of the information that the game evolves.

As in westerns, love interests are largely ignored; they

get in the way of the story. While your detective can be in love, the relationship, unless it specifically impacts on the investigation, is usually mentioned and forgotten, though some writers are now pushing at the boundaries. If they're successful, some future edition of this book will delete this paragraph except as an historical footnote.

Language is polite; profanities tend to be limited to a well-placed "damn"; vulgarity and obscenity rarely appear at all. This may be because we have a view of the reader as being genteel in all ways. It may be sexist, but because so many of the readers are women, we believe they will be offended. Letters we receive tend to substantiate this, so when in doubt, leave it out.

The suburbs and countryside are the most frequent settings; that allows for a slower pace, fewer police officers to devote time to the case, thus making your character all the more necessary, and the kind of settings readers have come to expect, including the group isolated by a storm. Of course, the traditions can be, and have been, adhered to while setting the story in the middle of a city; the cozy is more a matter of attitude and the manner in which the investigator works than of time or place.

Mystery writers have placed their stories in all eras: there are medieval monks, Victorian archaeologists, and contemporary college professors of both sexes and varied disciplines appearing in the current fiction. A puzzle is a puzzle, after all; and that is what you're creating.

The traditional mystery as we've just considered it came to the forefront during the so-called Golden Age, which ended, as far as the purists are concerned, when the hard-boiled private detective came on the mystery scene and American writers took over from the British. There is an Anglophilia involved here, as there is in many of the arts. I'm xenophobic enough to argue the point at your leisure. The p.i. developed as a reaction to the cozy which grew as a counterpoint to the thrillers of writers like Sax Rohmer, creator of Fu Manchu, who were just stretching the envelope left to them by the writers who came earlier and created the genre. You've heard their names: Poe, Collins, Dickens.

The p.i. novel shares most of the basic formula with the cozy: The reader discovers the clues along with the detective, racing to a solution and trying to outwit the writer. The crucial difference is one of tone. Where the murders are offstage in the cozy, and the investigator rarely becomes involved in a physical confrontation with the bad guy, the hardboiled novel puts everything right up front. Raymond Chandler, in his essay, "The Simple Art of Murder," praised Dashiell Hammett (considered the father of the category though there were others before him leading the way) for putting murder back in the alleys where it belongs, committed by the kinds of people who really commit the crimes, for the reasons they really do it.

The writing style is tough, the language—influenced greatly by Chandler—filled with metaphor and simile. The p.i. carries a weapon, which he uses frequently, has a love/hate relationship with the local police, operates more often than not as a loner, and solves the crime in spite of the law enforcement agencies around him.

In the real world, private investigators rarely become involved with murder investigations; most of them are dealing with security matters, missing persons, fraud, theft, and the ever popular cheating spouse. Those kinds of stories have become part of the literature, though murder still leads the pack.

A private detective is licensed by the state to perform his duties; he may be self-employed or on the staff of an agency, which can be part of, for example, an insurance company. He is hired by an individual—or assigned by his employer—to get to the bottom of a situation, during the course of which other crimes may evidence themselves, thus offering a multitude of motives. And the opportunity to do the same thing the cozy writers do: comment on society. The hardboiled school isn't as satiric; it is, though, infinitely more cynical. And, traditionally, in the first person. The use of that voice keeps the reader and investigator completely equal. We see only what the hero does, as the hero does. We are privy to all the thoughts and thought processes. The challenge is in getting information to the p.i.; he cannot be aware of anything that happens out-of-the-scene unless he unearths it during the course of the investigation.

One of the most exciting developments of recent years is that we're seeing more and more women in the role of licensed investigator, just as they've always been a mainstay of the amateur crimebuster ranks. Some of them are as tough as just about anyone except Mike Hammer; they do not burst into tears when things go wrong; they don't flutter helplessly; they carry weapons and use them when they have to; and they tend not to spend as much time ruminating with a bottle of bourbon that has been conveniently tucked away in the bottom drawer. And they are gaining in popularity every day, as proven by regular appearances on bestseller lists. It makes sense, given the fact that women not only are the bookbuyers, but that men and women both are beginning to tire of the macho posing that is part and parcel of the character of the private detective.

That isn't the only way in which writers are expanding the category. There are private investigators who have escaped the mean streets of the city to open offices in towns that are just wide places in the road, but where there is enough crime to ensure that they can keep working. Any category is doomed unless writers and publishers are willing to take chances, looking for ways to broaden the canvas on which they are working. If writers remain chained to a formula, writing—and the category—becomes stagnant. It may very well be one of the reasons the western became moribund. Change is also a risk too many publishers are unwilling to take. All a writer can do is try. And try again. In the sixties, Honey West might have operated as a private eye, but she was a caricature, unlike the very real women created by Marcia Muller, Sue Grafton, and Sara Paretsky.

The private investigator and the amateur both use the official law enforcement agencies as a foil. Both can do things that the police cannot: they are not bound by Miranda and the rules of evidence; they can, if they so desire, use wiretaps and other technologies without getting a court's permission. They rarely find themselves on the receiving end of a court order telling them to stay away from a suspect. And while they have their own stoolies, they don't have the advantages of large staffs, medical examiners, and the other forensics resources available to the state, although they may have contacts inside the various departments who will give them information.

The reader gets a sense of the real inside dope through the better examples of the third of the more traditional forms, the police procedural. As the label suggests, these mystery novels have law enforcement personnel as the central characters. They investigate a crime in the way real police officers and detectives do (within the parameters set by fiction and mystery editors), subject to the same limitations. The puzzle remains central, which means that the solution rarely hinges on a tip from a disgruntled partner-in-crime, although tips are what provide the information needed to effect most arrests; usually, it serves a confirmation of what the investigating officer has already discovered.

Like the p.i. novel, procedurals tend to be hard-edged and they are, when written by someone who has done enough research or a former member of the force, filled with an almost vicious black humor. It isn't that violent crime is funny; it is that gallows humor is the only way professionals can deal with what they face on a day-to-day basis. The cynicism of the private investigator is enhanced by the unending frustration of the detectives that caught the case. Not only do they have to do everything by the book, but they have to contend with a bureaucracy that is often more concerned with quick solutions, public image, political ramifications and the rights of criminals than things that may matter more, and their private lives suffer in ways that civilians cannot imagine. Having served my time, I speak from bitter experience.

In today's market, the procedural has become less a category entry and more a novel. All that means is that while the standard length for a category mystery novel is between 55,000 and 70,000 words, the procedural these days has gotten longer, and tends to pit one detective against one heinous criminal, probably a serial killer. At that point, the novel is sold into the marketplace as suspense—or some other catch-all—and transcends the category. The sales are not necessarily any better, nor is it the only route to follow. While Ed McBain has gained a certain amount of acceptance outside the genre, the 87th Precinct novels are still category length.

There are a couple of other classic forms in the puzzle mystery, but I haven't seen anything new in either of them for years and years. The first is the "armchair detective": the hero does not visit the scene of the crime, never leaves the chair in which he's sitting when we meet him, and comes up with the solution based entirely on information he receives from the people to whom he speaks.

Finally, there's the locked room, or impossible crime, subgenre. (When it is solved by an armchair detective, it becomes the purest of the pure.) The victim is found in a room locked from the inside, no way for anyone to get in or out. Whodunit and how? There are rules and traditions here (outlined by John Dickson Carr in *The Three Coffins);* researching them is fun, informative, and useful. As well as powerfully intimidating. Whether you will be able to sell a locked room or armchair detective novel these days is debatable; readers, even the cozy kind, want a little more action in their stories. The elements of both might, in the hands of someone with the talent and patience, be exploited and create a new wave of interest in the mass market.

Keep in mind that the mystery, like science fiction and horror, has specialty publishing houses at which it is possible to both experiment and re-create a style. The editors are steeped in the traditions of the category, the readers more knowledgeable than someone who might be picking up the book at an airport. For a house like that, a locked-room mystery might be the key to opening a career.

The cozy (or novel of detection; a rose by any other name still has the same thorns), the private eye novel, and the police procedural are all traditional in that the puzzle element is the central focus for the reader. They are all games played between the author and reader and, while most people like to win games, if the reader beats you too often, he'll lose interest in the game.

But there are other forms, with traditions just as rich. Which brings us back to something that is at the heart of all good fiction: suspense.

The novel of suspense, the thriller, is generally considered part of the mystery genre, thus making suspense writers eligible for membership in the Mystery Writers of America. The most crucial and obvious difference is that the whodunit aspect of the puzzle is downplayed. The reader usually knows early in the story who the antagonist is; indeed, if in the traditional mystery form we never know more than the detective, in suspense we rarely know less than the bad guy. The story is driven by the attempt to prevent further depredations and capturing or killing the criminal, be he spy or serial killer.

To a great extent, these novels are also fueled by a cat-and-mouse game between the hero and the perp. The protagonist knows who he is after; the antagonist knows he is being tracked. They may even speak to each other, send messages back and forth: an example of this is the serial murderer who lets the cops know when and where he is going to strike next—something that happens often enough in real life that it is in risk of becoming a cliché.

Why aren't they simply called mysteries? That's really a marketing ploy. A mystery is category fiction. An espionage or suspense story is a *novel*. Mysteries are consigned to a small section of the book racks; the quantities taken by any dealer are based on his concept of how the category sells for him, and he won't take every mystery being offered by publishers. (Among other problems, there are too many being published right now.) Too many books in any category in a given month can hurt all of them. But a novel will, more often than not, be placed on the fiction shelves, right up there next to Ludlum or Follett. Or, for that matter, Marquez or Updike.

What else constitutes a novel of suspense? They are longer than category fiction entries, usually having a minimum of 85,000 words and reaching into the six figures comfortably. (Not six-figure advance—six-figure word length!) Characterization plays a much greater role in the storytelling, and while you will continue to use the cliff-hanger and other techniques designed to force the reader to turn the page, you do have the leisure to bring in more subplots, more narrative—everything you would expect from a larger canvas.

The themes vary. Most of today's suspense fiction falls into either the international intrigue or multiple killer subset; the technothriller, clearly a suspense novel in the formal sense, is marketed as fiction. As we've seen, the more traditional spy novel is currently in disrepute. That doesn't mean that it isn't being published, just that it is more difficult for a newcomer to break in that way. That still leaves a wide world of nefarious action and derring-do for the writer to exploit. It also means that if you're clever enough to hit on a "new" theme—ecological and world trade concerns might be something to consider, along with industrial espionage—and tell a dynamite story, you could be the example people use in the future of what a particular subgenre should be . . . just as Tom Clancy is used today.

Another genre worth considering is the "crime novel." (I know, I know: right now you're saying, "But aren't they all?" Yes, they are. But we're dealing with subtle issues here.) *The Godfather* in books, and movies like *Scarface* and *Goodfellas* are excellent models for you to follow. The morality of romanticizing criminals is something you can debate with members of your writing group; the reality is that people are fascinated by the "inside" look at the way these people live, at the Robin Hood face authors give some crime lords, and that's something you, as a writer, might want to exploit.

Finding the right crime family is a challenge. The Mob

was a favorite for a while, but became overexposed. Drug dealers don't have quite the same cachet: I think readers recognize the evil out of Colombia while forgiving the *capos*. It doesn't make sense, except when you consider that the crime families seem to have a code of honor which can be used to great effect in your novel. The cartels aren't seen in the same light and, too, they are too much with us, a clear and present danger.

The crime novel also serves the writer in another way. While most of the fiction in the genre is considered "category," and a substantial amount of it appears as paperback originals (no matter what the scope of the story), there seems to be a willingness on the part of the publishers to try this subgenre in hardcover. You have to remember that the hardcover publication of almost all category fiction is really aimed at getting library sales: There are many publishing houses that print a limited quantity of hardcover mysteries (or whatever) with only a small part of the printing going into the bookstores; the majority of the copies sell directly to libraries, with the hope being that a reprint deal with a mass-market house will happen. This hardcover publication also makes it easier to get review attention outside of the fan press.

While it is possible for a private eye or cozy writer to make that crossover—just look in any bookstore—the so-called crime novelists seem to have a better chance of doing it . . . and when they do, the results can be stupendous. While fans, for instance, knew the novels of Elmore Leonard, it wasn't until Arbor House published *Glitz* that readers across the country suddenly discovered him.

Variations on this theme are endless: Robert J. Randisi started out as a paperback writer, and was eventually moved into hardcover, though his breakout book is yet to come. Robert B. Parker started in hardcover and built slowly but surely. John D. MacDonald started at Fawcett Gold Medal as a paperback author and became one of the avatars of crime fiction. His solid sales prompted his acquisition for hardcover, where his market—and thus his sales —continued to grow. More often than not, however, the writer has to do something somehow "different" in order to break out. A surprise success in hardcover (consider *The Hunt for Red October)* will fuel the market for all similar fiction, creating a sudden urge on the part of mass-market editors to find writers to do the same thing for them as paperback originals. Whether it is the tail or the dog doing the wagging is left to other sages to explicate. For us it is enough to know that we have as many options and possibilities as we have the imagination to create.

In addition to these putatively bigger books, there's a whole range of other fiction that should be considered here. Most men's adventure—the *Destroyer* and other action novels of that kind—are found in the mystery section of the chain bookstores: there doesn't seem to be any other place where they comfortably fit. They have also become tired, and sales have fallen off dramatically, though rumor has it that some paperback editors are beginning to look for new titles. Cautiously. I've always considered these books to be nothing more or less than romances for men, fulfilling the same escape/fantasy needs. They are also derivative of the traditional western: a loner (or a posse) riding hard for justice. Category length, concentrating on plot and action (and among the better examples, redolent of a sense of the absurd), the action novel will never go away completely. Right now, they are using elements of the technothriller; next week . . . well, for next week, you come up with something.

Gothics, romantic suspense, and some books published by Harlequin under various imprints and logos are certainly legitimate entries under a mystery heading. However, because of the romance elements and the hint of the supernatural in the gothic, the marketing, and some rather blatant cultural and societal biases, they are now part of the romance genre, and we'll look at them next. One rediscovered form, however, should be looked at now, and that's the woman-in-peril novel.

The model for most publishers in this particular field is Mary Higgins Clark, but the tradition goes back much further. Helen MacInnes developed a following there, as did

Evelyn Anthony. In form, these books are contemporary gothic novels. The author places a woman (always single, sometimes a parent) in jeopardy. She doesn't know who or what or why, only that someone is out to get her. Usually working with a strong male character, the heroine saves herself, finds love, sometimes gets rich, and lives happily ever after. It is important that the central character does not consciously do anything to bring her problems about: a female police officer being stalked by a criminal is not viable; the executive mistaken for someone else, is.

The reason I've included the *womjep* here is that many mystery and suspense writers have turned to this particular subgenre now because of the crowded traditional mystery field, because the books are often treated as being out of category, and thus mainstream fiction, and because they seem to be selling strongly. It also provides a perfect segue into our next category.

•••

The Romance

Every demographic study done relating to book sales confirms that most books are bought by women. This remains true whether we are discussing hardcovers or paperbacks, bookstores or the so-called "nontraditional" book markets, which are, for mass market, rapidly becoming very traditional—K-Mart, for instance. So it comes as no surprise that romance novels, as a category, outsell just about everything else. What may come as a shock is the fact that lots of men read them, though rarely in public—sexism has several faces—and some even write them, too.

Most of the titles released each month (and Harlequin does more than sixty, in a wide variety of subcategories, and other specialty houses like Silhouette and Meteor make their own contribution) are paperback originals. Today, though, many publishers are moving their bestselling authors into hardcover, at which point, apparently, the books are no longer romances, but fiction. (They aren't treated with much more respect by the mainstream review sources, however.) The process began in the seventies, when Avon began releasing some of their new titles in trade paperback format. Less expensive than hardcovers, but having more of the feel of a "real" book and, because it was a format chosen for the publication of other books that wouldn't have been cost-effective as hardcovers (I'm thinking particularly of certain literary and other midlist fiction titles), it created an atmosphere in which these romances received more attention at every level of the industry. It is the same process we've observed in the western and mystery categories, and it happens for the same reason. If you can sell the same product twice—and remove some of the onus that automatically attaches to extremely popular mass market fiction—you have a better chance of recouping your investment.

The romance market, publishers and readers alike, are hungry for product. That makes it a potentially lucrative genre for you. While the writers producing these books probably receive less respect than any other—with the possible exception of those penning erotica—if you have a grasp of the formula and can tell a good love story that accurately reflects a woman's point of view, you'll have a bank account that you can respect. You'll also have thousands of loyal fans (which translates into readers) and editors eagerly awaiting your next manuscript. (I can cope with that.)

When someone mentions romance, they are probably talking about historical romance, the infamous bodice-rippers that defined the genre when it began as a contemporary publishing phenomenon (Jane Austen, after all, wrote romances) based on the cover art that adorned and still adorns the books. (Some people—romance writers, in fact—refer to them as "nursing mother" covers.) The biggest problem publishers have, aside from finding enough product, is giving a particular line or imprint a distinct identity. When a given look has a discernible impact on the market, everyone else rushes to follow suit—or torn shirt in this instance. At the ABA—American Booksellers Association—convention in New York in June 1991, one of the most popular "stars" was the male model on an Avon cover. So, it has become increasingly difficult to tell one book from another on the racks, and publishers are always looking for ways to make their titles stand out. Zebra made inroads with their "hologram" covers (a hologram in the corner of the cover, with an image that wasn't always clear); once it ran its course they switched to something called a Lovegram. Same image, clearer presentation, less expensive.

Every publisher with a romance line or imprint issues guidelines, available for a self-addressed, stamped envelope. Less ritualized than the mystery, romance fiction is often defined by the idiosyncratic nature of the publisher. What is perfectly acceptable for one is strictly forbidden by another. If you are going to follow up on an interest in the category, you have to read a selection of each publisher's titles, and then get the tip sheet. You have to read the books because a guideline comment may be ambiguous. What does "hot" or "sensuous" or "sexy" mean to a particular editor? By studying what has been accepted, you'll begin to get an idea of the definitions you have to follow.

And once you've gotten the tip sheet, you have to follow it. One house demands novels of at least 107,000 words, and that's clearly stated. Recently, a writer submitted a manuscript of 55,000 words to the editor there, but in her cover letter she said that the book "met your needs as stated on the tip sheet for writers." The manuscript was returned with a form letter . . . and another copy of the tip sheet.

Because each publisher has a definite and distinct personality, it's difficult to present anything but a superficial overview here. What might work for one will fail for another. And by the time you read this, it will probably all have changed, anyway.

In the beginning, historical romances were brutal. The heroine was assaulted in one way or another as the action started, and she spent the rest of the novel trying to track the man down—not for vengeance, but because she had fallen in love with him. As we matured and became more sensitive to reality and began to understand the damage that was being done, that particular approach met a well-deserved end. It is interesting to note, however, that readers and writers both are still insisting on a macho hero. Every indicator we have makes it abundantly clear that Alan Alda wouldn't make it as the love interest. There's still a conflict between the man and woman to get things rolling, each perceiving the other as at least a threat, but the battlefield is no longer one of abject degradation.

The majority of historicals have an American setting, but the time frame surrounds a period from the early days of the colonies to the late 1800's. The South has always been popular and many publishers view it is as the strongest region in terms of book sales, but the West, particularly Texas and California, and the Boston-New York-Richmond-Charleston axis have their supporters, too. Unless the publisher you're romancing specifically suggests otherwise, go with the area you know best.

And you'd best know it well. Historical accuracy is one of the things editors look for (with varying degrees of success), and with good reason. You are going to get fan mail; the editor gets the angry letters from the readers. You'll be thanked for transporting your fans; the publisher will be told about the mistakes you made. Because of the regional nature of so much romance fiction, you'll discover that many of your readers know the area you're writing about, know the history, the clothes, the mores . . . and don't take kindly to being misled. So, when a tip sheet says historical accuracy is a must, the publisher isn't kidding.

Most of the romances I've seen—and I've seen a lot of them, although I've edited only two or three—have young heroines who are strong, independent (of mind), alone (either orphaned, kidnapped, or somehow separated from family), attractive, passionate, and involved in an exciting love/hate relationship with the hero.

He is older, wealthy, strong, a man of few words except

where she is concerned, given to action and going after what he wants.

Unless, of course, he or she isn't. One of the most popular subsets of the category is the Indian romance, with one or the other of the characters being either full-blooded or of mixed ancestry. While the historical events surrounding the action are supposed to be correct, the characters are, to my mind, sheer fantasy, a feeling shared by most of the Indians I've met, and certainly those who attended the first Red Earth Writers Conference in Oklahoma City in June 1990. Your best guide is to read the books currently in the marketplace and then make your own decision about whether you want to follow that particular lead.

No matter what kind of character you are creating (and pirates, gamblers, and other men with "danger" stamped boldly on their foreheads are always good choices), the important plot elements are conflict between the man and woman, passion, and a happy ending.

Does passion mean sex? Usually. How much? How handled? Your own taste should lead you to part of the answer, published material the rest of the way. One tip sheet says the scenes must tell all, but avoid being crass. I hope that clears it up.

In September 1988, I attended a gathering of romance fans and writers in Santa Fe, a function sponsored by Harlequin Books as a thank-you for their readers. During the question-and-answer period, someone in the audience asked why there was so much sex in the books. I'm told that I interjected—from my seat in the corner, and in a *voce* not at all *sotto*—that it was because people enjoyed fucking. I don't know what the answer from the panel was; I'd been hustled quickly out the side door by the friends who thought it would be fun to have me join them at this party. But I imagine it wasn't much different, though the language undoubtedly was. Many people do enjoy the voyeurism, as long as the scene isn't rubbed in their faces.

Another experience worth relating here: I received a letter from a reader complaining about the cover art on a particular historical romance. The woman was terribly up-set by the suggestiveness of the painting and felt con-cerned about leaving the book on her coffee table, where it might be seen by her grandchildren. But, she went on to say, please don't change anything *inside* the books; the sto-ries themselves were fine. I don't think that it's just a New Yorker's arrogance that makes me believe that we're deal-ing with a certain level of hypocrisy here.

If you're offended, as a reader or a writer, don't try to fake it. The editors and fans will know that you aren't sharing the fantasy, and your work will suffer for it. As will your sales. There are lines of romances that don't require heavy sensuality and, certainly, the Christian publishing companies with romance titles on their lists present an-other market for you.

The readers know these stories are fairy tales, just as fans know soap operas don't reflect "real" life. We are, however, as attached to one as the other, buy into the fantasy to the same degree, and that is reflected in the sales of historical romances. But that is not the only pub-lishing setting for love.

Category publishing tends to be cyclical. (All of publish-ing, is, actually.) What was popular once will come back, sometimes in the same form and formula, other times with variations. The plantation/slave novel *(Mandingo* comes to mind) once sold very well. Now, of course, the characteri-zations that were so much a part of the books would not be accepted. But a variation on the theme, using plantation life as a setting, might work. While success there remains to be discovered, two other forms of romance have re-turned in force over the last few years and seem to have settled in comfortably for a long run.

The gothic—which is a cousin to both supernatural hor-ror and mystery fiction—is not only back, but it has barely changed since its last appearance. The covers are still dark-blue or black, the house on the hill in the back-ground still has a light in the window, and the young woman is still running away while the wind blows and waves crash under a cloud-scudded moon.

There's a certain element of the "had I but known" school in the gothic, with the heroine narrating events. She's alone in the world, accepts employment or an invitation to a house that looms darkly over the landscape and, always, there's more than just a hint of something evil in the air. And a charming man waiting to sweep her away— if he isn't planning to murder her because . . .

That element of tension and suspense is crucial to the genre, and a supernatural red herring is never amiss. Events, though, are always moved along by natural causes —the gothic romance is rarely a pure ghost story.

History doesn't play a particular role in the gothic, except in terms of the society and attitudes which allow for the kinds of situations you are creating. So, while most novels in the category might be considered Victorian, with its stringent morality, we are seeing the development today of the woman-in-peril novel, which we discussed earlier as part of the mystery and suspense fiction.

From the heart-stopping events of the gothic, it is only a few years and a buggy ride into the city to get to the other comeback category—Regency romance.

Charming, possessed of wit and humor, and reflecting the world it represents, Regencies are, pure and simple, fun. They range in length from the classic category count of about 60,000 words to as many as 100,000 or more, although these latter are rare. (Book length, today, is as much a function of marketing needs and production demands as anything else.) The longer length represents a real challenge for the writer, because you must be able to sustain the "voice" of the period throughout. That voice includes the idioms, social concerns, and style of the characters. Obviously—and here it comes again—research is of paramount importance. Not only do you have to avoid the anachronisms that plague historical writers, but the customs and mores of the era are so vital to these books that the writer must be steeped in the social and political realities the characters are living.

Cleverness—of both the cast and the writer—is constantly under scrutiny. The parties that seem to be always going on are alive with chatter; think of them as being forerunners of our cocktail parties, if not of our singles bars. The dialogue must sparkle, be filled with repartee, quick wit, and flirting . . . and always stay in character.

If none of that scares you away, the rest of the story elements are best chosen by reading a publisher's output. Some allow sexuality, others frown on it. Some lines like a subplot revolving around intrigue, others want it kept simple. As they say, Ya pays yer money and ya takes yer chance; choosing the Regency will, if nothing else, guarantee that you have a lot of fun with your characters and your story.

Though the kinds of news stories we see in the media would lead you to believe that love is a thing of the past, romance readers know that even if the course doesn't run smooth, it does run. That's why the contemporary sub-genre has such a loyal following.

Contemporary romances are collateral relatives of the "glitz" novel (the kind of story we've come to expect from Judith Krantz or Joan Collins) as well as an assortment of others. In many cases, it is the publisher's particular strengths and weaknesses that dictate how a book will be released. Checking the guidelines and listed needs will give you what you need to make an informed decision as to the publisher you'll contact.

For me, the contemporary romance parallels the historical. Remember, this is a personal definition, not the guideline for any house with which I was, am, or will be affiliated. Indeed, all the descriptions and definitions of the categories reflect my feelings, how I would approach them as a writer. The editorial specifics remain very much a matter for each house to decide. But don't worry; I'm not leading you astray.

Word count here seems to vary; some houses—Harlequin and Silhouette, for instance—like shorter, "category"-length manuscripts and relatively simpler stories, while others are looking for longer and more complex books. The heroine is still on her own, though divorce sometimes rears its ugly head. The basic conflicts remain the same: The love interest is a little older, probably wealthy, or at least on the verge, and for whatever reason, he and she are not immediately blissfully in love. And remember what we discussed earlier regarding the kind of characters that seemed to be most appealing in the historical. If you can come up with today's equivalent of the Indian, in his role as noble savage, the gambler or pirate—someone who represents thrills and danger, kind of like a roller coaster—you should be on your way to creating someone who will appeal to a wide variety of readers.

Instead of the "exotic" settings provided by history, we see the opportunities provided by travel. Jetsetting allows you to introduce the places and lifestyles of culture heroes —Hollywood, Monte Carlo, today's tropical resort of choice. Don't forget, though, that your reader is aware of all these places and types, having seen them on television, the movies, or the pages of some slick magazine. That familiarity breeds expectation, so if you can't visit them yourself, make certain to get a good—and up-to-date— guide book and keep up with the gossip columns. Your readers here don't necessarily want the truth, they want the confirmation of their beliefs as the popular media have dictated them. A little goes a long way. You can use an impressionistic technique to good advantage.

More and more, the world of business plays a background role in these stories, providing subplots, tension, and a reason for the characters and action to move across your landscape. And both characters are involved; the woman does not sit at home knitting—she's probably challenging "him" for a promotion. She's not bitchy and hard, nor is she a pushover. And, yes, she can be a secretary or administrative assistant, although it seems likely that you'll want to have her higher up a particular career ladder; what is important is that she is always sympathetic and identifiable.

From yesteryear to tomorrow, with stops not only in between but in both, the romance offers as large a canvas as any writer could want. Some writers are experimenting successfully with time-travel and futuristic romances, pushing at the restrictive boundaries of the category. Even high fantasy has been tried. Some of these journeys are gaining acceptance with readers, and publishers are being forced to look at them seriously. After all, if every fifth manuscript received reflects that kind of interest, the publishers have to take note of the fact that the people are interested. But that doesn't mean they do. One publisher, when confronted with a "new" idea, simply said, "We tried one of those seven years ago; it didn't work." End of discussion. So, they won't necessarily move quickly (let someone else try it, first), but enough writers trying to do something is going to have an impact. As Tug McGraw used to say, "Ya gotta believe."

The problem for the writer is compounded, though, because not only do you have to be good enough; you have to be better. You have to take a reader who expects you to be playing by one set of rules and make her accept what amounts to a new genre. And you are going to be examined by critics not only of your category, but of others as well. Science fiction fanzines review time-travel romances and bring all the judgments they would bring to pure sf to their considerations.

The act of creativity becomes more difficult. Whether you are using history or the contemporary scene, you can count on your readers having a certain background, having a working knowledge of the setting. The willing suspension of disbelief works in your favor, and a lot that might have to be mentioned or explained can be alluded to: Just say that Sherman is marching to the sea, and the entire cast of *Gone With the Wind* become supporting characters in your story. But when you step over the line between the common fantasy that is all fiction and the incredible, you have to make the reader believe, as they tried to do with the Superman movies, that a man can fly. As much as we like to think that readers will read anything good, the truth is that most of them are wearing blinders. It is easier to get a science fiction reader to accept a time-travel romance than to convince an historical reader to do the same thing. The world you're creating defines your reader far more than you might expect.

If you're considering writing one of these nontraditional romances, it probably means that you've read some. (I hope no one is running out now to find a sample to see if they *can* do it. If that kind of story isn't already part of your thought process, it's probably too late to get started now.) Having read them, you know who publishes them and how varied the list is. Do they have only one writer doing it or several; are they releasing six titles a year? More? Less? Those are indicators as to just what the needs may be. Put them together with what your bookstore manager is telling you about the next nine months and you can figure the odds for yourself.

Those are the basic romance categories, at least as I see them. As I said earlier, it may very well be the most popular category; the one offering the writer the greatest possibilities. While the competition is stiff because so many people are trying, the market's needs demand that new product be constantly acquired. And in order to avoid creeping boredom, publishers are going to be looking for the variations on the theme that will allow them to corner some part of the marketplace and have it to themselves, at least until everyone else manages to catch up.

■ ■ ■

Horror

According to *The New York Times*—and who are we to argue?—horror is the second most popular category of fiction in the country. Or at least it was in 1986. The proliferation of entries into the market that comes hard on the heels of notable success has brought with it the kind of questionable work that serves to kill the golden goose. Publishers rushed to acquire anything that they might label "horror" and the booksellers found themselves with more product than they could handle. That overabundance of riches was coupled with a marked decline in quality; while fans are avid and loyal, they do demand adherence to certain standards. When books didn't live up to expectation, the readers began to say, "Hold. Enough."

The result was that contemporary mainstays, people like Stephen King and Robert McCammon and Clive Barker and Dean Koontz (though he seems to be moving more and more into a pure suspense mode) continued to have their success; others, like Charles L. Grant, continued to sell, if not break out onto the bestseller lists (probably because they were working smaller, more traditional canvasses), and good, younger writers were given a chance to battle for a spot on the racks. However, the chains began taking fewer chances on new horror fiction in hardcover, holding out for the next book by one of the recognizable names and wholesalers began cutting back drastically on what they were taking in both reprint and original novels. And, as we've seen in other categories, the big guys are sold as fiction, period.

Now, in the early nineties, horror is considered "soft." That makes it a bit more difficult to get started, but not impossible, especially since the publishers with established lines, with credibility in the marketplace, and with editors who have some understanding of what drives the category (not all editors working in a genre have that sensibility, unfortunately; they are the ones who help kill a category), are continuing to acquire and publish. They might not be doing as much, but they haven't stopped; when the market turns around again, as it will, they'll be in the forefront of the next wave of success.

Contemporary horror fiction is subject to as much debate as is the mystery when we try to decide what it *is*, exactly. In the early days, ghost story, occult story, and supernatural story were used interchangeably, but even that didn't define it very well. *Frankenstein* is often considered to be one of the seminal titles in the category; to my mind it is much more science fiction (or Robin Cook-ish medical thriller), although it does have horrific elements, most notably atmosphere.

Generally speaking, horror fiction causes the intrusion of the supernatural into the everyday world. In the 1980's, we saw a new form emerge, the so-called "splatterpunk" school, defined by the works of writers like David Schow, Joe Lansdale, John Skipp, and Craig Spector. The ultimate expression of this crossover genre was probably the receipt of the Horror Writers of America's Bram Stoker Award by Thomas Harris for his bizarre serial murderer novel, *Silence of the Lambs,* a book which was ignored by the Mystery Writers of America. Whether or not it was a good crime novel is moot; that it *is* a crime novel, however, is not.

The splatterpunks are continuing to write novels that are manifestations of the fears we all have of random violence and psychotic acts. They are horror in the strict dictionary definition of the word, dealing with unspeakable acts as they do. But the otherworldliness of the traditional form is lacking, the battle between good and evil in the Judeo-Christian sense, the sense of the fantastical, the ephemeral spirit, are all missing. If you are going to write horror, then, you have to choose a field of battle and check the publishers' lists to see where their interest lies.

Like science fiction, I find horror more satisfying as a short form. While there were successful novels in the past —*Dracula* remains one of the most frightening books ever written—it wasn't until the publication of Ira Levin's *Rosemary's Baby* and William Peter Blatty's *The Exorcist* that novel-length horror fiction came into its own. Then, not so much with *Carrie* as with *Salem's Lot,* Stephen King created a new age and everyone was looking carefully under their beds and behind the closet doors to find something frightening. Many of today's best horrifiers admit that they write about what scares them; it may be the reason that the splatterpunks began exploring inexplicable violence.

No matter the form of the horror you want to write

about, word length is going to be a consideration. Category titles (the books written to fulfill the basic needs of the genre without necessarily going into extensive characterization or subplots—in other words, traditional and less "novelistic"—as is the case with all genres), weigh in at about 72,500 words. The books being treated as fiction, the ones the publishers feel have a chance at being accepted in the mainstream, by the people who don't read horror, and the publishers will make that decision, are getting longer and longer. Have you tried to lift a copy of *The Stand,* even before King put back all the words originally cut? Not every publisher issues a formal tip sheet for the category, but most will respond to a query letter and provide the information you need, not only about the physical aspects of the work, but about the subject matter as well.

I spent the summer of 1990 judging the horror category for several contests and discovered one intriguing point: Writers in the Southwest seem to be very concerned with devil worship, witchcraft, and other cult-related subjects. Checking in the bookstores, I could find very little in category horror, and virtually nothing at all in the longer form, that focused on those themes. When I spoke to the writers at the various conferences sponsoring the contests, it became clear that they were writing out of the headlines: the local media had been filled with stories about kids experimenting with drugs and the devil. And as often as not, tying the whole thing in to heavy metal music.

In New York, where the publishing decisions are made, however, the subject isn't one that comes up very often—even though there's the occasional story about evidence of a "voodoo" sacrifice in Central Park. When you add to that thought the fact that devil-worship and its related storylines are tired, have been used so often that there's almost nothing new to say about them in the course of your novel, you begin to understand why it might not be the best direction in which to move. It seems to me that if lots of writers are toying with a subject, and the writers are out in the heartland of the country—where the customers are, too—then it might make sense for the publishers to pay attention. It is not an attitude that's met with much favor in the editorial boardrooms, where the only valid information seems to be the competition's list and input from wholesalers and chain buyers.

Other areas that don't seem popular at the publishing houses, or with the booksellers, are voodoo, the Ancient Ones of H. P. Lovecraft, or pagan gods wreaking vengeance on their followers—unless they're the spirits worshiped by American Indians. As is always the case, if a novel using one of those subjects suddenly makes it big, and someone is almost always willing to publish anything, the picture is going to change. Fortunately for the writer —and the reader—there are still enough subjects available to provide not only plot lines, but growth of the genre.

There are some standard characters, the category's equivalent of the private eye or loving rogue: The werewolf (or shape changer) and vampire come immediately to mind. Both had fallen into disrepute through overuse combined with boredom; the stories being written were simple variations on the theme that offered nothing new. Anne Rice brought about a drastic change with *Interview with the Vampire*. While remaining true to the traditional form of the undead, LeStat revealed an underlying humanity that had been drained from most of the characters. The floodgates were opened.

Today's vampire is a revisionist's dream. They appear as police officers, scientists, the girl next door; and while they are, by definition, still evil, that is becoming as much a representation of a psychological ill as it is a curse of the devil. The same can be said of the werewolf and most of the other creatures of nightmare that populate the fiction.

At the same time, they are being successfully used, again, in their more familiar role: Robert McCammon's *They Thirst* is a grand display of the vampire *qua* vampire; Garfield Reeves-Steven's *Bloodshift* combines elements of both. The trick for you, as a writer, is to play "what if" with an open mind. Experiment, place the creatures in new and unexpected settings. Don't jump on bandwagons; create them.

Spirit possession is a theme that never seems to go out of style. Again, psychology seems to play a role: not wanting to accept the fact that people can commit some of the acts we know they perform, we allude to some evil choosing the character as a vehicle for its actions. It is easier to accept Hitler as the tool of a demon than as a human choosing to do what he did. A lot of what is being published in this area today has a child in the role of antagonist, allowing for an intriguing juxtaposition of innocence and evil. Most of these novels are of the standard category length.

Children are always excellent foils in horror fiction, either as the evil force or as the target. Because they seem so defenseless, their victimization carries a stronger emotional impact. For the same reason, women are often depicted in the same way, paralleling what we see in mystery and suspense fiction. Throw a mother and child into a situation together, and you have the makings of a salable, category horror tale.

While vampires and their cousins might be defined as monsters, there are dozens of more blatant examples in the literature: scaled creatures, awakened after centuries of slumber and breathing noxious fumes; others that are supposed to be protectors of sacred land now fulfilling their role. It's nice when they prove victorious over the far more evil land baron who wants to build yet another mall (unless, of course, you're a building contractor) and, sometimes, demons called forth from whatever hell they happen to inhabit in the writer's mind.

The popularity of slasher horror (as opposed to splatterpunk) movies, as exemplified by the *Halloween*s, *Elm Street*s, and *Friday the 13th*s, has resulted in attempts to duplicate the effects in novels, usually with a remarkable lack of success at any level. Dependent on shock, which is much more easily achieved through camera manipulation than writing, the books tend to be catalogues of blood and gore, with no story to carry them along. Unfortunately for the category, these books sometimes get published; it contributes to the glut on the market and makes it more difficult for worthwhile novels to get their chance.

While we're on the subject of successful movie and TV projects, it would not be amiss to mention here that you cannot simply decide to write a Freddy or Jason story, or a *Star Trek* adventure. Protected by copyright, trade mark, and other legal registrations, the creators of these properties jealously guard those rights and you have to work through them if you want to use their worlds for your writings.

Ghost stories seem more popular today in the short story form; whether anyone is going to attempt it as a novel right now seems questionable. I know that I haven't seen any manuscripts in the last few years; maybe it's time to try to duplicate Peter Straub's success.

Novels such as *Psycho* by Robert Block and Harris's *Silence of the Lambs* fall into the subcategory of psychological horror. As I indicated earlier—and maybe due to the fact that I've concentrated on crime fiction for most of my editorial career—I see these novels as being more a part of the mystery/suspense or criminous genre. The Harris, of course, was published simply as a novel, as fiction. It would be interesting to see what would have happened if it had been released into a category. There's no question but that both of these books are frightening, as are the better examples of splatterpunk, but where they belong in the scheme of things remains a matter of taste, style, and marketing savvy.

The moral and allegorical underpinning of horror fiction has been the subject of lots of fascinating discussions at the various conventions the writers attend. David G. Hartwell, in the introduction to his anthology, *The Dark Descent,* offers one of the best analyses of the genre that I've come across, and I recommend the book to you if you are planning to scare the daylights out of your readers.

▪ ▪ ▪

Fantasy and Science Fiction

Fantasy has always been with us; as a category for *contemporary* publishers, the vogue began with the publication of J.R.R. Tolkien's *Lord of the Rings* trilogy, still a standard against which much of the genre is judged.

The word "fantasy" means different things to different people; ultimately, all the fiction we're writing falls into the category. But for our purposes here, fantasy indicates entry into a world filled with magic and otherworldliness, one in which none of the rules of science, none of the things that are part of real life, apply. However, a *consistent, believable, workable,* and *rigorous* physics does exist. Part of the challenge in this most challenging of categories is developing such a world. Before horror became a publishing event unto itself, it was considered under this general rubric and is still one of the forms discussed and honored at the World Fantasy Convention. When we use the term fantasy today, however, we're generally talking about a couple of specific forms of storytelling. The labels by which we identify them are useful for critical writing; they are not particularly recognized in the industry outside of the editorial halls. If a book is being published as fantasy, it is simply identified that way. Of course, packaging gives the reader a very clear idea of what kind of book is being offered.

Heroic fantasy, or sword-and-sorcery, is best exemplified by the Conan series, one of the earliest forms of the category as we know it today. Barbarism rules the world—supported by magic—and the hero must battle both despots and magicians, who may or may not be the same person. Strange beasts abound, some with wondrous powers, and the hero can tame them. There's often a woman to match our hero and occasionally, as in the Red Sonja stories, it is she on whom the fate of the world depends. Most of the novels in sword-and-sorcery are shorter works, although a publisher will now and then try to do something special for an extraordinary novel. (Keep in mind that "most" never means "all.") And, too, most of the work appears in the form of paperback originals.

There is a definite market for fantasy fiction, but it is not represented on most publishers' lists. The editors working in the field say that it is selling very well for them; the problem for the writer is finding the theme and editor, otherwise writing fantasy can become an exercise in frustration. There's a cult following and a limited amount of space on the racks. While the video games based on the heroic fantasy concept are popular, as are the role-playing games that are also related to the category, these have not translated into a growth spurt for the books, undoubtedly because the kids are so busy playing, they don't have the time to read.

The second major label in the genre is high fantasy. These are books that have always reminded me of fairy tales (well, to be honest, the entire category does; personally and professionally I probably read less in this area than anywhere else). Again, magic—and that rigorous physics mentioned earlier—is a key element, but the stories seem to rely more on the use of magic than on physical action. The various creatures of fairy tales are present in the stories in one form or another, and I find the ones I like best to have an allegorical aspect to them.

Arthurian fantasy is another face of high fantasy. Because the stories of King Arthur depend so much on magic, because we have noble heroes doing battle, because the elements are so much in place, tales about the Round Table have gained their own place in the scheme of things. Marion Zimmer Bradley's *The Mists of Avalon,* a book which has gained a following as Arthurian fantasy as well as general and feminist fiction, was a great success and inspired a lot of writers to follow in her footsteps. Most of the editors I've spoken with feel that it is an overcrowded field but that a new approach, which is what made Bradley's book work, would be worth considering.

Anyone can use the world of Arthurian legend as the basis of a novel. Something which has developed in both the fantasy and science fiction categories is called the "shared world." Usually done in the form of short stories or novellas, these books are created with the permission of the creator of a particular world: the characters, settings, and rules of life are utilized by other writers working around a particular theme. *Star Trek* and *Thieves' World* are examples of this; another approach that has been the subject of some heated debate is the writing of new novels (sometimes called pastiches) based on characters created by authors now dead. While no one is complaining about the Conan books that are being published today, there have been questions raised about the ethics of an estate allowing new Nero Wolfe novels to be written, while Dame Jean Conan Doyle has been fighting the publication of new novels focusing on the characters in the Sherlock Holmes canon. And some writers are making it clear in their wills that their estate is not to give permission for someone else to continue with their characters. As was mentioned earlier, before you rush off to share another writer's universe, you have to check and get permission; whether that other writer is alive or dead has absolutely no bearing on the situation.

With certain notable exceptions (Stephen Donaldson and Robert Jordan come immediately to mind), contemporary fantasy publishing is pretty much limited to paperback and to a very relatively small section within the science fiction racks of most bookstores, while some of the specialty bookshops might rack them separately.

It should go without saying that this is a category with which you have to be intimately familiar before you decide that it is something for which you might have a flair. The writing challenge itself is one of the more difficult: in addition to creating a story, you have to create a world that is only metaphorically related to ours, create a system of magic and a population that can use it, and then maintain a suspension of disbelief by never varying, never allowing our world and its science and physics and realities to intrude. Unless your idea is so good, and your writing truly outstanding—and your background and interests completely interwoven with these worlds—I don't know how successful you can be here these days; to my mind it is one of the most difficult genres to master.

Science fiction is only a bit easier to conquer and remains lucrative, although some of the top editors in the field are beginning to worry about an overabundance of product. Something that has always impressed me is the quality of editorial judgment and ability in this area. It is directly attributable to the fact that publishers have had the good sense to hire people for those positions who have grown up within the fandom. While anyone might, with effort and commitment, learn to write or edit in most categories, the knowledge and understanding that only comes from years of involvement has always marked the best in every area; in science fiction and fantasy, in all of their manifestations, this experience has a marked effect on the success of a book or a line. Knowing the traditions in any field is important so as to not reinvent the wheel; because sf (it is not called *sci-fi* within the community or, at least, I've never heard that abbreviation used except to label unimaginative or derivative work. That *The Times Book Review* and other mass media insist on using the label should be ignored) is all invention, that background is even more urgent.

Science fiction is pretty much a product of our century, although the roots can be traced back to the works of Jules Verne and Edgar Allan Poe, who also created the detective story and was no slouch when it came to horror, and certainly H. G. Wells. As I mentioned earlier, I also think of *Frankenstein* as being part of the phenomenon. Hugo Gernsback, after whom the annual fan-voted awards are named, got it all started for us as a publishing entity with his magazine *Amazing Stories,* wherein he called it "scientifiction." The late Robert Heinlein, certainly one of the deans of the form, is credited with having first used the term "speculative fiction" for the category, and just as crime fiction strikes me as being better for the more commonly called mystery, so, too, does Heinlein's term seem more accurate, more encompassing, and truer to the function of the genre.

SF—which avoids having to choose between the two—is a category devoted to vision, speculation, and fact, all drawn from the scientific knowledge of a particular period. There is an often repeated story about a writer in the thirties being called in by the government because he was writing about atomic power, which was supposed to be top secret. However, based on information available, the writer *speculated*. It is in this genre more than any other that the storyteller's requirement to talk about "what if" is brought to the fore.

In the beginning, sf was an extension of the adventure story, developed as pulp writers began to find new markets: bug-eyed monsters were running off with beautiful Earth women, with the hero in hot pursuit. As the category matured, so did the themes. Hardware played a large role in the story: rockets, weapons, and assumptions about the utilitarian objects around us were used with abandon —and many of them have become part of our everyday lives. The parallels to established forms were quickly set: the books were called space operas, derivative of the western's "horse opera" and radio's "soap opera." Today, the novels and stories which concentrate on hardware are thought of as *hard sf*. As in the technothriller, which lives on the border between sf and mainstream, the hardware is often the hero. There is also a popular school of military sf writing in which future warfare is the central issue.

Another stream branching from the river is "soft" or anthropological science fiction. As the second adjective indicates, the stories are more concerned with the interaction between humans and the beings we discover, or who discover us. It is the life sciences, rather than the physical ones, that are central. Here, the idea rather than the technology is the hero. While some writers continue to create warlike creatures, today the extraterrestrial of choice seems to be kinder and gentler, almost a mentor to us. Politics and sociology continually change; with those changes come new directions in all fiction. And the more we look at these new directions, the more we realize that the themes have been used before. Check "The Day The Earth Stood Still" if you doubt that.

For a brief period in the 1960's and 1970's there was a movement called new wave. It always struck me that these works were part of an avant-garde literature; the quality of the writing, the use of language, the themes (if you could figure them out) went far beyond anything that was being done in popular fiction. If they hadn't been labeled, the reader might have expected to find the works in the so-called little magazines where experimentation was not only welcomed but encouraged. While the style did not last, it has had an impact in that the overall quality of writing in the genre has improved and the more adult concerns dealt with have filtered into the body of the work, generally.

The latest change is "cyberpunk." The writers seem to be younger, the writing itself very hard-edged, contemporary, and tough. While William Gibson's *Neuromancer* is generally acknowledged as the first of the breed, books like Philip K. Dick's *Do Androids Dream of Electric Sheep?* which became the movie *Bladerunner,* are legitimate ancestors.

As always, one thing leads to another, and there's been what might be seen as a soft revolution, with feminist sf— written by authors such as Ursula LeGuin, Joanna Russ, and Pat Cadigan—gaining attention and popularity.

Almost all of the major paperback houses have an sf line or imprint, publishing anywhere from two to six new titles a month. Most of the authors are established, but editors are always on the lookout for something—or someone— new. The novels tend to be longer than the standard category lengths we've discussed; it would appear that 75,000 words is the minimum; however, as always, check the guidelines and published titles. You're looking not only for mechanical guides, but also for taste and direction: because there are so many variations possible, and because a list very much reflects the tastes and visions of the editor, the basic research into what is going on is extremely important.

And speaking of research: SF readers are highly educated and know not only the category, but the physical and other sciences on which the stories are based. While there might be an editor around who will still let a writer get away with something as farfetched as, say, sending a man to the moon in a shell shot from a giant cannon, most will not. It has also become important to create worlds that are legitimate speculation: the social structures, physical attributes, and hardware of the culture you place somewhere has to be very carefully thought out. Just because it is speculative fiction doesn't mean you can be ridiculous, and that is a lesson a lot of newcomers haven't learned.

Category fiction is the beating heart of popular fiction, of mass-market fiction. It is popular because, as we saw earlier, the books speak to the concerns of a majority of readers. We always have to remember that in his day Charles Dickens was considered to have been writing potboilers, which is also how Louisa May Alcott started. We have to remember that Ernest Hemingway got lousy reviews. Don't sit down to create "art"; that comes later. You are an entertainer, you are perpetuating the myths of your tribe, and the categories we've just discussed are the most accessible and salable of the forms available to you.

Art and commerce are not contradictions, you can be literate without being obscure. Tell your stories and let the world judge you. It will, anyway. While you are working, however, try to avoid the self-consciousness that tends to creep in when style overwhelms substance.

That little lecture delivered, let's see if there are any other directions available to you as a writer.

■ ■ ■

Other Voices

There may be a perfectly valid reason for you to avoid popular fiction. You may have an intellectual distaste for it, you may find it boring, too challenging, or so far out of the realm of your experience that you would rather start with something with which you're more comfortable.

You may not like writing fiction, preferring to offer your potential reader the benefits of your insights, knowledge, and expertise in some area. Or you may simply want to look at other options before you commit yourself to several months of hard work.

All of these considerations are sensible. Too many people simply rush into what they think will be writing careers without giving any thought at all to anything. So let's stop and think a moment.

The fiction market is obviously larger than just the categories and, as we've seen, genre titles sometimes go "mainstream." What does that mean, exactly? I wish there were an easy answer.

When you go into a bookstore, you'll notice that books are usually displayed by some label or another: there's a mystery section, a biography section, current events. The choices are endless and the bigger the store, the greater the variety. There's also a section called FICTION. You'll find some titles that you think should be in category—a new novel by Elmore Leonard, maybe, or something by Robin Cook or by Rosemary Rogers. They, and others like them, have established a following among readers generally, those people who might not look at the category racks, but who will buy books by these writers and others like them. In fact, for many, like Dean Koontz or Sue Grafton, they've literally become eponymous categories—they have their own logos and their own readily identifiable typeface. Remember how *The Godfather* type became synonymous with mob novels? Achieve that level and you're a star. Customers come in and ask for the new "King" or "Parker" and don't bother with titles at all.

There may be a new technothriller, or trial novel, capitalizing on the success of Scott Turow's *Presumed Innocent,* a book that a publisher feels will be more successful if it isn't boxed into a genre. (They're not always right about that, but if you lead enough horses to water, one of them is going to drink.)

And then there are all the other books: Michael and Kathleen Gear's "American Prehistory" series, Leslie Marmon Silk's *Almanac of the Dead*, Charles Durden's *The Fifth Law of Hawkins*, a new release from Philip Roth or Joseph Heller, or Joyce Carol Oates. Some of these novels might fit into a genre as well, but many do not.

So, when we try to define mainstream, what we're really talking about is everything that, for one reason or another, doesn't fit comfortably under another label. It becomes even more interesting when you think about it a little further. First, the word mainstream is defined as "the prevailing current or direction of activity or influence." Fair enough. Now throw this fact into your considerations: According to an article in the January 6, 1992, issue of *Publishers Weekly*, a study done by the Book Industry Study Group between March 1990 and April 1991 reveals that popular fiction accounted for 66 percent of all books sold. For future consideration, 63 percent of all copies sold were in mass market (paperback) format. We may be getting into an argument of semantics here, but it seems to me that mainstream should be defined as what people read, and that's obviously popular fiction.

Publishers have another expression that creeps into acquisition decisions: "midlist." A publisher's schedule is generally divided into LEAD, MIDLIST, and CATEGORY slots. Lead titles are obvious; they're the ones the publishers expect to do best with, the ones they're trying to get the most copies of into the distribution network, the ones they're counting on to make some big bucks.

Category titles don't have to be worried about; they do what they do.

And then there's all that stuff in between, in the middle. The midlist. One of the worst things someone can say about a book during an editorial discussion is that it's midlist. It's sort of a limbo in spades. It's almost impossible to estimate what the sales are going to be, what the returns are going to be, what the reaction of the marketplace is going to be. It's a catchall. And it's where most general fiction winds up.

The picaresque coming of age novel that so many young writers start with, the deeply felt story about an immigrant family coming to terms with America, the novel about a coal miner's strike and its impact on a community—they're all common enough versions of the midlist novel. Every once in a while, one of them breaks out, suddenly shoots to the top. It has captured the public imagination for the same reason it captured the author's and the publisher's. *The New York Times Book Review* of January 26, 1992, lists fifteen titles on the hardcover fiction bestseller list. The authors include Alexandra Ripley, Dean Koontz, Stephen King, Danielle Steel, Ken Follett, Robin Cook, Tom Clancy, Dr. Seuss, W.E.B. Griffin, Sidney Sheldon, and Jonathan Kellerman. The only surprise might be Seuss, whether it belongs there, debatable. The other books, from *Scarlett* at the top to *Private Eyes* at the bottom, are easy enough to understand.

We also have, though, *Griffin & Sabine* by Nick Bantock, *Lila* by Robert Pirsig, *Disney's Beauty and the Beast,* and John Grisham's *The Firm.* What's brought them to the list?

The Bantock novel was released by a small publisher (Chronicle House), which means it didn't have the marketing clout of a major house behind it; the book made it on its own. In this case, that means the way in which it differs from most novels. The story is told through a display of illustrated cards and letters. It's an instance of reviews really helping to sell a book, at least at first. If it stays on the bestseller list for several weeks, word of mouth will have kicked in, and the book could stay on for some time after that, even becoming a cult favorite, like *Jonathan Livingston Seagull* or *Zen and the Art of Motorcycle Maintenance.*

Which brings us to Pirsig's novel, *Lila. Zen and the Art* . . . was a bestseller about a generation ago and has maintained a cult following. The new novel, philosophical musing on a sailboat cruise down the Hudson River, made it to the list because of the author's reputation. Does anyone doubt for a minute that if you or I had written it, it would not only not be on the list, it probably wouldn't have been published at all?

Beauty and the Beast is a commodity, not a book; a tie-in with a motion picture and, like the Seuss, a children's book; it's taking up room on the bestseller list that might better serve a deserving novel.

Finally, *The Firm.* Ever since Shakespeare admonished us to begin by killing the lawyers (remember what I said earlier about the classics lasting because they spoke to real people about their concerns?), the legal profession, and doctors, too, for that matter, have been popular targets for novelists. It probably has something to do with our resentment at having to put our trust in them, but the reason doesn't matter; what counts is the fact that this novel about a lawyer uncovering shady doings in his law firm has been on the hardcover list for close to a year and will undoubtedly continue as a mass-market bestseller. Grisham took a good topic, told a good story, found the right editor and publisher (by luck or careful planning), and wound up getting rich. The same book in someone else's hands may have been a failure; without question we'll see several more lawyer novels hitting the shelves in the next year or so, and the sales results will indicate whether or not *The Firm* is simply an individual success or the foundation novel for a new category of fiction that will sell strongly for a few years.

With that thought in mind, you can examine the bestseller lists to see what is selling and then, if you have the right background, try to duplicate it. There are problems with that approach, though. If you hit it right, you get in on the phenomenon created by Tom Clancy; if you play it wrong, you try to cash in on a *Mists of Avalon* or *The Witching Hour* by Anne Rice—as a category—and wind up with a novel you can't sell; the success of those two books was strictly a one-shot affair, although the Rice novel did have the cachet of her bestselling name.

If you have a manuscript that seems to fit in with what you perceive as a new direction, by all means, get it into the mail. If you don't, and if you have to learn about something in order to get one done, you're better off going with what you have and know. It's a time for hope and confidence and for remembering that the only thing we can be certain of in publishing is that things happen and we don't know why as often as we should.

There are also some smaller categories that may appeal to you: The Christian inspirational market continues to be a nice market for writers with the know-how and ability to tell the uplifting, positive kinds of stories it is looking for. The books appear in all formats, and while most of the distribution is through Christian Bookseller Association stores, some titles not only appear in the chains, but some can go on to bestsellerdom. In the seventies and eighties, many of the mass-market houses had inspirational lists, but as times—and the public perception of some of the televangelists—have changed, that market no longer exists.

Erotica, as most definitely something separate from pornography, seems to be a growing market today, with a number of paperback publishers looking for titles. There's little to go on in the way of guidelines so far (and editors seem strangely reluctant to publicly discuss what their plans may be), but the indications are that Victorian settings are in favor. Anonymous is one of the bestselling authors, and that fine line separating good taste from the prurient will have to be danced upon.

There's also a hardcore market, where the guideline seems to be "go for it." Okay, so it isn't for everyone, and you might not want to show the books to your mother. Or your father. Well, your name won't be on the cover, so no one will ever have to know, and you don't have to keep copies of the book, even if the publisher supplies you with some. And you won't get very much money; good short story markets often pay more. What you do get, and it is important, is experience. Writing a novel is not simple, not a matter of just putting one word after another until you get 50,000 or 60,000 or 127,500 of them in order. You can learn by working on your great American novel, and if you ever get any response to it, you may find out what you've done right and wrong.

The smaller markets, the ones like adult or men's sophisticate fiction, give you the chance to earn as you learn and, believe it or not, receive some decent editorial input.

Spending a couple of hours leafing through the market guides will give you a very good idea of how broad and varied the markets for fiction are, and we're not even discussing short stories or children's and y.a. markets.

■ ■ ■

The Book Industry Study Group report that told us about the popularity of popular fiction also mentions another figure: General nonfiction represented only 9 percent of books purchased. It wasn't all that long ago that a reprint editor, having lunch with the subsidiary rights director of a hardcover house, would be hard pressed to find a good novel on the upcoming list. Everyone was concentrating on nonfiction. There were self-help books, biographies, business books, histories; no matter what the subject, it was being covered as nonfiction. While they are still a staple on major lists, it would seem that some of the public's willingness to buy these books has eroded, a fitting subject for a book, itself, but not this one.

Several topics remain viable: Given the economic situation we're facing, books on managing your money and protecting yourself from the coming financial disasters will be out there, with cover prices anyone interested in saving money will have to think twice about.

Self-help remains lucrative. If you know a way to help people have a better life, beat whatever addictions or codependencies or other problems they have, come up with a good buzz word to describe the ill and the public will immediately wonder how they've managed to live with the problem for so long and rush to help themselves out of it. And there is usually a publisher around willing to take a chance.

Cooking and crafts books are popular and always in demand, but you can't simply do another ethnic or regional cookbook, another knitting book. Part of your research will be to find the things that make your book different and that make you the person to write it.

Biographies form a part of every season's releases. Names in the news, sports figures, someone whose story is special—they all have books written about them. Obviously, unless you're Kitty Kelley, you can't expect to be able to write a bio of some figure and have it published. If you have the proper credentials, usually acquired through journalism, you can prepare a query letter and see what happens.

Every editor receives proposals for true-life adventures, accounts of the writer's experience doing something. Granted that what you've experienced is special, the market for books like that is slim. Unless you come into the project with *guaranteed* national publicity—not fond hopes —that kind of autobiographical writing may be a good exercise, but that's about all. Maybe you can turn the adventure into a novel. . . .

Regional publishers and smaller houses are often good markets for fiction and nonfiction alike. It is there that the biography of your grandmother, one of the first women in the territory, might have its best chance of acceptance. Many of the smaller houses specialize in topics that the bigger houses in New York realize that they can't do well; they also have more of an identity with their customers: Tarcher is known for self-help and so-called New Age books, Shamballah is known for New Age, as well. University presses also have identities; both the University of Oklahoma and the University of Nebraska are famous for their books about Native Americans and the history of the American frontier.

Writing, all writing, fiction and nonfiction, is about the variety of human experience. You've had experiences, you have insights into some aspect of life. It comes back to being the shaman of the tribe, explaining what's going on to the gathered clan.

The voice you choose to reveal what you know, the form in which you tell your story, is your decision to make.

Eventually, every *well-written* manuscript, every *well-told* story, finds a home. It may take time (let's not be coy, it *will* take time), and the process will be frustrating. If you give up now, you'll save yourself a lot of heartache and pain.

And you'll never know whether or not you could have done it.

The competition is stiff; publishers receive thousands of manuscripts every year and a very small percentage of them make it to the marketplace. But every year some 40,000 do.

The only way yours will is if you write it right, get it finished, and don't give up hope.

Chapter 5

....

DO YOU
KNOW THE
WAY TO SAN
JOSE?

That seems like enough background for now, doesn't it? Then it's time to sit down and get to work.

The first thing you've done is block out the time when you're going to write, let everyone know that you aren't to be disturbed, put the phone on low and turn on the answering machine. Everything you can do to isolate yourself from the world for the time you're writing should be done. This isn't just advice for the beginner, it is a work habit that you have to develop. I called Larry Block a couple of weeks ago; the message on his answering machine was to the point: "Larry's working on a book right now so he can't come to the phone. Maybe he'll get back to you."

Your work area is ready: all the pencils, pens, papers, notes, dictionaries, typewriter ribbons or computer disks, paper clips, coffeepots, and security blankets are within easy reach so that when you sit down to write, you don't have to get up for anything.

That's the way it is, right? Good. In that case, we can get started.

It all starts with an idea. It's become something of a tired joke now, but you'll run into it, probably at the same party at which someone is telling you about her dream of becoming a writer. Someone else will show up at your side and ask, "Where do you get your ideas?"

I buy mine from a Greek pretzel vendor outside the Plaza Hotel on Central Park South in Manhattan. Nice guy; all you have to do is whisper the pass word and he slips the idea to you written on a napkin wrapped around the pretzel. Just look out for the mustard.

Bob Randisi once shook his head in dismay as we sat talking about his next project and his plans for future work. "For every idea I put down on paper, three more pop up to replace it. I've got more ideas than I know what to do with." He's not the only one, though. There have been writers who seem to have had the opposite problem —they may have only one *good* idea or one book in them. We know about them because that one was something special: Henry Roth's *Call It Sleep* is a perfect example. Given the choice—and most of us have it—I'd prefer to have Bob's.

Anyway, you have your idea. It's something so vivid, so alive, that you can see it, hear the dialogue, almost take it in your hands and taste it. If you're smart, you haven't talked about it with anyone, not beyond the basics, at any rate. That doesn't mean that you're ready to sit down and starting putting it on paper, though.

It's time to start talking about the outline; not the one you're going to use for submission, but a writing outline, something to work from. I've only met two or three writers in my years in the business who could write effectively without some kind of notes to guide them. Anytime I hear a writer come up with some excuse for why they don't (it's generally something like, "I find outlines too restricting, too rigid. I know what I want to do, and that's fine"), I know that one of two things are at play.

The first is laziness. It takes some time and effort to create an outline that's really effective, and there's always the very real possibility that as you start tracing the idea on paper you'll discover that the pieces aren't coming together the way they should.

The second reason is because most people don't understand the form and function of an outline, thinking of it more as a blueprint, a model that must be adhered to or the entire structure will fall. If that's *your* problem, I'd suggest that you think of it more as a road map.

Look at it this way: If you want to drive from New York to California, you can find a direct route, some series of linked superhighways that will get you from here to there in a minimum amount of time. And with a minimum amount of fuss. But you have an option: You can always get off the highway, make a side trip. If you like what you find there, all well and good. If you don't, you just turn around and get on with your journey.

Writing, especially fiction, is like that, too. A story is a vital thing, with characters who live and breathe and sometimes make demands on us. While we're ultimately in control, which is one of the nice things about writing, we can and do give our creations a certain amount of free will.

Your outline, then is simply a map. You'll mark out the stops you want to make along the way—instead of visiting the Football Hall of Fame and Mt. Rushmore, you'll be putting in the scenes that are necessary to make the piece work—but you know that you can always stop somewhere else and, because of that, maybe skip one of the stops you've planned.

Keep in mind the words of Carlos Castañeda in *The Teachings of Don Juan:* "Any path is only a path, and there is no affront, to oneself or to others, in dropping it if that is what your heart tells you." The advice serves to guide you as a writer both personally and in structuring your story.

Having convinced you of the necessity of preparing an outline, then, the next question to be addressed is what kind of outline is best for you? Most of us learned the basics back in elementary school, the straightforward, old-fashioned, formal or Roman outline. At least I think most of us know it; I discovered that my teenaged daughters had never had it explained to them. So, to be on the safe side, here's a sample:

■ ■ ■

Living the Dream

I. INTRODUCTORY MATERIAL
   A. FRONT MATTER
      1. title page
      2. dedication
      3. acknowledgments
         a. Kevin McDonald
   B. INTRODUCTION
      1. "I've always wanted . . .
      2. Commercial
      3. . . .
   C. IT'S ABOUT TIME
   D.
   E.
   F.
   G. GENRIFICATION
      1. Western
      2.
   H. OTHER VOICES
II. WRITING PORTION
   A. OUTLINES

    1. Roman
    2. Index cards

Which gives you a skeletal look at the outline for this book to this point.

The same thing can be done for any piece you're writing. Your first entry might be INTRODUCE JONATHAN followed by AT THE BAR, TALKING TO KAREN and whatever other incidents are necessary to get the character into the story, beginning to establish him as a person, or initiating the action that will get the novel going: HE SEES GUN IN PURSE.

The outline can get as deep as you need it to be, Roman and Arabic numerals, upper and lower case letters, and whatever other indicators you're comfortable with. Each line follows on the one before, each entry tells you what the next bit of business is going to be. And as we said before, if something doesn't work, just make it go away. That's why they invented erasers, crossing out, and the delete key in the corner of your keyboard.

While I still use that formal outline at times, I'm more comfortable using a stack of index cards. I keep several sets: some of them contain descriptions of characters I'm using in a particular story, or want to use; others contain descriptions of places that I think I might use effectively, bits and pieces of dialogue I've appropriated from people on the subways or the streets, facts I want to have on file, even emotions and feelings created by a particular context. They're filed according to key words and sometimes duplicated in other sections of the card drawer.

For a story or an article or anything else I'm going to write, I'll put each scene on a card, maybe just indicating that I want Karen to meet the vampire in a hotel dining room, maybe using several key words to describe the meeting. The next card will indicate something about the kind of dialogue I want them to have. The nice thing about the cards is that I can shuffle them. If I don't like the way the pieces are coming together, I'll move a card closer to the front or farther to the back.

Here are the cards for a story I'm working on now, in

between chapters of this book, something called "Virtual Reality." First, the card for one of the characters, the "hero," insofar as there might be one, then a couple for key scenes, and finally the joker in the deck, which we'll talk about a bit more later on.

> PETER SHAW: late '40s, well dressed, hair and beard long (mountain mannish) and gray. Vivid dreams, creative imaging *a la* Silva, est, etc. Determined . . . and suddenly scared.

Those notes, simple as they are, give me enough to go on. I've "lived" with Shaw for some time, of course; in this instance he was created to fit into a particular story. The hair and beard play a role, his dreaming and imaging are central issues. His fear is what the story is about.

Now, some scenes:

> PARK OPENING: Woman in park with young son and dog. Dusk. Rats. See Shaw running from tree to tree, hand shaped as "gun." Her fear, expressed in movements and actions, rather than words. She leaves. Shaw sitting on bench, looking at risen moon. His comments: "A good night for . . ."

That's the establishing shot, the image that will begin the story, and start the reader considering just what kind of person Shaw is and what danger he represents. From there, we'll go into a scene that shows him unobserved:

> AWAKENING: Shaw's bedroom; his dream [erotic?] Awakening. First imaging: strong. Parallels dream. Beginning to define Amy. Each imaging takes it farther toward what happened. Realization for reader that imaging vision precedes the dream sequence.

That's what I need to know in order to get the story going. It isn't going to mean quite the same thing to you as it does to me, but you're not writing the story. And that's the point: The outline has to serve your needs, allow you to move from one place to the next without losing your way. Obviously, every detail of the story isn't there (that comes in the writing), but the blocks are present. And possible side trips are built in, that's what the "[erotic]" note is for; the story is supposed to have a certain amount of sensuality to it, that's part of what Shaw fears, but I won't reveal what and why at this point, either in the story or to you. (That's another matter for later discussion: how much of what you're writing you want to talk about during the writing process itself.)

Oh, the "joker" I promised:

> dusk scurried in on little rats' feet
> the ever less reluctant night
> "they all look alike, don't they?"

These are all lines that I've had stored for different amounts of time, comments overheard in bars (wonderful places for lines), things that have just literally popped into my head at one time or another. The sources are unimportant; what matters is as soon as I had the opportunity, I wrote them down. The first line on the card, the one about the dusk, gave rise to the story completely; once I had it in mind, and knew I was going to use it, I just waited until it led into the line that would follow and the one that would follow that.

The last line, the quote, is something overheard which I'm going to use to help define a character. Every thought, every word, every image, should be noted in some way or another and drawn upon when they've fully ripened.

As I mentioned earlier, the particular beauty of the card system is the ease with which they can be shuffled. If I'd used the formal outline, and saw everything set down in what is really an arbitrary order, I would, like most people, see the words pretty much set in stone. To see the flow of the story with scenes switched I'd be forced to redraft the outline. However, by putting the cards in a different order, I immediately see how the changes will impact on the story.

As it is now, we meet Shaw as an eccentric, weird but harmless, as he moves through the park, near a woman, but not posing a real physical threat to her. On the other hand, if we see him in the dream/imaging sequence first, and if the images are not only vivid but strongly sensual, then his movements near the woman take on an entirely different spin. My decision will be based on what kind of fears I want to plant in the readers' minds as the story begins.

There's another thing I'll keep in mind. By starting with the woman seeing Shaw, the reader also gets to see him through a character's eyes; the reader is being shown the character, rather than being told about him. You've heard that old saying about showing, not telling, haven't you? That's an example of it: the author isn't *telling* the reader about Shaw's eccentricity; he's *showing* it.

And by seeing the way the story shifts and other directions are made obvious when the cards are shuffled, we've also seen that outlines are not the rigid structures many people think them to be. In the March 1992, issue of *Writer's Digest*, Stephen King says that an "outline takes what should be a liquid, plastic malleable thing and turns it into something else." In the same issue, Nancy Kress, who writes on fiction every month, says that she prefers to go right into a first draft (which is a mess) and then worry about design and pattern in the second draft. When students ask her which way is best, she tells them that the one that works best for them is the way to go. Which makes every bit of sense.

At least it makes sense after you've learned something about writing, something beyond the theory of a writing class and lectures, after you've gotten to the end of a novel or two. I see the work of lots of writers every day, see it and reject most of it. And I guarantee that I know which of those writers didn't think an outline was necessary.

Chapter 6

PEOPLE WHO
NEED PEOPLE

Everything you write is about *something* (though there was a joke making the rounds when Joseph Heller's *Something Happened* was published. Nothing happened). That thing may be an incident (a murder, a trip to the moon on gossamer wings), a concept (semiotics, as in *The Name of the Rose*), instruction (a cookbook), and in almost every instance, whatever happened happens to, and whatever is conceived is explained by, a character. (Cookbooks just make you fat . . . and sometimes rich.)

The character may be a person, a thing, an animal—even a place or a time—to, or in, which something happens, and something else results from that. (Broccoli, unlike asparagus, has no character, so the fact that President Bush refused to eat it is not an incident.)

Now, the scenes you're planning, whether you've blocked them out in outline yet or not, will have to have characters in them: your central character, of course, but also the people that character will play off of, interact with, receive information from, or otherwise relate to. All too often, the characters editors meet in manuscripts are nothing more than pawns, cardboard, put in the story to advance the needs of the author without having any life. Lacking life, in fiction, they lack believability. If the reader doesn't believe in the characters, you might just as well go back to writing about broccoli.

Characters have a history—a past, a present, and, depending on their role in the piece, a future—and emotions and feelings and mannerisms. What they do is based on that history; if they just act as you want them to because you need them to, you've failed the reader. Not to mention the character.

Developing all of that, creating the character of your characters, is characterization.

Like us, your character is the sum of all his or her parts. Put together well, the character lives beyond the pages. Dracula was nothing but a character and, in spite of what the Baker Street Irregulars might have you believe, neither was Sherlock Holmes. Travis McGee and Miss Marple and HAL, the computer in *2001: A Space Odyssey,* are all creations that took on a life of their own beyond the stories in which they appear. (In the mystery story, especially, this is becoming a more and more important factor. The readers, and so the booksellers and the publishers, look for the continuing character. They want the series, and many excellent hardcover novels are not taken for paperback reprint if they don't offer that potential.)

So, what goes into your characters?

Many of the manuscripts I see have a character's physical description early on in the story: *I looked into the mirror and saw . . .* But I realized something a while back during a discussion with an art director about a group of covers we were planning. I had no idea of what the central character in most of the books I was dealing with looked like. It didn't matter if they were originals or titles acquired for reprint; the lead in the story existed in a descriptive vacuum. And it hadn't affected the reading of the book in the slightest. There were broad sketches and lines, perhaps, but none of the kind of detail necessary to paint a portrait.

On another occasion, though, I was editing a major action novel, the beginning of a series for a prominent paperback publisher. There were hundreds of characters in the story, good guys and bad guys and some guys who were just there so they could be blown away in the next action scene; a scene that was never more than five or six pages away. And every time a new character entered the action, we got something like this:

> The Captain turned to Santana.
> He was a tall man, in his early forties, with dark hair and a paunch, but still strong. Sweat dripped down his face, leaving tracks in the dirt. His uniform was made up of bits and pieces salvaged from the guys who'd gone before.

The action came to a complete stop as we were given a word portrait of Santana, a man we would never see again in the story. This happened not once, but each time someone spent a couple of minutes with us. It added nothing to the story, and even the details like the sweat and the ragtag uniform were beside the point, because we'd already been treated to long scenes describing the conditions the men were working under.

And what Santana looked like had absolutely nothing whatsoever at all in any way to do with his role.

Don't get carried away, then, with the thought that every character needs to be lovingly described in detail. Sketches will do, and more important, the sketch should be offered up in pieces, through the thoughts or dialogue of other characters. In that way, you're not stopping the action, you're making the description part of the scene, of the events taking place. The description means something to the viewpoint character and is thus made to mean something to the reader. Here's a quick sample, taken from *Harry's Last Tax Cut* by Jim Weikart (Walker and Company, 1992):

> Her brown curly hair was held back with two of the rainbow-sprinkle barrettes she loved, but the cold had knocked the twinkle out of her blue eyes. Wearing flannel pajamas with little teddy bears all over, she hopped up into my lap.

Weikart could very easily have stopped everything when he introduced Jennifer, the narrator's seven-year-old niece who was now living with him. Instead, he has used the scene to break the tension that surrounds it and added a couple of details about the girl, whom he loves very much. At another point we learn about her height, at still another about other features. As a result of this approach, the reader begins to know Jennifer over the course of the story. If you think about it, most of us don't take in everything about the people we meet all at once, either. That makes this approach a very natural one.

Jennifer plays a role in the novel, but it isn't based on her looks; more important is her age, and the fact that she's in school, and some of her observations, which are important to the action. What I particularly like about the quoted scene is what it tells us about the narrator himself, from his allowing her to jump into his lap to his noticing the twinkle that was missing from her eyes.

Someone who combines description with action (or, at least, movement) within her story, and letting us see it from a character's perspective, is Kathleen O'Neal Gear. These two sequences are taken from her novel, *Sand in the Wind* (Tor Books, 1990):

> "Wounded Bear?" The soft feminine voice came from behind a nearby pine tree.

He turned slowly, feet unsteady, to see Yellow Leaf. Her long black hair fluttered in the wind. She was bundled in a heavy buffalo robe, gathering kindling by breaking dead twigs from the trunks of live trees. She walked toward him, smiling.

He tried to smile back, but his frozen jaws made it more of a scowl. His eyes wandered over her beautiful face. The old women of the village whispered that Yellow Leaf would be an old maid forever. She was already twenty.

Colleen Merrill rolled to her side, her thin arms thudding dully against the bed of the wagon. A web of long blond hair fell over her heart-shaped face, fluttering softly with each incoherent phrase she mumbled. Her brown eyes opened suddenly but quickly closed again, her mind still deeply asleep.

In the first scene, the movement of the hair, the description of the clothes, and Yellow Leaf's activity not only offer an image of the woman, but let the reader know what's going on: We get a sense of the weather, the life of the people being discussed. And her face is beautiful.

That's an impression that's coming to us from Wounded Bear. There's no definition of that beauty offered by the storyteller and none is needed; what the warrior thinks is beautiful is probably very different from your impression or mine.

The last quoted lines in that scene, Yellow Leaf's status as an old maid, and her age added separately give the reader a quick lesson in the culture of the people while allowing the author to tell us the character's age. We're then free to make any comparisons to our experiences without having anything forced on us.

And, again, in the second scene, rather than saying that Colleen had blond hair, a heart-shaped face, and thin arms, the information comes to us in the context of an activity, in this case, the observations of a woman in the throes of a nightmare. Because it is framed that way, the details aren't imposed upon us but become something we experience.

As for the definition of "heart-shaped," well, again, each reader brings her own vision and understanding to bear. We don't see the same woman, but we don't have to; it is enough that we have a sense of the character's physical aspect. We can then create a "reality" that meets our needs.

Too many writers offer descriptions of characters in terms of people it is assumed we know. There are several traps there.

When the description is of someone currently "hot," you face the possibility that two years from now that celebrity will have had his fifteen minutes and disappeared. I fell into that trap a few years ago, when I was stretching for a metaphor to describe some Manhattan neighborhoods. I said that the West Side was like Sophia Loren, while the East Side was more like Phoebe Cates. There was no problem with the comparison to Sophia Loren; even at the time I wrote the description—when Cates was starring in a miniseries based on a Sidney Sheldon novel—people couldn't make the leap.

The same thing happens when you use celebrities to limn your characters. If you told me someone looked like Veronica Lake, I'd have an impression of a hairdo and that's all. But I'm old. Offer that mirror to a twenty-year-old reader, and you're going to get blank stares.

Of course, one of the reasons people resort to making comparisons is because describing someone is enormously difficult. We may be able to visualize the features, but translating that into words is something beyond the powers of 99 percent of the writers at work today.

When in doubt, then, leave it out.

Granted, there may still be some (and maybe more than some) who still judge people only by their looks; more important than physical details, however (unless those details define the character somehow. Kevin Robinson has created a wheelchair bound detective named "Stick" Foster; his description is more than a passing detail), are your characters' mannerisms and habits. These will help provide the reader with the kind of information needed to form an opinion about the character or the event. And bringing it all together, it will make the reader *care*. Caring, the reader pays attention. Once you have the reader's attention . . .

One of your biggest challenges is in making it possible for the reader to differentiate between your characters. They must be distinctive, not interchangeable. When "Joe" shows up at the door, the reader has to remember who Joe was, what he's done, why he's done it (unless keeping that secret is part of the storyline), and how the other characters react to him.

You do that by giving the character traits, mannerisms, and all the other things that allow you to identify the people in your life. Combine those traits with the kinds of labels we use to remember the folks we meet, and you'll have a character well on the way to becoming flesh-and-blood.

Traits and mannerisms are easy. I know you've come across the character who always looks away when he's lying or the one who begins stammering when she's nervous. They show up frequently because we all have people in our lives who do the same thing, and it becomes an easy way to identify them in a story, to allow the reader to know what's going on in the character's mind by showing the trait.

In his novel *Mall Rats,* Kevin Robinson has a character called Soda Speak by the kids hanging out at the mall. When we finally meet him, and listen to him speak, we know where the name comes from: The man is constitutionally unable to speak a sentence without adding, "So to speak . . ."

I know that you and I don't do this, but there are many people out there who put tags on people, identify them with some characteristic or another: This one's a slut, that one's a pig, the other one's a jerk, and that JAP's coming to the party. The tags are not necessarily ugly: Someone is described by all who know her as charming, her husband is gentle, and isn't it a shame about their punk son.

Whatever tags you use in life become the tags your characters use in talking about each other. Once a character is labeled, *show* the reader why, let us see the character doing whatever it is that has earned him the tag. It is also possible, of course, that the tag is unwarranted; that it becomes an arrow pointing at the character who applied the label and may be used in the development of the story as the unfairly tagged person proves the lie.

I can feel a hole being dug here. All the references to your real life, all the suggestions that you look at your friends as you come up with the tags, labels, and other things you're going to use to develop and describe and bring to life your characters . . . *You know that I'm not saying* that you should base characters on your friends and acquaintances, don't you? If there's been any misunderstanding about that, let's clear it up right now.

Too many writers, when told that something doesn't ring true, that a situation or a character seems forced, false, or phony, respond by saying, "Well, that's the way it happened," or "But that's what she really said." The requirements of fiction, however, demand that events be less strange than truth: you do not have the benefit of the fact that something happened. Simply because someone said something does not mean that it serves the proper dramatic purposes called for by your work, and just because a character is a clone of someone you know doesn't make it a good character for your story. Characters must have the same broad, dramatic gestures of an actor.

The characters you create are there to serve the purposes of the story, a dramatic function. Fiction is not reality, it is not supposed to be reality, and the intrusion of too much reality erodes the suspension of disbelief. While a core of "truth" serves as a foundation, the building on top of it is the fantasy you have erected in order to entertain and enlighten us. In the words of Eric Bentley, in *The Life of the Drama:* "Paths cross that swords may cross. This is the paradox of 'drama and life': life is dramatic but its drama cannot be defined and presented without departures from life's usual procedures. In our usual 'life as it is lived,' inhibitions reign."

And as in drama, your characters must make broad gestures, must be seen and heard from the balconies. Our natural inhibitions prevent us from doing that effectively with our friends and acquaintances.

There's another, less philosophical, problem with using your friends and neighbors to fill character holes: if they don't like the portrait, they can sue you. It might be a nuisance suit, but the nuisance is something you don't need and often can't afford. Our sense of that possibility is, I think, one of the reasons we are so ineffective when we design characters based too closely on those we know well. The little touches that fiction allow us to use as window dressing are, we know, things that might offend someone. So, when a character needs a personality trait that we're uncomfortable with because of our friendship, we drop the trait rather than change the character. And at that point, something flat and unworkable prints itself across the page.

Your characters need motivation, and that motivation simply cannot be your needs as a writer. Granted, your investigator may need someone to show up at the right time with the right information, but the snitch has to have a believable reason to show up. The heroine in your romance may need a friend to confide in; that friend can't simply be moved into and out of scenes on whim. She must be part of the tapestry of the story. Otherwise, the character is a pawn, someone the editors recognize (and most readers don't, because the books don't get published) as having been created for the sole purpose of a scene.

You must give that character a life—a sufficient degree of background, personality, and motivation—so that the reader accepts without question that character's presence. That doesn't mean a full biography, though you may want to create one for your own needs, just enough so that this story person is real to both of us.

Every character in your story requires the same kind of attention; it is in the degree of attention that the stars are separated from the supporting cast. Even if you don't use the bio that you build for each character completely, if you are going to mention someone, use them in some way in the course of your storyline, you—and your editor and your reader—must be able to recognize that character, relate to him to the degree necessary to make him effective, care about her in either a positive or negative sense to the degree that her role demands. When you are doing it right, you use that background, that biography, even if you don't reveal it to your reader.

Your characters must be motivated, and recognizable as individuals. They must serve the purpose for which they've been created. If they don't, redraw them.

Your characters must be suitable to the story and, to some degree, fulfill the expectations of the readers. Jane Marple is an excellent detective, but she'd make a lousy p.i. on the streets of San Francisco, and a worse heroine in a contemporary romance.

And the entire cast is there in support of your central character, the "hero" or "heroine" of your story. *That* character is another story altogether.

Chapter 7

HEROES ARE
BORN . . .
NOT MADE

By the definitions offered in my *Webster's Third New International Dictionary* a hero is: a) a mythological or legendary figure endowed with great strength, courage, or ability, favored by the gods and often believed to be of divine or partly divine descent. Or: b) a man of courage and nobility famed for his military achievements, an illustrious warrior. Or: c) a man admired for his achievements and noble qualities and considered a model or ideal. Or (finally!): d) the principal male character in a drama, novel, story, or narrative poem and e) the central figure in an event, action, or period. For "heroine" you simply replace all the references to "man" or "male" with "woman" or "female."

What we're talking about here refers to either, but I'm looking to save some keystrokes.

Today, in America, we're desperate for heroes, and we're not looking for principal characters in a drama. We are really rather cavalier in our use of the word, applying it with equal ease to athletes and politicians, soldiers and stars of stage, screen, and television. I am not arguing any heroic qualities possessed, for instance, by the men and women who served during the Gulf War, but I don't think they were all heroes, as we labeled them in the media. I do not see any reason to think that a rock star or baseball player has to bear the weight of being a role model or ideal for anyone.

But that is the way we think, and we think that way because we don't have any heroes in our fiction, any characters of mythic quality, anyone to inspire the reader.

In the late 1940s, Irving Stone wrote a novel titled, *Men To Match My Mountains*. Think about that image for a moment, see the purple mountains' majesty and picture the kind of men and women who might match that power and strength. That's the kind of hero I'm talking about here, and I'm not thinking only in terms of an overwhelming physical presence. Whatever aspects of heroism you decide to emphasize in your writing, if you give your creation the attention necessary, you might very well be the writer who will give us the hero to lead us into the twenty-first century. If your hero isn't quite that large, though, at the very worst you've created someone who will capture the imaginations of editors and readers. And that's no mean feat in itself.

There's another definition to keep in mind here: Plot. For me, plot is not *what* happens; that's the story. No, plot is *how* happens—the intricate gear-meshing of the action and character interactions. To make story and plot come together successfully, your characters must be *motivated,* not *manipulated;* they must drive the action. A hero makes things happen; the failure of many of the manuscripts that I see each week is that things happen to the hero, not because of him.

Creating the contemporary mythic hero, using the blue-print left to us by writers like Homer, makes it all come together, makes you a better writer, and demands that the character drive the story. All that's left then is that you give your hero a vehicle worthy of his abilities.

There are eight basic steps, stages of development, in this creation, and you don't have to use all of them all of the time, especially if you are creating a series character. Series get boring because the hero is just, well, there, re-peating moves and actions. It's like playing chess with someone who makes the same moves game after game; after two or three sessions, you need a different opponent because the challenge is gone and you're bored stiff. And while it is true that most category readers want the com-fort of familiarity in their stories and characters, the next to the last thing you want to do is bore your reader. The last thing you want to do is bore your editor.

It all begins once upon a time, at the beginning.

▪ ▪ ▪

Birth

Unless you're writing an epic or a saga, the day the hero slips from his mother's womb is beside the point; unless you are writing fantasy, the Venus-on-the-halfshell ap-proach, the hero simply appearing full-grown on the scene, is not credible. No, the hero has to be born to the event. That's the one time the hero isn't necessarily the cause of the action.

Consider The Batman. Whether you're a fan of the original *noir* rendering or came along later, when the dark aspect of the character had been relegated to the memory of a few, one constant is there. Batman was born at the moment the child Bruce Wayne saw his parents being murdered. A particular event gives birth to a series of ac-tions, and the person who will perform those actions.

The ancient Greeks taught us that the only constant is change; birth is the first in a series of impacts between character and action, one that begins to define the hero, that serves to shape him as he begins to move your story. And that means that you have created the first of the series of conflicts and resolutions, of scenes and sequels, that are so important to effective storytelling. Something has happened, it results in something else, and will lead to yet another event. Most important, you've *shown* the readers this birth, not simply *told* them about it.

Your hero is now in your story; what's next?

■ ■ ■

Initiation

All too often we come across a character who just seems to know everything, to be able to do anything. That may very well be the kind of hero we want, and there's always a place for someone like that in our fiction. But—and it's an important *caveat*—these abilities must be hard-won; the hero has to undergo a period of initiation, of learning, of honing the skills and talents needed to accomplish the goals you've set for him.

Now we have another layer of motivation: because the hero wants to accomplish something, he has to ready himself. On the action level, of course, this is easy. The Karate Kid stood on one leg atop a piling next to the sea for days on end, learning The Crane. We, as observers, knew this was an important lesson because the Kid was going to use it in battle. But there were other lessons involved in the exercise: perseverance, patience, stamina—all attributes this hero needed.

In action writing, as in fantasy (the young Arthur studying with Merlin, for instance), this period is rather easy and obvious. But it plays a role in all forms. A young man learning about the business world, a young woman learning about business in a contemporary novel or about dealing with life on her own in a romance; any character learning the things it will be necessary to know in order to accomplish the tasks, Herculean or otherwise, you are setting.

It is during this period that the hero is also making the decisions that will set the events of the story and the plot elements you are going to use. You have the opportunity here to foreshadow, to begin the growth process—laying down some of the ground rules for the character: how and why your hero will react in certain ways to particular occurrences—and full development of a well-rounded *person*. We sometimes forget that characters are people, and a person's actions and reactions are predicated on everything that has happened in a life up to the point we are witnessing. *Nothing happens in a vacuum.* By creating a realistic past you are simultaneously establishing the psychological, sociological, and historical motivations that serve to maintain the reader's willing suspension of disbelief.

Fools, we are told, rush in where angels fear to tread. (We're also told that he who hesitates is lost. Sometimes I think we're told far too many things.) There's something to what is said about fools: how often have you watched a movie or read a book and shaken your head in disbelief, if not despair, because a character goes into a room where everyone knows the story's particular boogeyman is hiding? That's why the hero must go through a very important growth stage.

● ● ●

Withdrawal

The mythological hero—your mythic hero—should always sit back for a minute, look the situation over, and say, "Hey, hold on here. This is really crazy; I don't want to do this." He withdraws.

Pulling back, which is an action, is subject to the same rules of physics as is everything in our world. There is a definite, equal, and opposite reaction. And when things are going two ways at once, you've created another conflict. By not being at a particular place at a given time—by choice—we are *causing* an event. It is not the expected one: a love interest is not met, a deal is left unconsummated, a shot left unfired. The hero is still causing action, because you are going to have to resolve the conflict through the use of another sequel leading to the next scene.

You've done something else, as well. Remember when the first (contemporary) *Superman* movie came out, and the advertising promised "You will believe a man can fly"? I never believed it and I don't think anyone over the age of consent did, either. We want our heroes to be larger than life, to be something to emulate even as we know we will probably never reach their state of perfection. "Probably" is the key word there. By giving the hero that one small wart, the moment of fear and introspection, the questioning and self-doubt, we make the character just human enough that the reader has the hope of being able to see him reflected in his mirror.

While the hero is withdrawn, the story continues, things happen because of that moment. A situation may become clearer, a crisis worsen; their momentum unchecked, events speed up. The hero must do something.

■ ■ ■

Quest

All popular fiction, certainly, and virtually all the fiction we read, deals with a quest, a search. Sometimes it is the obvious thing—wealth's always a good one—while in others the goal lies more in the realm of the philosophical: What is the meaning of life? Because fiction is a storyteller's attempt to make the world clear to the reader (remember the shaman?), the quest has been at the center of everything.

All popular fiction, all the novels and stories thought of as category, depend absolutely upon it. Each genre has its particular Grail. We are all, every one of us, searching for something, for some answer. So does the hero you create.

This is the center and the focus: this is what your novel is all about. Now the hero is the direct cause of the action, forcing matters, pushing, prodding, acting with a very real goal in mind. Everything the hero does advances the story, sets up the next conflict, makes things happen. The pace quickens. When you hunt for dragons, you go into their lair; to get there you have to search and searching means pushing people to give you answers; answers they're reluctant to offer because of the threat to their own well-being. And so the hero's every action is a pebble thrown into the pond of your story, sending ever-widening ripples in all directions.

Things are happening, and it is because your hero is on the scene, center stage, causing them. You've created a character to match the mountains; make certain, though, that they are not molehills. Don't send Hercules to defeat a child, unless that child is the daughter of Dracula. The conflicts abound, the challenge is met.

When the surface of the pond stills, the story will be done. But your hero is not done growing.

■ ■ ■

The Underworld

War is hell and the hero, in one way or another, has to visit the underworld, has to pass through the realms of "death." Fiction is a series of beginnings and endings and the hero is at the start of another period. He has been born, studied, backed away, and finally accepted his role and begun the quest you've created for him. Each one of those steps has represented change; with the change comes a new vision, as the hero sees what is possible. He no longer has to fear rushing in because he knows his capabilities.

In terms of your story, you have been creating a series of escalating conflicts. Now you are nearing the end. The battles are getting larger, the stakes more worth fighting for, the threats more fearsome. Everything is arrayed and aligned against the hero; this is what your story is about, the fear to be vanquished, the injustice to be corrected, the fire to be brought back to the world.

Again, the metaphors I've been using have an action/adventure tone to them, but with a moment's creative thought you can find the parallels that pertain to any fiction. This is the point in the story when the hostile corporate takeover is about to become a reality, the time when the businessman has been fired, when the lover leaves, when the failing grade is received; it is the conflict your book is about, the lesson your story is going to teach, the thing that made you want to sit down and tell this particular story in this particular way at this particular time.

Your hero is in a fight for his life, really or metaphorically. He is not simply battling events, things that are happening so that the story can continue, which would be manipulation; he is fighting someone. And given the locale I've chosen for this battle, the antagonist is self-evident.

■ ■ ■

Meeting the Devil

Sometimes the bad guy is clear: the killer, the rival lover, the politicians, the censors. (The editors.) There is always an "enemy," a character representing the other side of the story. There's no reason why the devil cannot be some aspect of the hero's self; it's certainly done in introspective fiction all the time. No matter who this supreme antagonist is, though, the hero is embarking on the ultimate battle; this is the final conflict of your story.

Everything you've had your hero learn now comes into play; all the background material, all the factors you've put into place to support the character's motivation and actions bear fruit. The reader believes the hero will win, but wants to see how, wants to know how the lessons of the earlier pages will be utilized, how the actions and events which have brought the three of you—reader, character, and author—to this point will be resolved. Because you have made everything "real" and made the world you've created from the chaos of a sheet of blank paper a place the reader can enter, because each event was driven by your hero's decisions on how to act, and not by the kind of random factor that does exist but is inexplicable, the reader *cares* and is cheering the hero on.

And since the hero will go on, he cannot emerge from this battle as he entered it. The character will undergo a sea-change, shedding his skin, growing.

▪ ▪ ▪

Rebirth

The passage through hell is the start of yet a new beginning. Having been tried by fire (literally or figuratively), the hero emerges into the light, victorious. Everything now is approaching the finale, the moral. The ripples have reached the shore, the war is stilling. The conflicts are finished, the final resolution awaiting statement; the last scene, depiction.

One of the most serious problems in series fiction—most evident on television because of the rapid turnover time between episodes—is that the hero never reaches this stage of development. He doesn't change, doesn't grow;

past events are forgotten by everyone. Remember the series, *Hunter*? When that began, Hunter had a family that was connected to the mob; he was a rogue cop, a vigilante, partnered with a woman known as The Brass Cupcake. They wouldn't give Hunter a new car because he wrecked them before he got out of the lot. All of that stuff disappeared without a trace, without any explanation.

But life isn't that way; everything changes us. This doesn't mean that a static series can't be successful—the evidence to the contrary is all around us—but it does mean that your character will rarely cross over into the realm of hero and legend. Your hero is not lasting. And your lessons are lost.

Rebirth is enlightenment; your hero, having learned, serves to guide your reader to the same insights. All the conflicts, including those that may have seemed chaotic, random, now make sense. Your story is told.

▪ ▪ ▪

Transformation

As good as your hero was, hardened by the fire he is better still, tempered steel in a rusted world. He is also ready to begin again, bringing everything he's learned and experienced to the next phase. It's all a circle, and it's time to begin again.

The story is finished; the acknowledgment of this transformation is the final resolution. Don't forget: All the conflicts in your fiction are the result of human action and interaction, the story is about people and how events change them. All of the characters in your stories are affected, but not all of them are heroes; their actions and reactions are meaningful, but secondary to those of your hero.

By making certain that the reader can recognize your hero, and letting the reader share in the events that make the character a hero, you've not only given us someone memorable but ensured that your story will evolve in the right way, driven by the character. Each of the growth periods, the changes, the events that shape the hero are major pivotal points in the fiction, notes to help you create the "how's" that help make up your plot and guideposts to the "what's" that keep your story on track.

Most importantly, you will have brought together the three things an editor is looking for—story, character, and plot—and done it by following the method used by the storytellers whose work is timeless.

And sometimes, unfortunately, by those whose work leaves a lot to be desired. *Dances with Wolves* was filled with anachronisms and poor writing. But Dunbar, the central character and a man very much a hero, fulfills the needs of the role. It's entirely possible that at some unconscious level it was that awareness that first made the movie a success, and then allowed the book, published several years earlier, to go from its publication to an overwhelming silence to bestsellerdom.

There's a final thought to be expressed. Most fiction doesn't come anywhere near living up to the ideal I've just described. Obviously, it doesn't matter. But if you can improve your work by trying to draw a hero in this way, if it will make your work stand out in a positive way, if you can make it happen, it's worth the effort. And if you can't, it's also worth the effort, and if that has to be explained, you're in the wrong business.

Your business is storytelling, and the story begins now.

Chapter 8

HOOK 'EM
HORNS

No, we aren't taking a break now to discuss the vagaries of Texas football, though I've got some friends down there who might be in favor of it. This is about something only slightly less important.

I know that there are several editors in the book business who read every word on every page of every manuscript that lands on their desks. Their flesh tends to be doughy, their complexion slug-white. Their muscle tone is a matter of memory and their physiques—well, they tend to look something like a toy that was popular a few years ago, a little roly-poly thing called a Weeble.

You'll probably never meet one; they don't usually leave

their offices; they can't really, not if they're going to do all
that reading. They also don't have time to do much editing or anything else, for that matter. Anyone who tells you
that they *do* treat all the submissions they receive in that
manner is lying. Or incompetent.

If you haven't done this lately, go down to a big bookstore, maybe one of the chain outlets. It will work just as
well at the racks in an airport news kiosk, but the impact is
so much better in a large store where the selection can be
overwhelming.

Watch the way in which people are choosing the books
they're going to buy. Or not buy. If they haven't come in
with a particular book in mind—a current bestseller or a
gift item—if they are just browsing the way readers do,
they will start in a particular section of the store and begin
their search. Something attracts them to a certain title: it
may be the cover art or may be a title or an author's name.
And have you noticed the way hardcover wrappers are
beginning to ape the approach used by mass-market
houses for years now, using embossing and foil and all the
other eye-catching devices the paperbackers have developed? Whatever it is, the customer picks up the book,
reads the cover—or flap—copy, and then turns to the first
page. She scans the first paragraph or two, perhaps flips
through several pages, maybe even looks at the last
page(!), and makes a decision. You have that long to capture a potential reader's attention.

And in the final analysis, that's how long you have to
capture the interest of an editor.

When I first moved over from the sales side of the industry to editorial, I had the good fortune to work with
one of the best editors and critics in the country, Theo-
dore Solotaroff, who was then editing *New American Review*. While he wasn't kind enough to tell me to go back to
sales (in 1991, the average salary for an editor-in-chief was
$49,411; for the vice-president of marketing—the equiva-
lent position in most houses—it was $65,844), he did look
at me sitting at my desk, surrounded by four five-foot-
high stacks of unsolicited manuscripts (all short stories

and articles, so you can imagine the number of pieces being considered), shook his head, and said, "Michael, there's a prurient interest that will drag you to the end of every manuscript you start. If you're smart, you won't give in. Because if you do, you'll never get anything done."

You have to realize that Ted is someone committed to finding and nurturing new talent; that was one of the raisons d'être of NAR. But the truth of the matter is that he is right and that he was able to do more of what he wanted to do because he didn't read more than he had to before making an acquisition decision.

It wasn't easy for me to accept that. After all, here were people who'd spent weeks and months on a story. Was I to simply wave them off? Maybe the story got better as it went along. Maybe I had time to edit every manuscript that came along. Maybe reenlisting with the 310th MP Battalion was a good idea.

So, I learned the lesson and have taught it to every assistant I've trained in the last twenty years, and I've watched the same disbelief and fear on their faces as I displayed when I was young and learning not to mewl about the injustice of it all.

And I teach the same lesson to writers, because it is a hard, harsh reality and if you don't learn to come to terms with it immediately, right now, the road ahead is going to be a hell of a lot bumpier than it need be.

The message is simple: you have to hook the editor, you have to hook the reader, from the first word on the first page. If you don't, they'll never stick around long enough to discover what a brilliant ending you've constructed.

There are things we all look for at the beginning of a book, a signal that tells us that this is something worth our time and our money. We look for narrative drive—storytelling power. We listen for a "voice," for something distinctive in the way the words are strung together. We look for some idea of what this story is going to be about, perhaps, about where the author thinks she's taking us. We look for involvement and these days we look for it immediately. That's why so many writing teachers preach the gospel of hooking the reader by hooking the characters immediately upon the horns of a dilemma.

There's nothing new about it; Homer did it, and we learn about the technique. It's called beginning *in medias res*, "in the middle of things." There's an immediate involvement: our hero is already involved in something serious, we know there's a danger or threat or something to concern us. Something is going on and, it is hoped, we'll turn the page to see just what it is.

Here are the first paragraphs of Bill S. Ballinger's *Portrait in Smoke* (Harper, 1950):

If I shoot off my mouth to the wrong guy, I'm a goner.

And besides, who'd believe me?

But the whole thing doesn't make sense. It doesn't make any sense at all. I been thinking about it and talking it over with myself. And then on top of that I get dreams. And it still doesn't add up. I can't understand why it happened. I go over the whole thing, step by step, and then after awhile it gets hazy. It's like trying to paint a picture with a bucketful of smoke.

At first the picture of Krassy starts out clear and distinct. Then the edges move a little and it starts to get fuzzy. Then all the lines overlap and the edges curl up and start forming crazy whirls and swirls . . . and you don't have a picture anymore. I try to take my mind and grab the lines and pull them back straight, but the lines are really smoke and they slip away. And then all I have is hazy blue smoke which stretches all over the picture.

That's the way it is, and maybe I'm making it up in my mind. About the smoke part, I mean, because the day it started was a smoky, hazy Chicago day.

We know immediately that the narrator, Danny April, has a problem, that there's been—and continues to be—

some kind of trouble and it's haunting him. The voice is *noir,* dark and brooding. The author repeats the images of smoke and haze; they obscure the vision.

What's going on? What's plaguing the narrator? Who is Krassy, and what has she done to him?

The next opening is from Marc Behm's second novel, *The Eye of the Beholder* (Zomba Books):

> The Eye's desk was in a corner by the window. Its single drawer contained his sewing kit, his razor, his pens and pencils, his .45, two clips of cartridges, a paperback of crossword puzzles, his passport, a tube of glue, a tiny unopened bottle of Old Smuggler scotch, and a photo of his daughter.
>
> The window overlooked a parking lot two floors below. There were eleven other desks in the office. It was nine thirty.
>
> He was sewing a button on his jacket and watching the lot, where an old guy in overalls was rifling a yellow Toyota. The bastard seemed to have keys fitting all the cars and had already hit a Monza V8, a Citroën DS, and a Mustang II. He took a carton of cigarettes out of the yellow Toyota now, closed and relocked the door. Nobody could see him from the street because he was crawling on his hands and knees. He scampered over to a Jag XJ6C.
>
> The Eye dropped the sewing kit into the drawer, pulled on his jacket, picked up the phone, and called the basement. A few minutes later three thugs from the guards' squad closed in on the thief. They took his booty and the keys away from him, dumped a bucket of water over his head, and threw him out of the lot.
>
> It was ten o'clock.

Another detective sitting in another room. This one seems to be biding his time. When we learn about his desk, the first thing we're told about is his sewing kit. The author has created a ticking clock by bordering actions by announcements of the time. We don't know where he's working, but we know that they have a security team. We don't know the character's name, either.

We never do; throughout the novel he is, simply, The Eye. And at noon he is called into the boss's office, and his story begins.

Danny April and The Eye might just as well be the same person: each becomes involved in an investigation that brings him into contact with a woman who takes possession of his soul.

Behm's approach is less florid, but the *noir* roots are still visible. The Eye, as much as Danny, is a man whose life is not entirely under his own control.

Both writers have also managed to begin drawing their central character. Neither portrait is complete, of course, but we're beginning to get an idea of the type of men we're going to be spending the next couple of hundred pages with, and that image will change as we learn more about them, as we see them in action. Danny April will reveal himself through his narration and we'll only see as much of him as he'll allow; The Eye will be offered to us scene by scene. But even in those few hundred words, we have an idea of what to expect. Whether or not the authors will surprise us can only be discovered in the reading.

The people we'll be reading about are not the only hooks for readers. Remember my saying that time or weather or place can be a character? They can also serve to draw your reader in, as in the following examples.

Patricia MacDonald is an Edgar Allan Poe Award-nominated writer who doesn't write mysteries so much as novels of suspense. Her 1989 novel, *No Way Home* (Delacorte Press), begins like this:

> For three days running the weathermen on the Nashville TV stations had been warning of a "storm watch" in middle Tennessee. And everyone in Cress County knew they weren't talking about a little rain coming. It was tornado weather, and

country people weren't fooled by that network doubletalk. In order to forestall panic, the TV news never mentioned the word tornado until one had actually been sighted. But fast as a tornado traveled, by then it was too late anyway.

From the afternoon shade of her front porch, Lillie Burdette scanned the sky uneasily for a faraway funnel of dust and wind. Usually tornado weather came earlier, in late August. It was a little freakish this last weekend in September, but it was impossible not to recognize it. The air was humid and utterly still. Everything you looked at seemed unnaturally sunlit, and yet the sky was hung low with dark clouds. It was hot as blazes, but, now and then, a cold breeze would trickle over your skin and make you shiver.

MacDonald has immediately set a mood, a sense of threat, as well as a sense of the place and the people. Using a phrase like "hot as blazes," with its rural connotations, pointing out that the country people didn't believe the network doubletalk, gives the reader a feel for characters we're going to be dealing with and at least one of the conflicts they're going to be facing.

Mickey Friedman's *Hurricane Season* (E. P. Dutton, 1983) was called "A Novel With Murder" on its front cover because Friedman, like MacDonald, is not a mystery writer, per se. But whatever label we feel compelled to stick on her work, she offers passages like these:

Hurricane season comes when the year is exhausted. In the damp, choking heat of August and September, the days go on forever to no purpose. Hurricanes linger in the back of the mind as a threat and a promise. The threat is the threat of destruction. The promise is that something could happen, that the air could stir and become clammy, the heat could lift, the bay start to wallow like a huge humpbacked animal.

If a hurricane came, there would be something to do besides drink iced tea on the front porch and take long, sweat-soaked naps in the afternoon; there would be something to talk about besides how hot it is. So hurricanes linger in the back of the mind.

Across the bay, a dark green line on the horizon, is St. Elmo's Island. During the twenties St. Elmo was a resort, with a reputation that spread as far away as Atlanta and Birmingham. There was a boardwalk and a hotel, the Elmo House, with gingerbread trim and red-and-white striped awnings, and a seawater pool near the ocean.

The great days of St. Elmo were brief and have been over a long time. The Elmo House is boarded up, loosening at the joints in the wind and blowing sand. Adventurous lovers and beer-drinking teenagers have found their way inside and left crude messages. The pool, drained long ago, now contains only sand, occasional rainwater, dried seaweed, discarded egg cases from marine creatures.

The Elmo House sags nearer to the earth. Every year, people wonder if it will survive another hurricane season.

Friedman doesn't offer us a human character to react to the threat of the weather as MacDonald did, but we know the people are there, the folks who are drinking that iced tea and watching the dark green line of St. Elmo's. We also know that somewhere down the line that hurricane is going to hit, and that when it does, something will be happening at Elmo House. By creating the threat of the storm, and foreshadowing events, Mickey Friedman started her first novel with all the flair of a seasoned storyteller.

Another bit of foreshadowing—and scene setting—is displayed by Aaron Elkins in *Old Bones* (Mysterious Press, 1987):

So still and silent was the fog-wreathed form that it might have been an angular, black boulder. But there are no boulders, angular or otherwise, to mar the immense, flat tidal plain that is Mont St. Michel Bay. When the tide is out there is only sand, more than a hundred square miles of it. And when the tide is in, the plain becomes a vast, rolling ocean from which the great abbey-citadel of Mont St. Michel itself—St. Michael's Mount—rears like some stupendous, God-made thing of dark and gloomy granite, all narrow Gothic arches and stark, medieval perpendiculars.

The mist eddied, then shifted, and the figure was revealed to be a lean, elderly man in a fur hat and a heavy, well-tailored black overcoat, kneeling in the sand and hunched over a limpet shell in his leather-gloved left hand. But though his head was appropriately inclined, the old man was not looking at the shell.

He stared without seeing, his thoughts far away. His right hand was thrust deeply into the pocket of the overcoat. For many minutes he remained so, unmoving, lost in reflection, and then he tensed suddenly. His head jerked up, then cocked to one side, the better to listen. The wide, aristocratic forehead was inquisitively wrinkled, the thick, white eyebrows arched. A terrible, white scar that began at the left corner of his mouth and disappeared under a black satin eyepatch seemed to tighten, so that his thin mouth was jerked out of line. His right eye, gray and clear, held a look of strained disbelief.

The old man, who never spoke to himself, spoke to himself.

"The tide?" he whispered, and again: "The *tide!*"

Even for those readers unfamiliar with the tidal plain at Mont St. Michel, Elkins has, by describing the differences between tides, let us know that there's a certain amount of danger present, a danger emphasized by the use of words with a gothic echo. Then he introduces his character, a man with "a terrible, white scar" and an eyepatch. Why those elements of description? Because they indicate something about the character, something which is going to play a role in the story we are about to read. There must be something in this man's past that is going to have an effect on today's events.

The reader is left with haunting questions immediately: Will the man escape the tide? He is elderly and, if not feeble, certainly not as strong—or as fast—as a man in the prime of his youth. What is the secret of the terrible scar? Who? What? Why?

Turn the page.

There's something else that should be noted about the openings we've looked at thus far. While they're all taken from novels that are nominally category fiction—mysteries —it is only in the passages from *The Eye of the Beholder* that we know we're dealing with crime fiction. The others could be anything.

As might the two that follow. I'll tell you the books they're from after we look at the openings. The first is from the Prologue of a recent bestseller.

> The taxi, an old Rover smelling of old cigarette smoke, trundled along the empty, country road at an unhurried pace. It was early afternoon at the very end of February, a magic winter day of bitter cold, frost, and pale, cloudless skies. The sun shone, sending long shadows, but there was little warmth in it, and the ploughed fields lay hard as iron. From the chimneys of scattered farmhouses and small stone cottages, smoke rose, straight as columns, up into the still air, and flocks of sheep, heavy with wool and incipient pregnancy, gathered around feeding troughs, stuffed with fresh hay.
>
> Sitting in the back of the taxi, gazing through the dusty window, Penelope Keeling decided that she

had never seen the familiar countryside look so beautiful.

The road curved steeply; ahead stood the wooden signpost marking the lane that led to Temple Pudley. The driver slowed and with a painful change of gear, turned, bumping downhill between high and blinding hedges. Moments later they were in the village, with its golden Cotswold stone houses, newsagent, butcher, The Sudeley Arms, and the church—set back from the street behind an ancient graveyard and the dark foliage of some suitably gloomy yews. There were few people about. The children were all in school, and the bitter weather kept others indoors. Only an old man, mittened and scarved, walked his ancient dog.

A lot of local color, a feel for the countryside (obviously England), a combination of the upbeat—the magic day with a shining sun in a pale, cloudless sky—and a hint of something else: the gloomy yews around the graveyard, the old man and his ancient dog.

The second opening also uses setting as character, but the approach—befitting the place—is quite different:

Great speckled birds forever fly over the delta, over the reach of this alluvial sea. Early-morning lights go upward to make a horizon where there was none, and the dappled birds become crazed, crazed like many of the delta children below. Bird and child rise up in horizonless morning to fight the fire creatures of their dreams. And the great oleander birds wind southward toward home.

The willows bend their souls in this land. The sun learns how to shine. This is the land of the mosquito and jacksnipe, the swamp of the moccasin and gar. Friend and foe, friend and foe, friend and foe.

It is a new land with a better promise, a land of new men and new laws. Time was the delta held its children like ghettos hold their starvelings. Time was the delta gave darkened wind for hope, and its children learned to cease dreaming, to yearn for nothing at all. Ghosts like the fire creatures in the wavering sky ran races along the flatland and rested in the whispering willows, and the scorching winds below blasted those who worked, who labored, who dared not dream. Darkened wind and delta chariots, and children facing into the wind like stone statues.

Daylight kills the delta madness. The children grow up in light, come out upon the weltering flatland and walk the country roads. The sun proves there is a boundary where there was none in night, and the sound of the delta begins.

The delta, as much a state of mind as a place, is obviously more than simply a setting for the story that's going to follow. But what kind of story is it? What's this one going to be about? Murder? A chain gang? The Civil War? The possibilities are endless, but the sounds and sights in the description resonate, holding the reader.

The first paragraphs are not the beginnings of a gothic or a romance, nor are they leading us into a traditional British murder mystery. They're the opening scene in Rosamunde Pilcher's bestselling saga, *The Shell Seekers* (St. Martin's Press, 1988).

The second quote is from *The Burning Season*, by B. C. Hall (Berkley, 1974), a rich, elegant, subjective novel of "the New South." In its way, then, this is also a saga. Both novels, as a function of their length, as well as the nature of their story, allow for longer, less action-oriented openings. There may be hints of what's to come in the novels, but the most important thing for the reader is knowing that the land will act as a character in the story.

There are times when you can take chances with an opening. Joan Hess has been entertaining her fans for some years with her novels set in the town of Maggody, Arkansas. Having her audience well defined allowed Hess to break the mold a bit with the opening of her 1991 *Mortal Remains in Maggody* (Dutton). The first couple of pages are a script, clearly that of a movie. Reading scripts is not everyone's idea of a good time, so her agent, her editor, and her friends all had long talks with the author. She went with her instincts, and they proved right. Hess segues from the script into the following paragraphs:

> Ruby Bee was scared she was going to explode right then and there, splattering the walls and ceiling of Ruby Bee's Bar & Grill with blood and flesh and splinters of bones. Her eyes were as big and round as a matching set of harvest moons. Her body felt as though it were expanding like a liver-spotted pink balloon, and pretty soon her skin would have to give.
>
> It was a delightful sensation.

The author's done a couple of nice things here. First, she's balanced the graphic sense of destruction—blood, flesh, and splinters of bone—with the comic: Ruby Bee's thinking of herself as a liver-spotted pink balloon. Obviously, the explosion is one of joy and pride, so Hess has continued contrasting images, keeping the reader constantly on the lookout for whatever is going to come next. Not only don't we know what it is, but we don't know where it's going to come from, either. We have a sense of place and people—what those of us up here in New York would call "down home."

Another author who manages to keep his audience off balance is Ross Thomas. Here's the opening of *The Fourth Durango* (Mysterious Press, 1989):

> When the white bedside telephone rang at 4:03 A.M. on that last Friday in June, the 36-year-old mayor answered the call halfway through its fourth ring and kicked the 39-year-old chief of police on the ankle to make sure he too was awake.
>
> After a muttered hello, the mayor listened si-

lently for a minute and a half. She listened with mouth grim and eyes narrowed, forming what the chief of police had long regarded as her pothole-complaint look.

There's nothing particularly strange about a woman being mayor, and we've all heard of politicians being in bed with each other. But by saving the fact that the mayor's a woman until the second sentence of the second paragraph, Thomas still manages to take us by surprise. He did this in an earlier novel, *Briarpatch,* in which we read an entire chapter, taking it for granted that the character is one thing and discovering in the last sentence that our assumptions were dead wrong.

Sometimes, of course, a writer gives us exactly what we expect, exactly what we've opened the book to find. Here's how Loren Estleman begins *Every Brilliant Eye* (Houghton Mifflin, 1986):

> I drove the last twelve miles back to Detroit on the heels of a late-summer rainstorm that had the drains gurgling and my wipers swamping brown wash off the windshield from the tanker in front of me. I'd have passed it except it was doing seventy on the double nickel and I needed the help to get home without attracting red flashers.
>
> The truck was the first good thing that had happened to me all weekend. I had picked up a computer software salesman on a routine tail job in Drayton Plains Friday afternoon. It was now three-thirty Sunday morning and I hadn't been out of the car except to grab a burrito and visit a service station, having gotten my fill of the back side of Toledo and points in between while my subject ran his samples for vice presidents in Purchasing and took their secretaries to various motels to continue his pitch. If I'd been working for the guy's wife it would have been a productive weekend. But his firm had hired me to find out if he was running his

own game and so far as I could tell he hadn't left his assigned route. I had made the mistake of calling in my report and now they were shipping out a company man to pick up the baton. Sunday morning canned is a lousy place to be.

This is private eye fiction the way Chandler wrote it: sharp and crackling, filled with street slang (on the double nickel), with a character who is tired, jaded, wise. Estleman's p.i., Detroit's Amos Walker, has an enormous following, so his readers know what to expect, and anyone new to his work will know immediately, as well.

Thomas D. Davis is new to the marketplace. His first novel, *Suffer Little Children,* was published by Walker and Company in 1991. Here's what his readers got:

> The baby was baptized one Sunday in May. We were in a church full of flowers, the baby lying in Katie's arms, a children's choir singing "Jesus Loves Me."
>
> We came home, had Sunday dinner, put the baby down, then lay down ourselves, making love as an excuse to be close. I woke hearing Katie scream. She was across the room, staring down at our crib-dead child.
>
> Katie's grieving never stopped. She held onto her pain as if it were a second child she was determined never to lose. No one could take it away—not me, not her friends, not the doctors who treated her after her first suicide attempt.
>
> She got what she wanted, finally, on another Sunday, lying in a hot bath with her wrists slashed. I thought by then I'd mourned her already, but I was wrong. That first night alone I cried until I couldn't breathe, then stumbled outside into the darkness. I ended up on my back in the grass, staring into the heavens of the God who'd let my wife

and baby die. I said: Tell me again how great Thou
art, you bastard.
I don't go into churches much anymore.

That's the first page of the novel. Powerfully written,
full of emotion, but it doesn't tell us very much about
what's going on. And when we turn the page, we get this:

But this was business.

Dave Strickland, the narrator, is also a private investigator, but he's nothing like Walker. Or The Eye. Another
individual voice, another character.

Davis has also taken a risk: While we should recognize
that the words are those of the character, not the author,
far too many people confuse the two, never separating
them. It happened to Stanley Ellin when he was trying to
publish his highly praised *The Dark Fantastic,* which we'll
be discussing later, and it is likely to happen to Davis in
this instance. We (that's the famous editorial "we") might
have accepted Strickland's pain, but his blasphemy—necessary to the character, to the story—is going to be mis-
read by some.

Charles Durden takes somewhat the same risk in the
opening passages of the last book we're going to look at,
The Fifth Law of Hawkins (St. Martin's Press, 1990).

The moment I saw Jesus Christ standing in the
bowels of the Baltimore train yard it occurred to
me that I might well be headed for serious trouble.
He had returned, just like all those Bible-thumping
turkeys had said He would, and there I was, four
fingers deep into a large jar of orange juice and
tequila and about four hours into a flight on the
magic-mushroom express. I definitely was not
ready to meet my Maker.
Jesus was wearing crisscrossed bandoliers
crammed with what looked to me to be gleaming
rounds of .30-caliber ammo, and He was waving an

M-16. He didn't look happy. In fact, He didn't look anything at all like those Sunday school images of Jesus-the-Lord-Savior I'd been force-fed by my Christian keepers in what passed for my youth. He did have the flowing robe and the sandals, the beard and the long hair, but the hair was matted, the beard needed to be trimmed, and his robe was made out of Mexican flour sacks. I knew the material. I had a pullover shirt made of the same material in my bag. *Chinga tu madre,* I muttered as I sat back and closed my eyes.

The train, on which I was entombed in something called a parlor car, collided with a force field. We had arrived at Whiplash City, one of Amtrak's many unscheduled stops on the run from Miami to Manhattan. My eyes popped open and I looked out the window as though I actually expected to find an explanation for the engine's sudden inability to move forward. And there stood J. C., laughing.

As abruptly as it had stopped, the train lurched forward and immediately smashed into a second, equally invisible barrier.

Fuck me, who's driving this piece of pig iron? I wondered. I looked outside again and there was Jesus, loping along, holding the rifle high over His shaggy head and shouting. Being locked behind soundproof, shatterproof, hermetically sealed windows, I couldn't hear Him, but His mouth was moving like a born-again Baptist missionary preaching to a Niger River revival meeting. He came abreast of my window, turned, and pointed the rifle directly at me. I grinned and responded with a couple of unmistakable Italian gestures I had learned from a friend in the backwoods of 'Nam.

J. C.'s knowledge of Italian semaphore was adequate. He lowered the weapon with a look of disappointment. I moved my head from side to side, my expression much like that of the disappointed parent who has secured a permanent seat on the High Horse of Superiority. God Almighty Himself would've had trouble jamming that .30-caliber ammo into the bore of an M-16 I thought, and I tried sending Him the thought telepathically. He may even have gotten it. He shrugged, as though to say, "What the fuck . . . it's just a game."

The train struggled forward, inching its way toward the station. Jesus was left behind, one more dumb shit lost in a timewarp.

"The inmates are running the asylum."

The source of the unsolicited wisdom was seated opposite me . . .

Blasphemous? Maybe; irreverent, certainly. The speaker admits to being in a state of chemically altered consciousness right up front, but while the drugs and liquor may have induced the vision, the reactions are the narrator's. And my feeling is that he's feeling just the tiniest bit sorry for Jesus.

If the reader can get past the language and the comments, however, the rest of the novel, the story of a reporter's odyssey through some shady and dangerous doings in Philadelphia, while never ceasing to challenge beliefs, is funny, passionate, and exciting.

Durden knows what he wants from his readers and they know, immediately, what to expect from him.

And that's what it's all about.

Each of these writers has chosen a different way to hook his reader and, if I'm the reader, they've succeeded. As an editor, each of these writers would have made me turn the pages, at least for a while. Whether or not the books maintain the pace, tone, or pull is another matter.

It would've been useful to give some examples of bad openings, but they don't get published often enough and there's a law or two about my quoting from manuscripts I've received and rejected. You will notice, though, that none of these books started like this:

The horse-drawn carriage moved slowly down the muddy streets, the horse's hooves clopping through the wet muck which the sun, trying to shine through the clouds coming in from the mountains due west of the little village, hadn't been able to dry, much to the dismay of Ella May Knott, whose blonde hair hung limp in the cold, humid air of this Godforsaken place she'd just inherited from . . .

I kid you not. Don't try to put everything into the first sentence, or even the first paragraph; you have a whole novel in which to do that. Give the reader something that will make her turn the page: a character, a place, an occurrence, and try to put some of your best writing right up front. Because if you don't, no one will get to see it when it finally does appear.

Chapter 9

THE FIRST
SIDE ROAD

Kick That Block!

One of the things I love about writers conferences is that
during the course of a weekend, every question, every
problem, every situation that might affect me as an editor
or a writer is bound to come up for discussion. And one of
the topics that comes up regularly is writer's block. As far
as I'm concerned—and as far as you should be concerned
—there's no such animal.

Sure, there are times when you can't write, when you
may be exhausted, or sick, or just plain not in the mood.
But don't glorify it by calling it block. Because what it is,

most of the time, is laziness or fear. You can give in if you want to, but don't come begging for sympathy.

The laziness is easy enough to understand. Writing's hard work and it demands attention, discipline, and a willingness to do what has to be done. All of us enjoy having written; getting there isn't necessarily half the fun. At least not for everyone.

There are times when the writing comes easy. When it doesn't, look to yourself for the answers. "The fault, Horatio, is not in our stars. . . ."

The fear has two sides. There's flop sweat, the panic that sometimes strikes entertainers before they go on, the gut-wrenching knowledge that they're going to blow it, that something is going to go wrong with the performance.

The other fear is a bit more difficult to deal with, and far more difficult to recognize. It's the fear of success and the demands that success will make on us, of living up to what we've done. I guess you could say it's the fear of having to worry about flop sweat.

None of this is terminal, none of it is really hard to beat. Unless you enjoy the angst, of course, love going after the pity of your friends. "Poor Joey, he's blocked, you know. Hasn't written a word in weeks." Even in a good workshop or critique group—*especially* in a good one—no one is going to pay attention after the first few days. They're too busy taking the chances that result in something getting written.

If you should, one day, find yourself sitting and staring blankly at the chaos of a sheet of paper or a cursor flashing merrily against the emptiness of your VDT—or even just doodling or scrawling the old Palmer exercises for penmanship (a lost art, that) instead of writing across the lines on the pad—don't scream or rant or rave or, worse, start feeling sorry for yourself. It's a lot like falling off a horse: you've got to start writing again. Immediately.

I've borrowed some effective exercises from Larry Block and Rex Burns and either one of them works very well.

Larry's approach, which he taught in his "Write For Your Life" course, consists of preparing a selection of simple sentences and keeping them in a box or a hat or an envelope or the back of a drawer. Write them out on slips of paper, one to each slip, during some free time, fold them up, and store them away until you need them. The sentences might be things like: "Michael went to the store." "Susan felt her lip begin to swell." "The sky turned gray." Well, you get the idea. Make up a lot of them, a hundred is reasonable. You could also cut the sentences out of magazines or books or newspapers, which has the attraction of something approaching spontaneity. You're not going to remember them as well as those you write.

Come the day when you can't get started, reach into the hole you've stored the sentences in, pull one out, write it down, *and just keep writing for fifteen minutes*. Don't think about what you're writing beyond a basic continuity. Now that your fingers and your mind are working again, getting back to your original project should be easy.

Rex Burns's approach is similar, but instead of complete sentences, he uses three little words: an article, a noun, and a verb. "The dog ran"; "A boy fell"; "The door creaked." The exercise is the same: pick a fragment, write it down, and keep writing. I used this approach in a class I taught to freshman English students at the U.S.M.A. at West Point. These were kids who were frustrated enough at having to take Comp 101; here was this civilian guest lecturer showing up to give them grief. There was probably even going to be a test! I let the students pick the three words, then had them start writing. Every one of the forty-five cadets I saw during the course of the day was able to write the effective beginnings of a story. Some, I'm told, went on to finish them.

The biggest battle here is fighting the little editor on the shoulder, the little voice that keeps telling you that whatever you've just written is wrong, that you should back up and correct this, that, or the other thing. You have to train yourself to be able to say, "Thanks for telling me, now shut up."

One of the tricks I use, when I'm working at a computer, is to turn off the screen, and not only when I'm doing the exercises. Seeing what I'm writing, and knowing how easy it is to correct an error, leads to the temptation to do just that. But it's just as easy to correct the errors later.

That's an advantage we have over the entertainers. If a comic blows a line in front of the audience, if the singer suddenly discovers flats he's never heard before, it's all over. They can't go back to fix it. There's no time or place for revision, for editing or, at least, there's none for that performance. But if we do something that rings false in our writing, we're in a position to fix it before anyone else sees it. *We don't have to correct it immediately.*

I guess it was Ernest Hemingway who came up with this next one, but it's useful even if he didn't. According to the story, Hemingway would stop his day's work in the middle of a sentence. When he began the next day, he picked up the thought he'd left the night before and just kept going from there. I find a variation of that even more useful. If I'm having trouble getting into stride, I simply take the last completed page and start retyping it. It usually doesn't take more than a sentence or two before I'm fully involved in the writing again and can go on with the day's work.

While some writers have told me that they can go blank in the middle of a project, I find that most often the problem occurs just before starting something new. The idea you thought you had doesn't gel or no idea at all comes to mind. There are ways of dealing with that, and we'll get to them down another side road, but a quick and easy fix is available and it serves a twofold purpose. First, something may come of it; second, it keeps you in the habit of sitting down each day and working. It's far too easy to avoid the problem by not writing at all, and soon enough that time you'd allotted to your writing has been taken over by something else.

What I have in mind is a variation on the Block and Burns exercises. Just sit down and start writing. Anything.

Let yourself go with the flow. This isn't for publication. It isn't for submission. It's for you. Don't let yourself be fooled into thinking that everything you write has to go out. Experiment. Play with words, use language that isn't a part of your daily writing vocabulary. Create a file of characters. Write scenes. Something out of each of those sessions is going to get used in your work eventually.

And you aren't wasting time, as I once heard one writer tell another. If you aren't writing effectively, not writing at all certainly doesn't help. By working, by maintaining discipline, and by letting your *self* do some of the writing while you give your overly critical intellect a chance to relax, you may even discover that your "block" was nothing more than boredom.

When a writer tells me he can't work I believe him. But I can't do anything to help. He's the only one who can. And the more he talks about it, the less he's doing to fight it. And that's a real blockage.

Chapter 10

HAS ANYBODY SCENE MY GAL?

Newspaper reporters learn early on that they have to find out Who, What, When, Where, and Why; their stories are all aimed at answering those questions.

As a writer of fiction, your job is pretty much the same, but you have to add one more question to your list of tasks to accomplish: How?

Now, a news story has all the basic information you need in the first paragraph or two; the reporter gives the answers to the questions, and the rest, as they say, is commentary.

It doesn't work quite the same way for us. After all, consider the following "lead":

As General Sherman and his Union troops continued their march to the sea, one of the casualties was the great plantation of Tara. Miss Scarlett O'Hara, who had been running the plantation, looked at the destruction and, when responding to questions from this reporter, said, "Well, I'll worry about it tomorrow."

At a press conference in the ruins of the great drawing room, Rhett Butler, whose name has been connected with Miss O'Hara's romantically, said, "Frankly, I don't give a damn."

After which, all that's left is writing the sequel.

You know by now that we want to start by hooking the readers, getting them involved with our characters, and pulling them along with us as we answer the questions. We do that by adding one scene after another, building tension, piquing interest, and creating more problems for our characters to solve.

And the scenes deal with one or more of the reporters' questions.

■ ■ ■

Who:

The who of our report are the characters. Not only the focal character, the "hero," but each of the people (or concepts: remember how weather and site can be effectively used as "character") whose involvement is necessary have to be introduced into the story. Their presence will be used to answer "what" and "why," as well as giving the reader something to read about and someone to whom they will relate. Remember, relating doesn't have to be positive, no matter what the local self-help guru says. A little negative relating is a good thing.

■ ■ ■

What:

Your story is about the *what*. What happened, what's the Grail? You'll want to get this stated early (even if it isn't in the first passages), and as a story gets more complex you might want to remind the reader of what the story is about. It hasn't hurt Dashiell Hammett's *The Maltese Falcon* that he didn't keep reminding the reader that what Sam Spade was searching for was the murderer of his partner Archer and that the statue was just something that got in the way.

■ ■ ■

When:

There's always someone who complains about the cop shows on television by saying, "You can't solve a crime in an hour." If we think about it, of course, we know that the story has spanned a greater period of time, but because time references are so sparingly given, it's possible that some viewers misunderstand. The problem is compounded in written fiction because so many events come under scrutiny that it is easily enough assumed that more time (or less) has passed than the author has designed into the story.

There are ways around this, simple, time-honored approaches: chapter heads can include (or consist of) calendars or clocks, characters can make reference to the time, or some clever literary device you create can fill the need.

You don't need the reference in every scene, but you do need it, especially if events are happening against a time frame. In a novel that I'm editing now, the author has presented a conversation in which two characters agree to meet between nine and nine-thirty on Wednesday evening. A hundred pages later, the meeting hasn't taken place, but the focal character has gone to bed at least three times. Since there was no reference point for me to use, I have no idea of "when" I am in the story. That's something we're going to fix.

The ticking clock seems to have fallen into disfavor these days, though it was a staple in the fiction of the *noir* writers, like Jim Thompson and Cornell Woolrich. Okay, maybe it's corny, but placing the character in a situation in which she is racing the clock—the answer must be found before midnight or disaster will strike—builds tension immediately and heightens it every time the author lets the reader know what time it is. (If you're a fan of old movies, you remember the close-up of the clock, the hands spinning, or the calendar leaves falling off screen right.)

••••

Where:

The reader has to know where the story is taking place. You can use misdirection if that serves the needs of your story (for instance, if events are only taking place in the character's mind), but a reference point has to be there. As you create your scenes, think about ways in which you can give the reader a sense of place. There are descriptions, there are labels, there are specifics.

Using "where's" adds to the sense of movement because we know we're someplace we weren't two pages ago and it helps maintain the suspension of disbelief. As long as we know that we're someplace that we can recognize (a kitchen, a church, Altoona, PA), as long as we can visualize the place based on the information you give us, it becomes easier for us to accept the fact that the place exists. If it exists, it is easier to imagine that the characters exist and that the events being played out just might happen there.

••••

Why:

Back in the summer of 1961 my Army reserve unit was activated because of the Berlin Crisis: the building of the Wall we just watched being torn down. At some point during the year that followed, the Army distributed a booklet to all troops. The title was "Why Me?" It explained why the government had found it necessary to pull me from my high-paying job at the William Morris Agency (I guess I was making $100.00 a week then) and send me to Ft. Bragg, North Carolina, and how I was helping to keep the world safe for democracy by being there.

If the Pentagon felt it was necessary to explain its motivations, can you expect to do any less? Probably, but you shouldn't. Why things are happening, why Mary loves Joe, and why Susan wants to discover who killed the old man next door, and why The Kid decides to rustle cattle and why . . .

Your characters have to be motivated to do the things you are asking them to do. If they aren't, the suspension of disbelief shatters. It is only in the world of quantum physics, where light is both energy and matter, that the irrational makes sense. Until the quantum novel becomes a bestselling category, you have to keep cause and effect in balance.

• • •

How:

That's the one you answer by telling your story, by weaving the scenes together in such a way that the reader has a picture of all of the events, all of the details that make a difference as your central character moves toward accomplishing the goal you've set by deciding "what."

But "how" also has to do with the way in which you structure your scenes, and the order in which you present them. Using the questions we've just looked at, it should be easy. (And since there isn't much that's easy about writing, this is going to be a pleasure.)

You know the questions you have to answer in order to make your story work. You also know that events are moved by cause and effect, motivation and response, and they are tied together completely. As the late Dwight Swain puts it in *Techniques of the Selling Writer* (University of Oklahoma Press): "Cause becomes *motivating stimulus* . . . effect, *character reaction.* A motivating stimulus is anything outside your focal character to which he reacts; character reaction is anything he does as a consequence."

When I take my break this afternoon, I'm going to have my left ear pierced and I cannot think of one good reason to do so, except for the fact that I want to have it done. Tonight, lying in bed and feeling my ear throb, I may start thinking about it more thoroughly, but for now my motivation is boredom as much as anything else. So far, cause and effect are guesswork.

In a week or two, my daughter is going to come home on Spring Break and she's going to see my ear and she's going to make a comment of some kind; knowing my daughter, it could range from "cool," to "Uh, don't worry, Dad, all you have to do is take the stud out and it'll heal shut."

On the other hand, when I go into the office on Monday, or arrive at the Left Coast Mystery Convention later in the week, the reactions are bound to be more varied and, possibly, violent. Those reactions can have a very real impact on my work, on my livelihood; the relationships I have—or may develop—with certain writers may be affected.

Now we've got a cause and effect: the cause will become someone's motivating stimulus and the effect will be a character reaction.

That's real life; everything is hypothetical at this point and I can worry about it or not. (Do they sterilize the instrument with which they're going to do the deed?)

If I decide to have a character get his ear pierced, I can

still get away with having him do so for no better reason than the fact that it was there to be done (granted, it's not like climbing Everest, but everyone has his own path). But there will have to be a reason, *in the story,* for the scene to appear. If it's being done to say something about the protagonist's character, that will have to be explicated. It can't just happen because I want it to, because the scene, like the ear, is there to be done.

Having people react to the character's decision will serve to create *conflict,* and that's another key element to keeping a story moving. Every story is about a conflict: if the heroine can win her Grail without facing any challenges, if nothing gets in the way, you don't have a story. Other characters may react negatively to my hero's self-mutilation (or adornment; notice how the choice of word changes the impact of the event?) and withhold needed help—creating a conflict.

Once you've created the tension of a conflict, you've got your own in terms of what to do next. Creating an immediate confrontation between characters has a certain appeal: the pace snowballs, the action becomes faster and faster. But the impression on the reader is that the characters don't think; they are reactive rather than proactive, dogs being wagged by the tail of the action.

It can happen that way, and there's nothing wrong with it as an occasional thing in a story. But more often you are going to want to create a "sequel" to the scene, a transition. It gives your character an opportunity to think about what's happened, to recognize that he's been beaten, and to make a decision about what to do next.

And that leads, inexorably, to the next scene.

It's something like a roller coaster: tension builds as you bring the reader up the first slope. She knows something is going to happen, but all she can see in front of her is the sky. Then there's the first drop, and momentum carries the reader halfway up the next hill. Speed falls off—a little —but the reader knows she's being pulled up and up and that what goes up must come down.

And so it goes, peaks and valleys, calms before and in the middle of the storms.

By playing with the readers' expectations in that way, you develop an extra layer of tension, one between you and the audience. When the readers don't know what to expect beyond the unexpected, the writer has them in the palm of his hand.

When you outline, and later, when you revise, look at your scenes. Do they offer the reader a sense of time and place? Does the reader know who is on stage? Does the reader know *why* they're on stage? What is happening? Is it motivated; are the characters' actions realistic in terms of the story? Is there a conflict, a struggle, something to keep the focal character from achieving the goal?

How are you getting from one scene to the next? Is there a transition, one in which causes for later actions are being created?

Can you get there from here?

If the answers are yes, you're on your way.

And as you're writing, if something *you* didn't expect happens in a scene, if your hero falls for a woman you hadn't thought about earlier, if your heroine puts herself in a position to gain control of the town council, that's fine. Because if it happens that way, something you've just done caused it.

Chapter 11

THE SECOND SIDE ROAD

Garbage In, Garbage Out

It occurred to me, about three thousand words into what is now going to be the next chapter, that it was time to take a break, take one of those side trips my outline allows. The first one was planned; this one is because of the struggle with what I was writing. It just wasn't coming together in the right way. Fortunately, my trusty Mac makes moving around in the manuscript a simple process.

Unfortunately, the very simplicity that makes manipulation possible carries a price.

Now, I know that you aren't guilty of any of the sins

word processing has made us heirs to, but I bet you know someone who is. I'm willing to make that bet because the evidence, empirical though it may be, lands on my desk every workday.

So we're going to talk about using technology as a writing tool and the pitfalls that face us. (If you're still using a typewriter—and thousands upon thousands are—you might like to take this excursion anyway. If not, you just go on to the next rest stop and we'll catch up with you there.)

Once upon a not too long ago, Tappan King, then the editor of *Twilight Zone* magazine, and I were having lunch and talking about writers and computers. Tappan defined the three kinds of people who are confronting the technology:

First, the old-timers. Many of them aren't comfortable with the toys the rest of us take for granted. Their biggest problem—and now a stale joke—is with the very name of the application used for writing: the "word processor." Somehow, that gives certain people the sense that they're using some kind of Cuisinart for the language. "I don't process words" is the battle cry, "I write them."

Well, fine. They're absolutely right. Unfortunately, there are too many others, people brought up with computers in the classroom, who *do* process them. Still, the process is intimidating; these writers need the feel of the paper. Nothing can be done about that.

But they have another complaint, one voiced by Donald E. Westlake: The way Don writes is the way good writers have always approached their work. He begins with a draft. He doesn't worry about typos, about misspelled words, about anything but the process of putting one word after another down on a sheet of paper. (He's a touch typist, of course.)

Then, he takes the stack of pages he's completed, sits down with a pencil, and begins to make corrections. He notes spelling errors, the misused word; whatever problems have cropped up are corrected on the page. And the next page and the one after that. Once all of the corrections are known, Don begins retyping. And a funny thing happens: he does some rewriting at the same time.

For Don and lots of other writers, that step is lost when they're working at a computer.

The second kind of word processor user is the person who was brought up with computers, who has been using them since grade school. They're completely comfortable with every aspect of the technology. They don't have to waste time rewriting because they make their corrections as they go along. Takes no effort at all, and it saves a load of time.

I don't know why they're in such a hurry. Because if the manuscripts being submitted are any kind of evidence, and it is all I have to go by, they're just rushing first drafts into the marketplace, and in today's market, no one needs a first draft.

Then there are the rest of us. We're old enough to have learned the old-fashioned approach but young enough not to be put off by the new tools. And we've learned how to use them as aids in the writing process, while not forgetting any of the tricks of the trade that make writing worth reading.

I'm going to share some of those tricks now. As I said, I know you don't need these lessons, but . . .

The first thing you have to learn to do when you're working at a word processor is to turn off the screen. Right. Absolutely. You are a touch typist, aren't you? There is no reason to have the words you're writing print out in front of you, especially because they're so easy to change while you're writing.

Think about it for a minute. When you're working at a typewriter, do you stop to correct every typo as you make it? Most of us don't. None of us should. It takes time away from the creative process, from the writing.

Now, consider what happens when you're watching the words form on the screen in front of you. Oops, there's a typo. I'll just back up and correct it; quick and easy. And, wait a minute, that sentence doesn't look right. Well, it's easy enough to bounce the cursor back there and change it now. And so it goes. Instead of moving forward, instead of writing, we're marking time. We keep revising that first sentence until there's nothing left of it, of the story, or of our patience.

If you turn your screen off, however, you're not going to be seeing what you're writing; instead, you'll be thinking of what the next word is, the next sentence. You'll be moving forward, toward the end of the piece you're writing. And that's the direction in which you want to be going.

When you're done writing for the day, print out what you've done and put it aside. Then, the next time you sit down to work, take up those pages, pick up a pencil, and go through the section word by word, looking for the places where changes are needed. Correct spelling, correct usage, add a scene or a bit of dialogue. Write them in in pencil.

Then, call up the file and enter the corrections. With a little bit of discipline, you may also be able to start doing what Don Westlake does: as you're putting in the new words, other new words may come to mind. So you add them, too.

You see, writing, straightforward as it is, consists of more than just putting the words down. It is rethinking and revising. And most people coming into the field today, it would seem, ignore that step. Because they've been making corrections as they went along, when they finish and print out, they think they've done everything they have to do. Of course they've revised, didn't they go back and change the blue eyes in the first line to brown? Uh-huh.

Whether you decide to read the printout at the end of every section or when you've finished the piece is of little consequence. I vary it, depending on the complexity of the work I'm doing. What's important is to remember to do it.

You'll also have noticed that I never mentioned using your spell check. I don't believe in them. I think they make you lazy and I know that people who become dependent on them let little things slip through in their manuscripts. Things like "there" for "their"; "can" for "wan"; "life" for "live."

That's one of the reasons for the next bit of advice, advice that counts whether you're flying a computer out of a John Clancy novel or working with pen and paper. Read your work aloud. It forces you to not only look at what you're doing, what's going down on the paper, but to listen to the words you've used, their rhythm, their flow. The simple act of reading will help you catch lots of the mistakes that creep in. It'll make you pay the kind of real attention that too many writers today no longer bother with.

After all, with their spell check programs, their grammar programs, their program to tell them how many three syllable words they've used and what reading level that puts their work at, with all the tools at their disposal, they're doing exactly what the old-timers complained about: they're processing words, not ideas.

The question of speed crops up a lot. A writer I know in Texas has just popped for more than three grand to buy a Hewlett-Packard IIIsi. Eighteen pages a minute! He's turning stuff out faster than anyone can read it. One after another, the manuscripts pour out of his machine. Hasn't sold a one, of course, but he's getting them done quickly.

And they look great. The pages I mean. He's got a desktop publishing program that let's him set up a page that looks professionally typeset. Doesn't read professionally written, of course. And that's another point that came out of the luncheon conversation with Tappan King: because writers are now capable of turning out pages that look perfect, and because their spell checks and grammar checks and all the other bells and whistles they've tarted their machinery up with have given them the go ahead, they think they're done, that all they have to do is put the manuscript in a mailer and get it to my desk.

This is a real problem and it doesn't only reveal itself in the work of amateurs. When I was pretending to make a living as an independent contractor—a freelance editor—I was asked by the publisher of a major house to take on the task of editing a novel by one of his company's bestselling authors. I mean a legitimate, *New York Times* bestselling writer. When I picked up the material, I thought the publisher had made a mistake, that what he wanted was a proofreading because the pages I held looked exactly like page proofs: running heads, single-spacing, designed chapter openings, the whole shooting match. I was wrong, of course; this was the way in which the author submitted his manuscripts. After all, he didn't need to do anything more, did he? Just look at the manuscript. It was perfect.

There's something else I've noticed about working at a computer, and it probably isn't a particularly clever insight, but I think it plays a role in how we approach our work. When I started to work on this book I was working at an old IBM Selectric. Not even an electronic typewriter, just one of the original beasts. I worked more slowly, not because the keyboard wasn't as responsive, which, of course, it wasn't, but because corrections were a tedious process. Instead of backing up on the screen to make corrections, thus slowing myself down, I was thinking and rethinking every word before I put it down on the page. And that is as harmful as the constant revising of words and misspellings because it, too, kept me from moving ahead. I questioned every word I put down, because if it was the wrong word, I was going to have to start futzing around with correction fluids, or retyping or whatever it took to get the page in shape for submission. No, the typewriter didn't have a correction tape; even if it did, I'd be doing the same thing I'm warning against, right?

By using the word processor in a way that doesn't interfere with your primary job (creating the story), by using it as a tool rather than a crutch, you free yourself to write without inhibition. Making corrections isn't a problem; there's no reason for them to be done during the writing process. Save it for the revision.

Chapter 12

HOW MANY PICTURES IS A WORD WORTH?

She had natural red hair, but she wore it wrong. It hung limp and lifeless around her face, without curl or wave, and Trace had always felt that red hair should be blowsy and breezy to look natural. Redheads were made by God to look as if they had just crawled out from under the sheets with a football team. Mrs. Collins' mouth was full, but she wore no lipstick and her lips just seemed to fade into her face. Her nose was turned-up pert and her eyes large and green, but they were just there. A little makeup would have made them worth traveling to see.

The house was as mousy and bland as its mistress. The living room looked as if it had been transported, whole, from the display window of a furniture store that still sold a sofa and two chairs for less than three hundred dollars, and would if you bargained hard, throw in a couple of wood-grained Formica end tables. The rug was a vague tan tweed color and the furniture, upholstered in an equally vague blue, was placed in a precise straight line against one wall. There was a fireplace, bordered with imitation brick and filled with electrical equipment designed to enable fiberglass logs to produce a light that looked red when viewed through cellophane. The few framed prints on the walls looked as if they came from a Sunday-newspaper magazine. Trace expected to find a print of President Franklin Delano Roosevelt.

The only attractive and personal touch in the room was a three-foot-by-two-foot tapestry of a unicorn hanging unframed on the far wall.

Trace sank back into the uncomfortable couch. He lit a cigarette and flicked it into the large plastic kidney-shaped ashtray on the plastic end table next to him.

That's a scene from Warren Murphy's "Trace" novel, *Pigs Get Fat* (Signet, 1985). Now, having read that, how many of you can come up with a description of how the room smells? (Murphy does go on to describe it, but you can fill in your own details.) From the information given us, even blind Homer could see the room, see Mrs. Collins, see the neighborhood in which the home is located. We also know exactly how Trace feels about being there. Murphy has given us a setting, and set us up for whatever action is going to take place in that room, between those characters. He's also done something else very important to note: by writing that "Trace expected to find" and "Trace had always felt," we see things through Trace's eyes, not the author's; we're *shown*, not *told*. We're allowed

to experience the room for ourselves and the description
of the room—important for the characterization of both
Trace and Mrs. Collins—does not stop the action; it is
made part of it.

Here's a first-person example by Jeremiah Healy from
his novel, *Blunt Darts* (Walker, 1984). John Cuddy, the
narrator, has to visit a courtroom. The judge's son has run
away and it appears that he doesn't want any outside help
in finding the boy:

> I became part of the wedge cutting its way into
> the First Session. The courtroom was like a church,
> with one of the cathedral ceilings I'd spotted from
> outside. The doors opened onto a wide center
> aisle, and the seating for the public was on high-
> backed benches, rather like Catholic pews without
> the kneelers. The center aisle ended at a gateway in
> a fence. The fence is the bar enclosure, so-called by
> lawyers because usually only members of the bar
> may sit within it. The fencing reminded me very
> much of a half-scale model of the balustrade on the
> stairway in the judge's house. Past the bar enclo-
> sure, which was sunken like a split-level living
> room, was the bench, raised like a pulpit.
>
> The congregation rose as the Honorable Willard
> J. Kinnington fairly scooted from a door to the
> right side of the bench and ascended. Possibly he
> moved so quickly because he was only barely me-
> dium height and didn't wish to advertise it. He had
> slightly graying, blondish-red hair and was wearing
> amber horn-rimmed glasses. He clutched a small
> loose-leaf book in his right hand; with his black
> robes this gave him the appearance of a new parish
> priest slightly late for his first mass. Once on the
> bench, however, he fixed the entire courtroom
> with a baleful eye. With the added height of the
> raised bench, he now looked as though he could
> jump center for the Celtics.

It probably doesn't hurt to know at this point that by profession Healy is an attorney, and whether that has an effect on how he describes a courtroom is something that can be argued long into the night.

In terms of the character, however (and it is the character who is describing the setting), we get a sense of awe and the power of the judge, a power that exists in contrast to the description of him as "a new parish priest slightly late for his first mass" and his slight size.

We know that Kinnington and Cuddy, just like Trace and Mrs. Collins, are going to be at odds; through his descriptions, Healy puts all the power on the antagonist's side.

Now, it is entirely possible that Healy could have simply had Cuddy say that walking into the courtroom made him feel as if he were walking into a church, but the scene would have suffered, just as Murphy's scene would not have been as powerful if he had simply said the living room looked like a cheap furniture showroom.

This doesn't mean that every description needs to be extended; if the room or place doesn't matter, if the character's presence there is not advancing the story but is just a stop along the way, it is far better to stick with the old K.I.S.S. principle. You know, Keep It Simple, Stupid.

There are a couple of other lessons in the descriptions we've been looking at. First, both writers kept a zinger of one kind or another for the end of the description: the impact of the judge being transformed from a smallish, aging man into a center for the Celtics by sitting behind the bench, and the sudden appearance of the plastic, kidney-shaped ashtray next to the uncomfortable sofa to put an exclamation point on Trace's reaction to the room, catch the reader's attention, and twist the imagination.

The second point—the more important one and the easiest for a writer to learn—is the way both writers use the little detail to make the scene more vivid. How do they do it, and what can you do to master the techniques?

I know that you've seen at least one movie or television show in which there was a scene depicting a director at work. He stands off to the side and gazes at the set through a gizmo that he's wearing around his neck. That little instrument allows him to see the scene as the camera and, ultimately, the viewer, will. He can adjust for wide angle and close-up, and focus on particular items on the set. If that statue on the table is important for some reason or another, the director will make sure that it is prominently featured in the scene being shot. If it isn't important, it will just show up as part of the background.

Most of us don't have the director's viewfinder, but there are ways in which we do much the same thing, and to the same effect. Do you have a camera with a built-in zoom lens? You can use it the same way: look at a room through the viewfinder while the lens is set at wide-angle. This is the reader's general view of the setting. Major items of furniture are obvious; the little details in the room, however, the touches that personalize it, may not be. Now, zoom in, moving to telephoto. What do you see now? What stands out? A kidney-shaped plastic ashtray, maybe? The handle of a knife sticking out from under a stack of papers? Is that a bra strap peeking out from between the cushions of the sofa?

See what I mean? Any of those details can serve the purpose of your story. All it takes is seeing them in the same way as the reader will. The better you think you know a room (or a character), the more important it becomes for you to make certain that the reader does. It isn't fair to suddenly put something in place because the plot calls for it; everything has to be set up beforehand. (Of course, the sudden appearance of an object in a room can become a plot device, but that's another story.)

Not everyone has a camera, but the cardboard core of a roll of toilet paper or paper towel will work, too. You remember how, as kids, we used them to make believe we had telescopes? By looking through a tube with one eye we increase our ability to focus. And because our view is suddenly limited by the diameter of the hole, we begin, again, to see the little objects that make a difference.

Justin Scott, the bestselling author of *Shipkiller* and

other thrillers, suggests that when you go someplace new, immediately write down the first five things about the place that strike you. It has to be done immediately; going back later will not offer the same visual impact. Those five items, or however many you note, become the telling details when you use the place as a setting in your work.

A little story, one of those anecdotes we're told bring writing alive. In November 1991, I was with Jeremiah Healy and several other writers in a restaurant in Philadelphia. The place is in an old firehouse, located across the street from an abandoned state prison. I remember the location, the weather, and the bourbon-tasting bar. I also remember a wine dispenser at the back of the bar, built from what appeared to be part of an old still. Mostly, I remember the bourbon.

As we stood at the bar, waiting for our table, I looked over at Jerry and noticed that he was scribbling away like mad, making notes about the place—where things were located relative to each other, the type of crowd, where the fire pole was . . . all the details that would allow him to bring that room alive for you, including those that were particular to it, that made it the popular place it appeared to be. Because I didn't bother making notes, I could create a bar, but it wouldn't have quite the same vividness, it wouldn't be the same place. Also, Jerry can write off the tab as a business expense. Research.

Here's a room created by Tom Robbins in *Another Roadside Attraction* (Doubleday, 1971):

> The Pelican, in Bryte, California, is one of those taverns that function as a neighborhood social club. There is a coin-operated pool table of less-than-regulation size. There is a shuffleboard table that seems as much too long as the pool table seems too short: it looks like a landing strip. There is a bowling machine and two pinballs. There is a library of punchboards: Black Cat, Texas Charley, Lucky Dollar. There is a jukebox stuffed with country-and-western hits and the kind of tin pan alley la-

ments that sound poignant to the jilted and juiced. There are revolving wire Christmas trees laden with beef jerky and beer nuts; there are jars of boiled eggs and hot sausages and a larger jar in which pickles lounge like green Japanese in a bath. There is an animated plastic trout stream advertising Olympia beer ("It's the Water"). There is a friendly middle-aged couple behind the bar.

Usually, I wouldn't like this kind of narrative halt for the sake of description, but because of the nature of the novel itself—and the role of The Pelican in the story—it fits the structure perfectly. By the time I got to the end of the paragraph, each use of the word "there" was as if the author were pointing the objects out to me, rather than reading like an inventory. Notice the things Robbins has chosen to mention: we get the punchboards and the games and the food; he leaves the tables and stools to the reader to fill in. He's given us the important details, the things that make The Pelican The Pelican. The important stuff.

Here's my file card on a local cafe, a place that I'm going to have one of the characters visit during the course of "Virtual Reality":

line to get in. Register on left; on right, "reserved" table, 3 fat guys. counter with "european" pastries. smell of cigarette smoke and of coffee. tables too small, crowded with napkins, sugar, vase: no room for two cups and two plates. sit all night. outdoor seating in summer. no cappucino with ices in winter.

It offers me everything I need to bring that room to life for you. When Shaw enters, he'll offer the names of the pastries, perhaps will describe the smells, that mixture of coffee and cigarette that typifies certain settings. The too small table will be part of the story. Or, I think it will.

Description serves a function beyond giving your reader

a sense of place or time; it can be an important tool in developing character and in foreshadowing events. Take another look at the room Trace is sitting in, and another peek at Mrs. Collins through his eyes. Now factor in these details: Trace is an insurance investigator, and Mrs. Collins's husband is newly deceased. Maybe. Trace isn't particularly comfortable in that room; his attitude about the widow Collins may leave something to be desired. What's going to happen?

We already know that John Cuddy and the judge in the scene from *Blunt Darts* aren't going to get along, but by describing the courtroom and Kinnington as he does, Healy creates the groundwork for the tension that will follow.

•••

We've already talked a little about character description, but there are some things to think about here.

Just as a short scene taking place in a parking lot won't take a lot of description, a parking lot is a parking lot, unless there's something a) special about it and b) whatever that special item is plays a role in what's happening, a character simply passing through the story doesn't require a lot of attention or detail. Remember that while the little details are important in making someplace "real," too much detail in the place of action (any forward movement of the story) brings things to a halt. Many, if not most, of the manuscripts I receive are written by people who think that my knowing everything about everyone and every place is going to impress me, that their eye for detail somehow defines their abilities as writers.

It doesn't necessarily work that way. Look at this description from Harlan Ellison's award-winning story, "Soft Monkey," the development of a character not only through physical attributes, but through action:

> Annie lay huddled in the tiny space formed by
> the wedge of locked revolving door that was open
> to the street when the document copying service

had closed for the night. She had pulled the shopping cart from the Food Emporium at 1st Avenue near 57th into the mouth of the revolving door, had carefully tipped it onto its side, making certain her goods were jammed tightly in the cart, making certain nothing spilled into her sleeping space. She had pulled out half a dozen cardboard flats—broken-down sections of big Kotex cartons from the Food Emporium, the half dozen she had not sold to the junkman that afternoon—and she had fronted the shopping cart with two of them, making it appear the doorway was blocked by the management. She had wedged the others around the edges of the space, cutting the wind, and placed the two rotting sofa pillows behind and under her.

She had settled down, bundled in her three topcoats, the thick woolen merchant marine stocking cap rolled down to cover her ears, almost to the bridge of her broken nose. It wasn't bad in the doorway, quite cozy, really. The wind shrieked past and occasionally touched her, but mostly was deflected. She lay huddled in the tiny space, pulled out the filthy remnants of a stuffed baby doll, cradled it under her chin, and closed her eyes.

She slipped into a wary sleep. . . .

There's not a wasted word in the entire passage. Through her actions we *know* Annie. Physically, we may know only that she has a broken nose, but Ellison, in one word of dialogue several paragraphs later, tells us everything else we may need to know about the woman.

Annie develops quickly: we know she's a "bag lady," and that she lives in New York. We know that she's street smart, a survivor. We see her taking care of herself, get an idea of her psychology ("She slipped into a wary sleep. . . ."), and begin to feel a certain degree of sympathy for her.

What else is needed?

Dean Koontz, in his novel, *Strangers* (Putnam, 1986),

does much the same thing. The big difference is that Koontz is working within the framework of "full-length" fiction, not a story, so he has a bit more room in which to work. But the effect is the same:

> Ginger was intelligent, pretty, ambitious, hard-working, and an excellent cook, but her primary advantage in life was that no one took her seriously on first encounter. She was slender, a wisp, a graceful sprite who seemed as insubstantial as she was lovely. Most people underestimated her for weeks or months, only gradually realizing that she was a formidable competitor, colleague—or adversary.

Koontz then gives us some back story, a scene in which Ginger fights off a mugger, and after that we get some further description. What the author has done is break up what might otherwise be boring exposition by building the physical character slowly, leading up to each bit of description by bringing us along in the story. We aren't forced to stop in order to get to know the character; the familiarity develops because of the action. And, even more importantly, that description is in terms of what and who Ginger *is;* it is not description for the sake of giving the reader a sense of the physical woman, it is description for the sole purpose of letting us get to know the character. And that is exactly what you want to do.

Strangers is written in the third person; Jonathan Kellerman's bestseller, *When the Bough Breaks* (Atheneum, 1985), is a first-person novel. In the bit that follows, Dr. Alex Delaware, the protagonist, is interrupted by the arrival of Milo, a homicide detective and old friend:

> Milo is a big man—six-two, two-twenty—with a big man's way of going loose and dangly when he gets off his feet. This morning he looked like an oversized rag doll slumped against the cushions—a doll with a broad, pleasant face, almost boyish except for the acne pits that peppered the skin, and

the tired eyes. The eyes were startlingly green and rimmed with red, topped by shaggy dark brows and a Kennedy-esque shock of thick black hair. His nose was large and high-bridged, his lips fully, childishly soft. Sideburns five years out of date trailed down the scarred cheeks.

As usual he wore ersatz Brooks Brothers: olive-green gabardine suit, yellow button-down, mint and gold rep stripe tie, oxblood wingtips. The total effect was as preppy as W. C. Fields in red skivvies.

We're seeing Milo, an important character, through the narrator's eyes; we're not only getting Milo's physical reality, we're getting Delaware's impression of him, and that impression functions to develop *both* characters. Later in the scene, during the course of other interaction between the doctor and the cop, we get to see more of Milo, learning about his hands (when there's a reason to bring them into the story) and other defining characteristics.

None of the authors has stopped the story to introduce their character; the introduction is part of the story.

■ ■ ■

Everything we've looked at so far has been taken from "realistic" fiction and the problems we face as writers—making the real, real—is relatively simple. The terms we use, the items we describing are, if not a matter of common knowledge, at least known to most of our readers.

People who are writing sf and fantasy, however, have to first imagine the fantastic, and then describe it in such a way that someone unfamiliar with what they're portraying can see it.

Not surprisingly, the writers who are most successful in the field manage to do that on a daily basis. Personally, I find the task of imagining and creating elves and Klingons difficult enough; the thought of describing a Jabba the Hutt or E.T. or the homes in *The Martian Chronicles* is absolutely daunting.

The best way to learn the techniques is to read as wide a

variety of the available fiction as possible and study what it is the writers you enjoy are doing to bring their worlds to life.

Your readers are willing to meet you more than halfway, and they are already familiar with the terms that you'll be using; much of the literature is based on what has come before. (Isaac Asimov's Laws of Robotics, for instance, were for a long time the guideline for all robot/human interaction.)

I've seen writers successfully do nothing more than use the word "skimmer" in reference to a vehicle, and I knew what was meant; I supplied the details—the pinstriping, the wheel covers, all the tarting—and never felt cheated.

If you're thinking of pursuing a career in the fantastic, you've been immersed in the fiction for a while—or you should have been. But as a reader or a newcomer, there's a book that should be required reading for you. Hugo and Nebula Award-winner Orson Scott Card has written an excellent guide to the categories, *How To Write Science Fiction & Fantasy* (Writer's Digest Books), that you will find invaluable, and that will tell you far more about the techniques you'll need to know than I can.

■ ■ ■

There's a line I'll never forget, read in some otherwise forgotten novel:

> A black shirt, black pants, and black boots hugged a broad-shouldered body.

No, it wasn't a description of Johnny Cash. But whoever the character was, I'm still trying to visualize the boots hugging that broad-shouldered body. I'm certain the author saw something dramatic and striking in those thirteen words, and maybe some of the readers did, too. But if I'd been the editor . . .

One of the things you want to accomplish is making your work memorable, you want the editor to remember it and you don't want her to remember it because you've done something silly. Finding new ways to offer description so as to not slow or stop the flow of the story would do that.

When I was teaching the writing workshop for fifth- to eighth-graders, one of my assignments involved a trip to a supermarket. What the kids had to do was watch a customer and then create a character based on what they had observed. Some of them became quite good at the game: they were able to tell what a person would be buying, based on what they'd bought; they were able to tell stories about these people and make them come to life for other members of the class.

Your assignment is pretty much the same. Just as you make notes about the five things you see when you enter a building or room that impresses you, make notes about the things that make the people you see stand out. Rarely is it a common physical aspect (Don Westlake once described a character as having hair-colored hair, which pretty much says it all), that makes the difference; it is body language and/or posture, it is the way they move, the way their clothes fit and what they choose to wear and how they carry it off—Milo looking as preppy as W. C. Fields in skivvies. Maybe it's the way they smell; try the New York subways one summer evening. Whatever it is that makes you notice someone is the thing that you should use to describe your characters—those items are the keynotes. Everything else comes in when it's needed for the story's purposes.

You're writing about specific people doing certain things in a particular place. Give your reader what's needed to get there with you and the characters, but remember that a good cook generally has a delicate hand when it comes to the spices.

Chapter 13

::

"WHO SAID I SAID HE SAID?" SHE ASKED

Dialogue is the most potent tool in your writing arsenal. And like any weapon, its misuse will create disaster.

Dialogue is a way of getting things across to the reader without taking up pages of exposition and flashback, pages that slow the pace and take the reader away from the story. It is a way of updating the reader on the activities of characters who have been away from the story for a chapter or two. It is a way of developing character, adding flavor, breaking—or building—tension, foreshadowing, describing, and advancing your story.

And all you have to do is create some boring blocks of dialogue, and you can kiss your reader goodbye.

There are several aspects to the creation of dialogue; as an editor the thing I hate most is the "Said Book-ism."

In a kingdom long ago and far away (but neither long enough nor far enough) someone came up with the oh-so-clever idea of creating The Said Book. The concept was simple: writers shouldn't be limited to saying "said," "replied," or "asked"; there were all these wonderful alternatives available. Words like "pouted," "hissed," "mumbled," "sneered," "argued," and "observed," as well as hundreds of others, were listed. And dialogue has suffered ever since. Indeed, there is a "creative" writing teacher in the Philadelphia area who distributes a "said book" to her students.

Said is an "invisible" word; the reader takes no notice of it. (As often as not, it can be left out of a line entirely; after all, the fact that the line is in quotes implies that it was said.) The same can be said for *replied* and *asked.* But a word like *hissed* calls attention to itself, the description overwhelms the comment. And it is thoroughly inaccurate. A hiss is, according to my dictionary, "to make a sharp sibilant sound as to make the sound by which an animal indicates alarm, fear, or irritation" and, further, "a prolonged sibilant sound like that of the speech sound s or z." So, " 'Get out of here,' s/he hissed"—a sentence that shows up at least three times a week—just doesn't work. If what is being said contains a lot of esses and zees, you might be able to add "he hissed," but why would you want to?

A *pout* and a *sneer* are facial expressions, not manners of speech; but they, too, show up tagged to the ends of lines of dialogue. The easy way around the problem—rather than the sensible one, which is to avoid such uses entirely —is to end the quote with a period and make *he sneered* a sentence.

There's another dialogue-tagging habit that grates as badly: *"Get out of here," he said angrily,* is one example, *"There, there. Relax," she said soothingly,* is another. Just as poets have learned to avoid adverbs, it might be a lesson that prose writers take to heart, too.

There are some variations on this theme that are logically acceptable, but no less silly. In a manuscript by a writer with whom I will never again work, the following appeared: " 'Have a seat,' he invited." In my editing, I deleted *he invited*. Have a seat is an invitation, there's no reason to explicate it further. The author put a flag on the page when he was reading the copyedited manuscript, saying, "I want this stuff left in." This stuff falls between the two examples we've looked at.

When I've asked writers why they do any of these things, they tell me that it makes the writing more vivid, makes things clearer, makes the story more exciting. In other words, without these tags their writing is muddy and dull. Well, the tags don't help.

In context, the manner in which a line of dialogue is delivered should be clear from the statement itself; if it isn't, rewrite the sentence. The invitation to have a seat is clear enough, and the rhythm of the sentence is not improved by the addition of two words. The same author insisted on saving this line of deathless prose: " 'Oh, God,' she observed." Unless she were looking directly at God, well, it's not an observation. It might, under certain conditions, be an expression of dismay, discontent, or pain; in the novel in question, though, it was an exclamation of discovery. My author thought it was funny.

There are times when a word or two of description might be important, and a sparing use of dialogue tags is nothing to worry about. Still, there are other ways of going about it, ways that help your story rather than not. Here's an example from Healy's *Blunt Darts:*

> "Hitchhiking," said Val as she squeaked open the Styrofoam chest. "John, I'm sorry, but I'm starving. Can we start just a little bit early?" I didn't like her voice when it wheedled.

Healy didn't write, " '. . . a little bit early?' she wheedled." He added the tag as a reaction on the part of the listener, giving the reader not only the tone of speech, but involving Cuddy. He did something else I like, putting an action in the middle of the dialogue, preventing "talking head syndrome." People don't usually simply sit still and speak to each other; there are movements—conscious or not—that take place during a conversation. Using them cleverly in order to bring some life to what might otherwise be barren is highly recommended.

Dialogue dangers abound. All too often, every character "sounds" like every other one. They use the same speech patterns, the same diction, the same vocabulary. The writers' argument in favor of that is that all the people come from the same social class—they're all prep school students or all Valley Girls—and they do all speak that way. Even if that were so, and I think it is moot, the needs of fiction demand that characters be differentiated and it is only in their words as we read them—or in the description of their mannerisms—that the reader can see the differences.

In an attempt to make dialogue "real," writers will quote actual conversations and/or fill sentences with the kinds of verbal pauses that pepper our speech. It's real, no doubt about that, but it's also tedious. Most conversations that we have on a day-to-day basis are boring, at least to others. There's a certain redundancy to them because so many of them are simply the result of chance meetings or courtesy. You don't want to have your characters stop to say good morning to each other every time they pass in the hallway; the inquiries as to the health of someone's mother-in-law's Akita generally don't do anything to advance your story. (Unless the plot involves the poisoning of the dog. Or the mother-in-law.)

"And, uh, well, what I mean is, see, we were going to the store, uh, you know, over near the theater, and, uh . . ." Yes, there are people who speak that way. Almost all of us use verbal pauses as we try to gather our thoughts in an effort to avoid embarrassment by saying the wrong thing or to make certain that the point we want to make is clear. We fall into idiomatic habits—*you know* or *fr shure* or other briefly popular slang terms—dialect, or

other common speech faults. All of them are absolutely
real; reporting them is accurate. But the reality of fiction is
not everyday life and you cannot expect the reader to put
up with those mannerisms as a constant on the page.

When we listen to someone speak to us, we start blocking out the mannerisms, an unconscious act. When I come
across them on the page, I skip the paragraphs, a conscious blocking out of what bothers me. Moderation,
again, is the key. The first couple of times a character is in
front of the reader, you might want to slip one or two
phrases in; after that, the reader will begin to supply them
without any prompting. The "uhs" and "ahs" can be
added in narrative: *Slade seemed to pause before each word as
if searching for something to say, as if his life would end the
moment the sentence ended.*

Tied into that is the use of dialect and regional speech.
Seven paragraphs in a row attempting to recreate a Scot's
burr or a Cockney's dropped letters and slurred L's, or a
deep Mississippi drawl are going to leave the reader gasping for breath . . . and grabbing for another book.
Again, drop in a word or two for effect and have one of
the other characters comment on how difficult it was to
follow what so-and-so was saying, and your reader will fill
in the blanks.

Eavesdropping is important. I've been known to sit at a
party, blending in as much as possible with the walls, just
listening to what's going on. With a little practice, you can
listen in on two or three conversations at a time, focusing
on the one that has the more interesting dialogue. There
are lines that stick with me, that serve as the basis for
something that will come later, but most often I'm trying
to absorb the patterns and rhythms. These aren't just the
regional differences, though they play a role, but the nu-
ances and subtleties of the way people speak. It isn't only
in the words, it's in the rising and falling of a voice, in the
mannerisms—the facial and hand gestures—and in the
way emphasis falls.

I've already mentioned a line I was going to use someday: "They all look alike, don't they?" I haven't given

away the reference, what the "they" is, and I haven't given you any idea of the tone of voice in which the line was delivered. (Do your own research.) When I finally use that line—or one born of it—in a story, everything that was in the speaker's voice will be brought to the readers' attention, and that will serve my purpose in delineating the character. Dialogue isn't just words spoken; it's how they're spoken, taking us back to dialogue tags; by choosing words carefully and letting the characters *express* them —not simply *say* them—I should be able to bring my character to life.

How are you going to use your dialogue? What's its purpose in your work? Here's the opening of a novel we've looked at a couple of times, Jeremiah Healy's *Blunt Darts:*

> "Name?"
>
> "Cuddy, John Francis."
>
> "Address?"
>
> "74 Charles Street."
>
> "In Boston?"
>
> "In Boston."
>
> "Social Security number?"
>
> "040-93-7071."
>
> "Date of birth?"
>
> I told her.
>
> She looked up at me, squeezed out a smile. "You look younger."
>
> "It's a mark of my immaturity," I said. She made a sour face and returned to the form.
>
> "Occupation?"
>
> "Investigator."
>
> "Previous employer?"
>
> "Empire Insurance Company." I wondered whether Empire had to fill out a form that referred to me as "Previous Employee."
>
> "Reason for leaving previous employment?"
>
> "I have a letter." I took the letter from my inside coat pocket and handed it to her. Opening it and

reading it slowed her down. I looked around the big, clattering room at the thirty or so other metal desks. Each had a woman filling out a form and an applicant answering the same questions. Most of the applicants were men. I wondered why we applicants couldn't fill out at least the first few lines by ourselves.

The man seated at the desk next to me sneezed. Brittlely old and black, he looked as though he should have been applying for Social Security instead of unemployment. He wiped his nose with a clean handkerchief that had a hole in one corner. When he was finished he folded it so that the hole didn't show.

"Mr. Cuddy, if you'll pay attention to me, we'll finish this procedure much more quickly."

I turned my head to face her again. "That's all right," I said. "I've got time."

She fixed me with the sour look again and tapped her index finger on the paper before her. "This letter from your previous employer is beautifully drafted, Mr. Cuddy, probably by a company lawyer. It nicely provides every fact the regulations require. Accordingly, I have no choice but to recommend you for benefits. I must say, however, that seeing a man of your obvious abilities here instead of out in the world earning his way makes me sick."

"I didn't think you were looking too well. Would you like me to complete the rest of the form myself?"

"No!" she snapped. I thought I heard the man next to me stifle a chuckle. She and I operated as a much more efficient team after that.

"Education?"

"High School, then Holy Cross. One year of night law school."

"Military service?"

"Military police, discharged a captain in nineteen sixty-eight."

"Employer prior to Empire Insurance Company."

"Just the army."

She looked up at me again. "Do you mean you worked for Empire since nineteen sixty-eight?"

"Since nineteen sixty-nine. I traveled around the country for a while after the service."

She shook her head, and we completed the rest of the form. I signed it and got a brochure explaining my benefits and rights. I also received a little chit that entitled me to stand in a slow-moving line ten or twelve people deep in front of a window like a bank teller's.

In a couple of pages of dialogue, Healy has presented his character (this is Cuddy's first appearance) giving us an idea of his background—education, military service, employment record—as well as his attitudes, his outlook, everything we're likely to need to know. Narrating backstory would have taken longer, wouldn't have been as interesting, and wouldn't've let us know anything *about* Cuddy. We will learn more—why he was fired, for instance—in the next few pages. That, too, is told and supported through the use of dialogue.

You'll notice, too, that there was only one tag: " *'No!' she snapped,*" and that the dialogue is broken up with activities, with the kind of wandering attention that afflicts us all.

Is the scene "real"? It was for me; I had no problem at all suspending disbelief. I wish I'd read it before I got on the unemployment line.

One more thing to look at: all the white space. People speak in bursts; the only time someone delivers oral paragraphs is when they're addressing a group. If for some reason you find it necessary to engage in that kind of polemic during the course of your writing, break the talk with the kinds of little actions that would normally occur. Throw in a line about someone sneezing or the sound of chairs being pushed around, or anything else you can think of to get some movement into the scene.

If the conversation is taking place between two or three people, have one or another interrupt with a question or a heckle—anything to prevent unrelieved blocks of text-speech. It is no more interesting to read than it is to listen to.

And speaking of interruptions, there are two techniques you should be aware of and use.

An interruption during a conversation is indicated by an "em-dash":

"So there I was, ready to kiss her and—"

"Ah, c'mon, I heard this already."

You do not have to say, "he interrupted," "he jumped in," or "he cut in," or any of the other little tags. The em-dash followed by the new dialogue tells the reader everything she has to know.

A pause in speech is indicated by an ellipsis, with no other punctuation. If the pause is coming at the end of a sentence, it is indicated by an ellipsis and a period. Like so:

"He didn't want to hit me . . . it was an accident, really."

"He didn't want to hit me. . . ."

You can add something like, *her voice trailed off* or *He stopped to gather his thoughts* or a line like that if you think it's necessary. It should only be necessary once.

Here's an example of dialogue being used to set up a story. It's taken from *The Ham Reporter* by Robert J. Randisi (Doubleday, 1986). The novel is about Bat Masterson during his later days as a newspaper reporter in New York City. Masterson is in the Metropole Bar with Damon Runyon:

> Bat took Runyon's arm and led him to the bar, away from the smiling Considine. "Listen," he said, "do you have any money on you?"
>
> "Yes, why?"
>
> "No reason," Bat said, patting the younger man on the back. "It's just a good idea always to have

money on you. You never know when you'll run into an unexpected expense."

"Like a horse dying on the backstretch, you mean?" Runyon asked, grinning.

"Beer?" Bat asked him, ignoring the remark.

"That's fine."

Bat held up two fingers for the bartender to see, and the man nodded and brought over two mugs of beer. Bat looked around the place to see if he could spot any of his friends, but his crowd usually didn't show up at the Metropole until after dinner, and today was no different.

"So you really think there's a fix in the making?" Runyon asked after they had begun to slake their thirst.

"Shhh," Bat said, "not so loud, lad." He leaned close to Runyon and said, "There is the scent of one—actually, with Ufer being Morris's manager, I should say there's a definite stench!"

"Yes, but if there *is* a fix in the making," Runyon said in almost a whisper, "wouldn't Herman Rosenthal be involved, too?"

Runyon had been in New York only a few months, but already he knew enough to invoke Herman Rosenthal's name whenever something crooked popped up, especially if it involved gambling.

Bat wrinkled his nose and said, "Now we're moving onto words like 'stink'!"

"How are we going to find out for sure?" Runyon asked eagerly.

"We?"

"Well, now that we both know about it, we have to act on it, don't we?"

"Al," Bat said, one of the rare times he called the other man by his first name—his real first name. "We don't *know* a goddamned thing."

"We suspect—"

"*I* suspect," Bat corrected him before he could

173

go any farther. "And if I *do* decide to do anything about it, I'll do it alone."

Runyon, looking hurt and chagrined, replied, "I was only offering my help."

"I understand that," Bat said, putting his hand on the younger man's shoulder in a conciliatory gesture, "and I appreciate it, but when I act on my hunches, I usually act alone."

"I understand."

"Some of my hunches have been known to be dangerous," Bat added, trying to soften the blow of refusing the younger man's offer of assistance.

"I'm not afraid."

Runyon's attitude was cocky, and Bat studied the younger man closely for a few moments, remembering when he was that age—was he *ever*—and felt the same way about danger.

"You'll have to learn to be," he told Alfred Damon Runyon.

"What are you gonna do, Bat?"

"The more I think about it, the surer I get that I'm right." Bat looked into his glass and said, "I think I'm gonna let the polecat out of the bag."

We know what the heart of the story is going to be—although it gets far more complicated than simply dealing with a fixed fight—and begin to get a sense of the way Masterson is going to be portrayed. We also know that Runyon is probably going to wind up paying for the drinks he's having at the bar during the scene.

While this is all a bit wordy for my taste (once we get out of the dialogue and into the author's voice), Randisi manages to teach us a little bit (Runyon's first name), and in the passages just prior to the quoted exchange, gives us a sense of a turn-of-the-century New York watering hole and the people who go there.

We get a look at a younger Runyon—someone we know will eventually be responsible for *Guys and Dolls*—and so have some idea of the world we're going to be dealing with

in the story. And while Bat is "out of place"—my generation, anyway, will picture Gene Barry running around
Dodge when we hear the name—we know this is a man
who can take care of himself. By mentioning the danger,
we also know he'll have to do so.

The one scene, and the dialogues at the heart of it—
there were some other conversations not quoted here—
begin the readers' involvement in the action.

Randisi also avoids the temptation—at least in this early
scene—to duplicate speech patterns, although the characters don't speak in the "voice" of the author's more contemporary, hard-boiled creations. Randisi, in his westerns,
does write in a traditional Old West fashion; why it doesn't
appear here was a matter for the author and editor. But it
does bring us to our next point.

As mentioned earlier, there are writers who attempt to
re-create period, dialects, and speech patterns in their
work. Here are a couple of scenes, the first from Ruth
Beebe Hill's controversial bestseller, *Hanta Yo* (Doubleday,
1979) and the second from W. Michael and Kathleen
O'Neal Gear's *People of the Earth* (Tor, 1992), the third volume in their "prehistory" series.

>"My son goes out with horsecatchers, but will
>anyone in camp know that this party invites a
>young Mahto?"
>"My father, I take traveling moccasins. Will none
>advise you?"
>"I know about the moccasins and so I under-
>stand that you follow out after the warriors."

That's the first; here's the second:

>"Brave Man is going to be working on Sage
>Ghost. Dropping hints, seeking to gain favor. He's
>going to want to marry you."
>"I'll say no. Sage Ghost, even if his heart is bro-
>ken, won't make me marry a man I don't want."
>Wind Runner frowned at the horizon. "You're

going to have to marry someday. The White Clay are running out of choices for you."

She laughed, flashing a smile at him. "There's only one man among the White Clay I'd want to marry."

Lowering his voice, he told her, "We've had that discussion before. You're my uncle's daughter. Among the White Clay—"

"—it's incest, I know. But I'm not your sister, no matter that your people call first cousins that."

Which sound would you rather hear over three or four hundred pages? My choice is the second. And, as long as the author is careful to avoid anachronisms, there's absolutely nothing wrong with it. The White Clay, in the second example (and the Dakotah Sioux in the first), when they speak their own languages, speak as colloquially as we do, as idiomatically. Their speech, rendered into English, would read *as English*. There's no reason, then, to force unnatural inflections into the conversations of your characters in historical fiction.

Generally. If you're writing American historicals, the Indian characters—raised speaking their native tongues—would probably not speak English with the same fluency as your whites. By the same token, a Frenchman or German or Pole—or any of the other nationalities that came to help settle the country—would not speak English as comfortably, either.

In fantasy fiction, by tradition, characters often speak a more courtly form of English. It is not mandatory, but it is widely accepted. And it can be used for effect—having one character speak in those cadences or using it occasionally throughout.

Even Arthurian fantasy, based on some of the most courtly tales of western European culture, does not have to read as if it were written by Malory. Here's an example from an Arthurian bestseller, Mary Stewart's *The Crystal Cave* (Morrow, 1970):

"Whist ye now, child! How do you know all this?
I'll be bound your elders don't talk of these high
matters in front of you? If it's Moravik who talks
when she shouldn't—"

"No. Not Moravik. But I know it's true."

"How in the Thunderer's name do you know
any such thing? Slave's gossip?"

I fed the last bite of my bread to the mare. "If
you swear by heathen gods, Cerdic, it's you who'll
be in trouble, with Moravik."

Stewart mixes a mild historical voice—the Thunderer,
swearing by heathen gods—with a very normal, comfortably idiomatic sound to produce something that's easy to
read. And that's what you want: something easy to read,
something that doesn't jar the reader back into the reality
of having to get the taxes done.

Anything that isn't "normal" in the mind of your reader
causes problems for you. And for your editor. Sustaining a
special voice, re-creating a dialect in such a way that a
reader both understands it and is willing to stick with it,
are very special skills. If you have that talent, exploit it,
but if anything about it strikes you as false, you can drop
the attempt without having your work suffer. If you have
to have people speaking funny in order to convince your
reader of a time and place, your manuscript has other
problems that you should examine right away.

Most fiction doesn't need anything but everyday speech.
That's the kind that uses contractions, that uses an occasional regionalism (and there's even a dictionary of regional English to help you research that area), but that still
falls easily on the ear. Listen to the people around you
speak. Pay attention to what they say and how they say it,
because they're also the people who are going to be reading your book.

The bottom line is this: If your reader doesn't want to
listen to your characters speak, anything they have to say
will be lost.

....

Chapter 14

WHAT THE POET SAID (and why he was wrong)

Poetry teachers are fond of saying that poets pay attention to words, to their rhythm, their sound; that poets use devices like rhyme and alliteration to make what they do special. "Otherwise," as the late Judson Jerome once put it in his column in *Writer's Digest,* "we might as well be writing prose."

Right.

I didn't bother writing a letter to the editor then, and I didn't bother when the person who took over his column said much the same thing later. One of life's little missed opportunities. But I'm not going to miss the opportunity to discuss the matter with you. Because Jerome was wrong and any poetry teacher who says anything that sounds anything at all like that is wrong, too.

I was talking to a brand-spanking-new editorial assistant recently about what makes a manuscript work for me. The discussion started when I told him to make a submission go away.

"What's wrong with it?"

A fair question. "It doesn't work for me, it just doesn't 'read'." Have you ever tried to describe a principle to someone who doesn't have any idea of what you're talking about? That's how I felt.

So we looked at the manuscript. It was flat. Everything necessary to the category (in this case a woman-in-jeopardy novel) was there: the characters were correct, the situation suitable to the genre. But the words were just words. The descriptions lacked detail and vitality. The dialogue fell like lead from the tongue. There was no *sound* to anything on the page.

I guess the writer thought that only poets had to pay attention to the words, to the way they went together, to how they sounded when said aloud. Maybe he believed Judson Jerome.

Good prose, however, fiction or nonfiction, always shows the writer's understanding of the language. (It's one of the reasons, I think, that translators should be paid more. They have to take something written with that kind of attention, but in a different language, and bring it into English while retaining that feeling but not changing meaning or sense. It's also the reason that so many translations read like translations.)

Words have meaning beyond what the dictionary says they mean; they carry a weight and baggage of their own derived from usage, which can vary from place to place. As a writer, you have to be aware of these senses. (One of the factors that goes into defining a psychopathic personality is the person's inability—or refusal—to recognize the meaning of words.)

These differences can be as blatant as a Londoner calling the subway the underground while calling a passageway underground a subway, while New Yorkers call their rapid transit system a farce, uh, subway. "El," once popular because so many of the lines were elevated, has fallen into disuse, even where there is an elevated line; in Chicago, they still use the expression.

What do you call a sandwich prepared on Italian bread? In New York, it's a hero. In other places it might be a sub, submarine, or grinder.

Those are very simple examples, the kind that might reveal poor research.

But what does the word "mad" mean to you? Do you use it as a synonym for "angry?" And by doing that, do you lose the more powerful meaning of the word? And what about "gay?" Unless you're writing Regency romances, having a character go to a gay party carries an entirely different weight. Frankly, I resent losing the word; "jolly" and "swell" just don't hack it. And what about "hack" in that context?

Language is vital (as in living, not as in necessary); therefore, it mutates. The changes it undergoes are important: if something is static, it is either dead or dying. We have a responsibility to the language then; to be aware of what words mean not only in the dictionary, but in the minds of our readers.

■ ■ ■

Here's an unfair challenge. Take a few minutes to think about it and then write a description of an intersection in a town or city that marks a change in neighborhood, a sociological tectonic plate. After you've written that one, jot down a paragraph about a late-night phone call. And having done that . . .

■ ■ ■

David Bradley (if you're one of those readers who reads every word, you'll remember that he's one of the two people to whom I've dedicated this book) is a writer who puts the lie to Jerome's statement that prose doesn't pay attention to words. Here's the opening paragraph of Bradley's *South Street* (Grossman, 1975):

> The street lay like a snake sleeping; dull-dusty, gray-black in the dingy darkness. At the three-way intersection of Twenty-second Street, Grays Ferry Avenue, and South Street a fountain, erected once-upon-a-year by a ladies' guild in fond remembrance of some dear departed altruist, stood cracked and dry, full of dead leaves and cigarette butts and bent beer cans, forgotten by the city and the ladies' guild, functionless, except as a minor memorial to how They Won't Take Care Of Nice Things. On one side of South Street a chain food market displayed neat packages of precooked food sequestered behind thick plate glass—a nose-thumbing temptation to the undernourished. On the other side of South Street the State Liquor Store showed back-lit bottles to tantalizing advantage and proclaimed, on a sign pasted to the inside of the window, just behind the heavy wire screening, that state lottery tickets were on sale, and that you had to play to win.

Now that you've read the paragraph, read it again. Aloud. There's alliteration there, and rhythm and word play (the unremembered memorial). The food is "sequestered," not just displayed or stored. The bottles, "back-lit" show to "tantalizing advantage."

The language resonates, the sounds the words make by themselves and together, echo in the mind and in the imagination. That's what a writer does, and it matters not whether that writer is a poet or a novelist.

South Street, by the way, is a first novel.

Here's the opening paragraph of Bradley's second novel, the PEN-Faulkner Award-winning *The Chaneysville Incident* (Harper & Row, 1981):

Sometimes you can hear the wire, hear it reaching out across the miles; whining with its own weight, crying from the cold, panting at the distance, humming with the phantom sounds of someone else's conversation. You cannot always hear it—only sometimes; when the night is deep and the room is dark and the sound of the phone's ringing has come slicing through uneasy sleep; when you are lying there, shivering, with the cold plastic of the receiver pressed tight against your ear. Then, as the rasping of your breathing fades and the hammering of your heartbeat slows, you can hear the wire: whining, crying, panting, humming, moaning like a live thing.

Again, Bradley uses all the devices language makes possible, combining words and sounds and meanings: "Whining with its own weight," "crying from the cold," "humming with the phantom sounds." There's resonance there.

But what struck me about that paragraph first was the use of the word "whining." Writers are fond of talking about the wires humming, the wires singing—all positive, upbeat images. But whining and crying are negatives, are the words that bring the fear of the late-night phone call with them; that hint of problems, of difficulties sooner ignored or, at least, left until morning. Again, reading the paragraph aloud is instructive.

There isn't one word in either of the quoted paragraphs that an average, adult reader would have to research in a dictionary; there's no pretension, no showing off. There's nothing standing between the reader and understanding.

Harlan Ellison's fiction offers hundreds of examples of using language—rather than just words—to affect the reader. Here's a brief passage from his story, "Paladin of the Lost Hour":

". . . When I go, that's the end of Minna. She'll be well and truly dead. We never had any children, almost everyone who knew us is gone, no relatives.

And we never did anything important that anyone would put in a record book, so that's the end of us. For me, I don't mind; but I wish there was someone who knew about Minna . . . she was a remarkable person."

So Billy said, "Tell me. I'll remember for you."

Memories in no particular order. Some as strong as ropes that could pull the ocean ashore. Some that shimmered and swayed in the faintest breeze like spiderwebs. The entire person, all the little movements, that dimple that appeared when she was amused at something foolish he had said. Their youth together, their love, the procession of their days toward middle age. The small cheers and the pain of dreams never realized. So much about him, as he spoke of her. His voice soft and warm and filled with a longing so deep and true that he had to stop frequently because the words broke and would not come out till he had thought away some of the passion. He thought of her and was glad. He had gathered her together, all her dowry of love and taking care of him, her clothes and the way she wore them, her favorite knick-knacks, a few clever remarks: and he packed it all up and delivered it to a new repository.

The very old man gave Minna to Billy Kinetta for safekeeping.

Any questions?

• • •

Choosing the right word can come in simpler modes. In *The Dark Fantastic* (Mysterious Press, 1983), Stanley Ellin writes:

"You think I could get to sleep after what you said? After what happened?"

Cotton-pickin' or midtown, that was quite a

voice. Milano sat down in his number one armchair, pulled off his shoes, and settled back the better to enjoy it. "Said what?" he asked. "And what
did happen?"

"That whole business about Lorena you didn't
finish telling me. Meaning that because I didn't
drag you right into the house, you got pissed off
and ran."

That was accurate enough to bruise . . .

Not "to hurt," not "to cut"; the comment was accurate
enough to "bruise," and the phrase is accurate enough to
stay with the reader long after the book is finished.

The Black Moon (Lynx, 1989) is a novel made up of sections written by five mystery writers. In his contribution,
"Dark Flight," Ed Gorman has his detective paying a visit
to a wealthy neighborhood:

. The names are beautiful, Indian Hill Road,
White Eagle Road, and High Stable Road, and so
are the homes that are hidden in the deep woods
on either side: clapboard, cedar, and red brick
glimpsed through the budding trees and heavy
green foliage. When you live near the downtown
area, the lives lived out here are almost unimagin-
able. You wonder what it's like to go for a sunny
morning walk when the grass is golden with dawn
sunlight and the mint leaves heavy with moisture.
You wonder what it's like to get into your Mercedes
and go to work. You wonder what it's like to un-
thinkingly hand over your American Express Gold
for whatever whim strikes you. Of course, this was
also the kind of neighborhood paperboys like to tell
stories about—at least the poor ones do—how
there are two Caddies in the driveway but never
enough cash to pay their paper bill.

I went up the three broad steps to the fine red
door and knocked. In the silence, the knock
sounded rude.

Not "loud," not any of a dozen other possibilities: the knock sounded "rude."

Using the right words is what writing is about. Using the right words, the words that bring images to mind—and keep them there—is what separates flat writing, the commonplace, from writing that impresses itself into memory, that makes an editor decide that the book must be acquired, that makes the reader haunt bookstores looking for the next book.

Words creating images; metaphor, simile, symbolism: tools—of the poets—and of storytellers whose work we go back to again and again.

■ ■ ■

Compare these sentences:

The table was against the wall.
The table was pushed against the wall.
The table was bare, except for a vase of flowers.
The table was bare, except for a vase of mixed wildflowers.
The table was bare, except for a vase of roses, red and white and yellow.
There was a bowl with some pieces of cereal floating forlornly in the milk.
There was a bowl with a few Cheerios floating in the souring milk.

A table against a wall is simply there; by describing it as having been "pushed" into position, you've added some past action; the reader sees someone putting the table where you want it.

A vase with flowers is ambiguous (which may be your intent); wildflowers give the reader one sense, the roses another.

Look at how the description of the bowl of cereal changes when you delete forlornly; consider how the impression changes when you describe the milk as "souring," how an idea of time and climate becomes part of the scene without requiring anything else.

■ ■ ■

The words in your fiction are all you have to work with. You aren't there to explain what you mean; the reader has only what you said, and if you what say isn't clear, if all the meanings—those on the surface derived directly from the definitions of the word you've used and those in the subtext derived from the subtle shadings of the combinations of words and their particular weight and meaning in the consciousness—aren't discerned, aren't sensed, if your words are just words and do not carry the reader on through the pages and into your future as a writer, if you are only telling us your story and not showing us the events because your words are ill-chosen, then there's nothing on the page.

Your writing will be flat, without dimension.

And you'll have proven the poets, already proven wrong, right.

Chapter 15

SHOW ME A STORY

We talk about "telling a story," but what we want, when it comes time to read, is for the author to show us the story —or at least as much of it as possible.

Storytellers—those folks who are out there these days at fairs and libraries and concert halls and who stand in front of an audience and regale them with tales—have facial expressions and the tones in their voice to help them. Writers have only the language and what they can do with it.

That brings us back for a moment to all the dialogue tags we were looking at before. Does saying, "he said angrily" show the reader anything? No, it simply *tells* the reader something. Readers are, we hope, working with us, meeting us halfway, accepting the premises we establish. We owe them the courtesy of making things as vivid as possible.

So: Rather than writing that *Ellen got angry and walked out of the room,* which not only isolates the characters but the reader, we try to do it this way: *Ellen's hand shook as she stormed out of the room, slamming the door behind her.* Ellen is now involved in the scene and so is the reader. We see Ellen, her reactions.

The point of view can be altered to meet the story's needs. If you're working in the first person, the narrator can say *I watched Ellen . . .* or amplify it further: *Ellen's hand shook as she stormed out of the room, slamming the door. I shivered in the sudden chill.* In a third-person narrative, another character in the room might react in the same way, shuddering, shivering, or shrugging away Ellen's anger.

However you choose to do it, the idea is to manipulate the readers' senses so that they are in the room with the characters. Let's try another simple scene, something that appears in one way or another in many novels. A character is being awakened by an alarm clock. It's easy enough: *Travis awoke to the sound of the alarm clock buzzing in his ear.* "Buzzing" brings something extra; maybe a bug hovering over Travis's head. But it doesn't do much beyond that. And it may not have to, if all you need to do is have the character wake up. (And if that's the case, we don't really need the alarm at all.) But let's assume that you're writing a horror novel like *Raw Pain Max* by Dean Andersson (Popular Library, 1988). Atmosphere is important to you. So you write it this way:

> The ripsaw buzz of a digital alarm clock chewed up the dream and jarred Trudy McAllen awake.

Another narrative situation. You have to establish a character's isolation and the vastness of the place in which he finds himself. All too often, what I see in manuscripts is: *Blake was alone in the middle of nowhere. There was nothing but sand and scrub in every direction, for as far as the eye could see.* Maybe Blake's eye. But I'm not seeing very much at all. Here's how John Byrne Cooke handles a similar scene in his Spur Award-winning novel, *The Snowblind Moon* (Simon and Schuster, 1984):

Here the countryside was broken, unfinished, as if God had deemed it unworthy of any further effort. To the south and west a range of mountains cloaked blue-black in evergreens rose into the gray clouds that stretched flat and featureless in all directions, but near at hand the land was unclothed. What few stalks of grass there were had clustered together for comfort, and the landscape was devoid of trees except for a few stunted specimens on the low buttes and a ribbon of tall cottonwoods hidden down in the bottomland of the North Platte, which hereabouts flowed in a shallow canyon a half mile off to Whitcomb's right. Even the brownish-yellow soil that served as the earth's poor flesh in these regions was insufficient, for on every slope and low summit the rocks—the bones of the planet— showed through.

The alien surrounds heightened Whitcomb's sense of loneliness. Overhead the twin strands of telegraph wire picked up the hum of the wind and he wondered if they were also carrying other messages, more comforting and friendly. He had only to follow the wires to reach Fort Fetterman, for they ended there, but as he topped each rise he saw only the telegraph poles marching onward and no glimpse of the fort. For a day and a half he had seen no living soul and had not company save for his horse, and so when he spied another rider approaching the wagon road from his left flank he greeted the sight with a surge of profound gratitude.

Cooke had something more to work with than simple sand and scrub, but he used every piece of that landscape, and then some. He gave the eye a place for the line of telegraph poles to end, and then took that place away; the reader, then, experiences the distances in the same way as Whitcomb. He doesn't just tell us how isolated Whitcomb is; he shows it to us by setting us down in the middle of the land he's describing.

Visual and aural cues work, but the sense of smell is one of the strongest memory triggers we have, and just calling scents to mind can create pictures that will allow readers to gain immediate access to the place we're hoping to take them. I could say that a character was entering a public school building. You'd have a particular image, depending on where you went to school. I might add that the building was built like an old castle or an urban armory. That would bring other details to mind. And then I'd say that it smelled of old hot lunches, wet wool coats, and dusty books; that I could taste the chalk dust, and that the stairwell I was in was dark as the afternoon sun fought a losing battle with the dirty windows. I'm showing you the building, involving your senses (I could add things about the echoing footsteps on the concrete floors as well, and add the echo of an English teacher parsing sentences. But that last would reveal my age.)

By involving the narrator (*I could taste the chalk dust*), by letting you know what she feels, by personalizing and letting you sense the place, or the person or the emotion— whatever it is we're dealing with can be handled in the same way, I transcend telling and move into showing.

It's exactly the same thing with character descriptions. Rather than cataloguing physical attributes, make them come to life. Instead of saying that Ellen had long red hair, give us Ellen moving, the ends of her red hair brushing her shoulders as she walks. If you want to let the reader know that a character was tall, have him duck as he walks under a tree branch. Don't just mention freckles, have a character think about playing connect-the-dots on his face.

It isn't going to be possible to "show" everything, nor is it necessary. There will be sections of narrative to which the technique doesn't lend itself, there'll be scenes and passages that have to be kept trim in order to keep the pacing. But even then, the judicious use of metaphor and simile, the intelligent use of language—all the things we've been considering as we looked at the creation of characters and the description of settings, all the elements that go into "poetry"—are tools that you want to use in every aspect of your storytelling.

And story showing.

Chapter 16

THE THIRD
SIDE ROAD

Writing For the Fun of It

We've been spending a lot of time looking at rules: do this, don't do that; write this way, don't say things that way; add this, delete that. Rules. Instructions. Suggestions. And if you sit down to write and try to keep all those things in mind, you're going to find yourself spending far too much time staring blankly. The suggestions—and that's what they are, suggestions based on what I've found to be most successful over the last thirty years—are meant as guides. They are not supposed to stifle you or get in the way of the creative process.

Whatever it is you're writing is an expression of your particular vision as it is applied to the category or tradition in which you want to write. Whatever it is you're writing reflects your style, and style is, first, last, and always, an individual thing. It is you: the way you think, the way you see things, the way you express yourself. William Safire defines it perfectly in *Language Maven Strikes Again* (Doubleday, 1990):

> You want to fix up your writing, parse your sentences, use the right words? Fine, pick up the little books, learn to avoid mistakes, revere taut prose and revile tautology. But do not flatter yourself that you have significantly changed your style. First, straighten out yourself so that you can then think straight and soon afterward write straight. Your writing style is yourself in the process of thinking and and the act of writing, and you cannot buy that in a bookstore or fix it up in a seminar.

Style is the way we think and use words, the way in which we express ourselves. The only rules are the ones we set, the ones we, as writers, can live with. Magazines have "style"—compare something in *The New Yorker* with a like piece in, say, *National Geographic*—and writers have styles. Compare any two whose stories stay with you.

You can develop an approach to writing that allows you to mimic the work of Elmore Leonard or Raymond Chandler or Stephen King or Dean Koontz or Rosemary Rogers or Danielle Steel or any successful writer you think you want to copy. What you write has nothing to do with you, though, and it usually won't be as good as the original, and who needs it anyway? Publishers don't: they may want the kind of story a certain writer produces, but they don't want the work to read like a rip-off.

Following guidelines does not mean giving up your style, though it may mean sacrificing a bit of your creativity. That's the choice you make, the decision you confront when you decide that you're going to be . . . whatever it is you've decided to be. You can, however, write in a category—or out of it for that matter—and sell what you've written, even if you don't follow the rules. It may be more difficult. It may be frustrating. It may take you longer. But if your writing itself is any good, if you can weave a tale, you will sell.

When we—as writers, as critics, as editors—insist that things be done in a particular way, we are doing all writers and all readers a gross disservice. While it is true that those who don't study history are condemned to repeat it, by insisting on formulas and rules, we're stopping creativity dead in its tracks. Yesterday's writing is just that. All anyone has is the present. The past is gone; the future conjecture. We must allow the *now* to exist so that the future may become.

"Wisdom," said Maimonides, "is the consciousness of self." (Which seems to be a lot like what Safire said about style.) The self, like the world, is in a constant state of Becoming, of change. Writing comes from the ever-changing self, from our ever new knowledge of the universe which is also always Becoming.

Writing worth reading does not come from repeating the formula or the accomplishments of the past. The contemporary author is not in competition with yesterday, he is creating his own benchmark. Otherwise, that writer and his work is not Becoming and is out of phase with the universe. It is the writer of whom we ask, "What are we to make of this," the writer who bothers us because we don't understand what is happening in the work, the writer who breaks the envelope, who should be searched out. He is the writer who knows the sound of one hand clapping . . . and tries to lead us to it.

The kind of writer you should want to be.

Here's how to go about it:

Don't worry about failing, don't worry about being wrong. Enjoy what you're doing for the sake of doing it; create bandwagons, don't jump on them. Write from who you are and let the rest of the world catch up to you.

Write because you love it and because you want to touch people with what you have to say.

Don't worry about the critics; write so that your words are read by people who need to hear what you have to say.

Write what you want to write and in the ways that you're most comfortable doing it. Don't write romances because everyone is telling you that they sell; don't stop writing hardboiled p.i. fiction because those same people are telling you that it doesn't sell. The people may be right, but that doesn't make the information right for you.

Write what you want to write because you want to get the charge that writing gives, that the act of creativity itself creates. When the writing is going well, it keeps on going.

You are writing today. That's all you have. Be aware of trends, and the fact that trends sometimes don't pan out. Be aware of trends and history, and write what *you* can write, what makes a difference to you.

And when you're done writing, when all the words are on the page, then look at them closely, examine each one and decide if it is the word that belongs there.

Is what you've written mathematically elegant, is everything that is supposed to be there in place, and has anything that doesn't belong been removed?

Is what you've written better than what you wrote yesterday? Is there growth?

Is there honesty?

Is there you?

■ ■ ■

And now that we've established why you should be who you are, it's time to consider being all you can be. And that means looking at other things that might be of interest to you.

There is going to come a time when you look at what you're writing, and you're going to ask, "Is that all there is?" After a while, doing the same thing again and again becomes wearing, if not downright boring, and you're going to have to do something to refresh yourself, to get the gears meshing again.

Some writers turn to other categories—lots of mystery writers pen westerns, lots of horror writers turn to the straightforward mystery—genres they've enjoyed and understand, but don't want to concentrate on for one reason or another.

In other instances, novelists try their hand at the short story, a different mind set. There's a saying that novelists are failed short story writers and short story writers are failed poets. Philosophically, there may be something to it, but it isn't a thesis I'd want to support. Still others turn to nonfiction. One bestselling mystery writer does screenplays (and has created a couple of successful TV series), travel articles, and does comic material for at least one major star.

The options are as varied as your interests; just take a look at the table of contents of the *1992 Writer's Market*. Every industry has its trade journals, every ethnic and cultural group its special-interest magazine, every hobby its publications. Looking through the lists of available markets is a mindboggling experience; it's hard to believe that there are so many different markets available at a time when writers are complaining that they can't find anyplace to sell their work—and that includes fiction of *every* kind.

Bill Brohaugh, the former editor of *Writer's Digest* magazine and now editor of their book publishing operation, has a flair for comedy. (At least he keeps telling me that he does.) And I guess he's proven it: he writes *shtick* for a drive-time dj. It keeps him fresh, gives him an opportunity to try out material that will probably find its way into one of the mystery novels he's outlining. And it makes money.

Turning to one of the other markets also allows you to regroup after finishing a major project, to clear your head and relax a little after the effort of maintaining the reality of your fiction for so long.

To give you an idea of just how important professional writers consider this, in issue #44 of *The Gila Queen's Guide to Markets* (a magazine I suggested that you look into earlier), the publisher and editor, Kathy Ptacek, who has a successful horror and suspense career going, offers a free subscription to the magazine to anyone who submits material to six featured markets in six issues. (The offer has expired, unless it's been reinstated.) That doesn't mean that you can submit the same mystery story to six different magazines; it means that you have to write six completely different pieces—different categories—and send them to six diverse markets. What Kathy wants you to do is write a mystery story for *Ellery Queen's Mystery Magazine* (so does its editor, Janet Hutchings), send a poem to *Cricket,* a humor piece to *Reader's Digest,* and so on.

Kathy's reasoning is simple and right on: "Writers should not stick to just one area or genre. Genres rise and fall with the times. So try your hand at something different—look into another genre, look into nonfiction (it pays *very* well), look into a different sort of market, say, greeting cards. Why? Because they're there, that's why."

You may discover something about yourself at the same time. In a universe that is always changing, it is more important to study that change, to understand that even with a map we are still traveling in a terra incognita, to encourage the change and visualize the next one, than it is to rehash that which has been done. It is more urgent to soar with the eagle and see the entirety rather than walk with the mouse, knowing nothing beyond the reach of its whiskers.

In other words, go for it.

The very worst thing that's going to happen is that you won't sell whatever it is you've just completed. That's happened to you before and it's going to happen to you again. But in the course of acquiring the experience you're going to learn something—there's no telling what it's going to be, but it *will be*—as long as you recognize that when your mind is empty it's ready for anything, open to everything. Beginners are filled with possibilities; experts have few. The good writer is a beginner, mind open, constantly ab-

sorbing. He is not searching consciously; rather, the subconscious is filing everything.

And when you touch the subconscious—as we will later
—those files are ready for you.

All of the you's that are you.

Chapter 17

REVISION AS A
FACT OF LIFE

I'm sure that you've noticed by now that this business is filled with stuff that "they" said. Things like, "Writing is sitting down and staring at the paper until blood pops out on your forehead." And, "Writing is the loneliest profession." And, of course, "Writing is revision."

Actually, "they" don't have it exactly right. Writing is writing, and revision is a very important part of the process. That's why I spent some time earlier discussing how to work at a computer; young writers are revising as they're writing, and that means that they forget to revise when they're done. Which is when they're supposed to be doing it in the first place.

And how do you go about revising? Well, this is what works for me, a variation on a theme. With the exception of one step, which I do use occasionally, it is exactly the same way I edit your manuscript when it arrives on my desk, ready to go. That step is reading. Out loud. Not moving your lips, not mumbling, but actually declaiming. It's funny how often we discover that what we've written just doesn't sound right when it's echoing around a room. Here's an example of what I'm talking about:

> Coming out of the women's side of the locker building, Val's legs looked a little thicker than they had in the other outfits I'd seen her wear to date.

That's from a writer—and a book—we've looked at before, *Blunt Darts* by Jeremiah Healy. Read it aloud. Are you struck, as I was, by the fact that Val's legs may have looked a little thicker, but the rest of Val seems to have disappeared? Val's legs are walking out, but where was *she?*

It's a little thing, and it doesn't seriously detract from the novel. But it's something that probably shouldn't be there. And if I'd been the editor, it wouldn't have been. ~~(Unless I missed it.)~~

You saw that, didn't you? The way those words in the parentheses were crossed out? Feel free to do that to your words, especially those that don't belong. Because if you don't, I'll have to.

Revision is the act of ~~rather~~ ruthlessly striking everything that doesn't belong. ~~The reason~~ it doesn't belong ~~is~~ because it represents ~~wretched~~ excess, ~~just~~ doesn't sound quite right, is an error, or, well, because you don't like it. Like that. Of course, I've just been sitting here having fun, putting in words and taking them out. Unfortunately, most manuscripts have problems like that, and you want to get rid of as many of them as possible before you submit your work. Not all of them, necessarily, because you'll find yourself worrying the manuscript to death and will never get around to getting it into the mail.

Here's an example of what can arrive on an editor's desk. First, the background. The manuscript is for a novel titled *The February Trouble,* the second David Garrett novel by Neil Albert, whose first, *The January Corpse,* was nominated for the PWA's Shamus Award as Best First Novel. When it was first submitted, there was a problem with one scene. Garrett was in the home of Bruce Chadwick, who'd hired him to investigate some threats against his new business. After a breakfast meeting with Chadwick and one of his partners, Garrett excuses himself to go to the bathroom (something characters rarely did back when I began in this business). The scene sets up a meeting between the detective and Chadwick's wife.

As it was originally written, however, it went on too long and pointlessly. So, I suggested to Albert that he cut it, and he did just that. However, some of the things established in the original version were now missing and the author didn't reread the entire scene when he printed it out for the final draft. After further revision, the passages look like this. (Words struck through are deleted; lines in italics are being added):

"Hi. I'm Dave Garrett, ~~the investigator~~."

She extended her hand; the nails were perfectly groomed and painted. "Nice to meet you —can I call you Dave? ~~Call me Anne. Everyone does.~~ *I'm Anne Chadwick. You're the investigator.*" *It wasn't a question.*

"Pleased to meet you, Anne."

She was a good deal shorter than Chadwick; and younger, too. Or perhaps she'd had a

facelift; Lord knows they seemed to have the
money for it. ~~"We were just running over to
the restaurant," I explained. "I need to see
what's been happening."~~

We started by deleting "the investigator" because it's meaningless. What kind of investigator? He could be from the Better Business Bureau for all this woman knows. And since Garrett doesn't know who she is—she might very well be another employee rather than his employer's wife —the introduction struck me as being just a tad arrogant.

Anne's comment, "Can I call you Dave?" begins to place her: she's a woman who's in charge, something confirmed by her now acknowledging Garrett's role in the household —she knows he's the "investigator."

Garrett's final line in the exchange, referring to what he was about to do, also seemed beside the point. The fact is mentioned several paragraphs later and, because the lines immediately following the excerpt are: "You must have just come in. Have you been here long? I know Bruce was expecting you," Garrett's comment is a non sequitur.

The errors appeared in the manuscript because of carelessness created by haste (and, too, because the author was working on a computer, editing on it, and not reading hard copy). That made them an obvious choice as an example here. But revision isn't always that easy.

Here are some of the pages from the story I've been working on, "Virtual Reality." Keep in mind that the story is still being written. Words that have been struck through are either deleted or changed in the second draft, and again the italicized words are additions or replacements:

Kara wept. She stood looking out *over the city*,
eyes blank and unfocused while ~~the~~

New York

~~city~~ /sparkled below her, and wept. Without
spasm or tear, she wept.

She looked up, ~~now~~ violet eyes focused now on
the full moon. She saw, regarded, disregarded, the halo of ice crystals and pulled the
glow around herself. Her hair,. *honey flowing
down to* bleached silver, ~~flowing down to its natural honey,~~ turned pewter. Humming; then
quietly whispering her name to herself. She
smiled, liking the small acid tingle of it. ~~Kara,
with rolled French "r" or sing "cara mia."~~
Kara mia.

Kara moved. Wrapped in white, fair skin fad-
ing back *pale* behind sultry red lips, she
danced, hips circling and making love to the
man who might have been her partner, to the
room, to the world. Caught in the lightning of
exploding strobes, her eyes glowed, amethyst
crackling. She danced and teased, easy laugh-
ter and showgirl face, quick smiles and but-
terfly touches as she wove around her partner. The men kept coming to her, courting,
smiling. ~~Lying.~~ And Kara moved, through

them, around them, she moved ~~and was happy.~~

an athletic   *grey*
Until /~~a slender~~ man with /~~light~~ hair moved into the circle; until she recognized that she recognized him. Then the evening began to end.

club
She left the /~~disco~~ abruptly, running ~~along~~ *through the streets.*
/~~the pavement of Manhattan.~~ Behind her, calling, reaching out, the ~~tall, athletic~~ man she had been dancing with tried to stop her. She turned her head, laughed. Her legs gleamed in the moonlight through hip high slits in her skirt. An ivory carving; dream flesh made quick.

Kara left, as she always did. It was time to leave, it is always time to leave when they close in, when the scent of rut grows heavy. The *man*/*athlete* turned away, bitter, teased, an image graven into his mind. A grail.

Kara's face melted, smeared, swirled down the drain. The showgirl rinsed away, leaving

Joanna, translucent, looking at herself in the mirror. Green eyes studied themselves, flashed. The innocent smile, full-lipped, as her perfect body reflected in the gold and white bathroom.

                                              massage
She turned on the shower, set the /~~Water Pik~~ head on slow, the water on hot. Soaping herself, her fingers traced the
racing from beneath her right breast to
pale white scar /low on her stomach: the only flaw, mark; a ~~secret~~ rosary told only by her fingers. The steaming water softened her hair, ~~drove the sticky stiffness of hair spray out~~ and the white and honey strands darkened, plastered

                                              her
themselves to her skull, her neck /~~and~~ back. She washed away the night, Kara, all the nighttime names, the sound of prowling dancers, the smell of drink and smoke. Joanna laughed as her fingers played along her body, her perfect body with its secrets of nighttime names.

Then, in the steam and heat, she shivered and hugged herself.

There are going to be more changes; Kara/Joanna, who started out as a victim, is becoming evil; the man is Shaw—before the transformation that creates the man for whom I showed the description card when we were discussing character. The changes he's going to undergo are a result of this meeting, which is being moved out of New York.

Are the changes necessary? *I* thought so. I think they improved the flow and sound for which I was trying, and that was my major concern. The final decision will rest with some ~~poor~~ editor somewhere when the story is ~~finished and~~ submitted. It's entirely possible—and even reasonable to imagine—that the whole passage will be reduced to four or five lines in the published version of the story. But I'll do little else with it until the story is finished and then the changes I'll make will be only those necessary to keep actions in line with character and incident.

That's important to keep in mind when you're doing your revisions: there comes a time when you just have to let the thing fly. I met a young writer recently who'd just finished the *ninth* revision of a twenty-two-thousand-word story. She thought that it would need one more pass before it was ready to go out. There are problems with the piece, but they have to do with length, not the writing. At twenty-two thousand words, it's neither fish nor fowl, story nor novel. And today it's almost impossible to place fiction of that length . . . at least in paying markets.

One of the things I did when I was beginning the revision process on the segment from "Virtual Reality" was to circle every repetition of a word on the page. The one that stood out was "wept." I don't spend an inordinate amount of time thinking about the effect of my words while I'm writing them, though I do spend days considering them before they reach paper. I like the sound of the word, though, the way it echoes "whipped," especially, and especially in this context. Whipped, in turn, brings to mind not only punishment, but a sense of being beaten, of having lost. And that's important in this story. I also wanted to emphasize the crying with the fact that there was no physical manifestation of what was happening. (The end of the passage, finally, has Joanna reacting outwardly—hugging herself and shivering.)

In most instances, however, it pays to delete as many redundancies as you can. If a character's name pops up seven or eight times on a page (or, as sometimes occurs, in a paragraph), spend some time seeing if you can substitute pronouns or get around it in another way. Remember, we said that "said" was an invisible word; you don't want to make your characters' names or other crucial words disappear, too, and their constant reappearance will always cause that to happen.

(I know, I know: there are programs for the computer that will count word occurrences. I still prefer doing it the old-fashioned way. By seeing everything in context, it is easier to decide where and what changes are best.)

Look back at the excerpts from the David Bradley novels and give some thought to how he's brought his words together, not only for meaning, but for sound. How does your work sound when you read it aloud? Are the words harmonious? Are all your sentences so long that you cannot speak them without stopping for a breath? Shorten them. Are they all so short that the effect is staccato? Make some of them complex, compound. Establish a rhythm and then use the longer or shorter sentences to break it, to give emphasis, to change mood. You are not sitting with your "listener"; you can't control the effect of your words except through their careful choice and use.

You don't have to—and you shouldn't—worry about that while you're writing. Your innate abilities and talents will take care of a lot of it. But during the revision process you have the chance to fine tune, to smooth things out. By reading your work aloud you begin to get a sense of how it sounds in the mind, something you cannot achieve by silent scanning. As the writer, you're automatically adding whatever may be missing, an advantage your reader doesn't have. Hearing the words, though, helps you focus.

Hearing the words is crucial when it comes to dialogue. We've discussed the importance of seeing to it that your dialogue is natural, appropriate to the character, and sounds like the things people say when they're saying the things your characters are saying. Virtually every rejected manuscript screams for attention in the dialogue.

Characters speak in formal cadences, ignoring idiom, cliché, contractions. The dialogue of the kid behind the counter at the local burger joint is indistinguishable from that of the mayor, the cop, and the schoolteacher. (Everyone sounds like the schoolteacher.) If you speak your dialogue or, better, "play" it into a tape deck and then listen to it, you'll see where you're making your mistakes. Now is the time to catch them.

Now that you've substituted pronouns for names, is who is doing what to whom still clear?

Is what is going on clear? Does the scene you're reading do anything for the story, anything *necessary?* It may read very nicely, and it may offer a point of view, but does that do anything for the story? Does it belong there, or should you save it for something else? The excerpt from "Virtual Reality" was originally written as part of another story. It didn't belong there, though, so I put the pages aside. Now I have a story in which they make a difference. And as noted earlier, by the time the story is completed, it may be shortened drastically. (It won't miss the cut this time, though, because the new story stems from it.)

If something doesn't advance the story in some way, if it doesn't have an action that makes a difference, if it doesn't add *substantially* and *urgently* to characterization, if you can read the story without those words and not miss them because nothing in them is important, cut them out. (If you don't, I'll have to.)

Another thing to look for with a critical eye are wishy-washy words, those nonspecifics we are prone to use. Examples? Sure. Did you write that the phone rang at "almost noon," "about noon," "perhaps noon," or a variation of that theme? How about height? There's a difference between being *almost* six feet tall and being *about* six feet tall. If there's a reason for the ambiguity, fine. If there isn't, consider changing the word.

You're the writer, you know what time the event occurred, the details of the characters' looks.

You know, the reader doesn't, and if you're not making it clear to her, you're not doing your job. One author recently complained about a change suggested by his copyeditor, who questioned a character's motivation in a scene. "I know this character better than you do," he wrote, "trust me, this is the way he'll act."

The copyeditor is part of the marketplace, someone who reads books, and reads them with care. If he didn't buy into what was going on, why should anyone else? If the author had been willing to divorce himself from his precious words for a moment, if he'd been willing to read what he'd written, the question wouldn't have come up—and the ensuing argument and bitterness wouldn't have become part of the process, either.

Whether that kind of objectivity is realistic, however, is another matter; your task, during the revision process, is to be as objective as possible, to consider every word, to think about what it means, and then to do something about it—even if that something is nothing.

After you've read through the manuscript and marked your changes and corrections on the hard copy, then go back to the keyboard and enter them. While the best way is to retype completely, let yourself feel free to keep typing after you've entered the new material . . . if the juices are flowing.

You're going to have an opportunity to make more changes after the book is acquired and may even be required to, but that's another chapter. But if you haven't done the initial revisions in a professional manner, you're not going to have to think about following editorial direction.

Chapter 18

THE GENTLE ART OF SUBMISSION

Okay, right about now you're starting to get impatient. You're thinking, isn't it time that I start figuring out how to submit this masterpiece? Well, that's a decision you have to make on your own, but since you asked . . .

There are a couple of questions you're going to want to answer immediately, beginning with, "Which house is right for me?" That's one of the questions we answered when we began this exercise, and by now you've researched the lists, checked with friends and booksellers, and done everything else you can from where you are to narrow the field.

The next question is one that brings a question of its

own with it: "Do I need an agent?" Oh, so: "How do I get one?" Whether you need one depends on you; there are authors who are quite happy representing themselves and some even do a good job of it. The problem is that for many beginners, as well as some writers who already have track records, finding an agent can be at least as difficult as finding a publisher. Let's begin by looking at what an agent can do for you.

Good agents know the editors, not just the houses. They know who is looking for what. They know the editors who treat the authors well and those who sign 'em and forget 'em. They know how much each editor is willing to pay for particular kinds of books, how quickly the contracts emerge from the maw of the legal departments, and how slowly the checks are spit out by the computers. They have an idea of each house's relative strengths in marketing and distribution, which houses may be undergoing a period of internal turmoil, and which houses are no longer looking for the kind of book you're ready to submit.

Of course, if a house has a "no unsolicited manuscripts" policy, the agent can still get your work through the door; on the other hand, and something important to remember, no unsolicited manuscripts does not mean that you can't send a query letter to an editor, so don't make the situation any worse than it is by creating difficulties that don't exist. There are enough that do. Consider this: There are agents who won't read unsolicited queries! And the reading fees . . . !

Agents are wonderful at taking rejection: if they're making the submission for you, you don't have to open that envelope with the tacky little note in it. And if a manuscript has been awaiting response for too long, an agent can make a call and get through to the editor; you'll probably have a bit more difficulty managing that particular bit of magic.

They're also more familiar with publishing contracts, know what can or cannot be changed at each house, and might be able to get you a better deal. That conditional "might" was a considered choice of word; I've acquired books from agents at exactly the same terms I've offered unagented writers with one exception: the agent *usually* retains both foreign and performance rights. That doesn't mean that your agent will be any more successful in placing those rights; it does mean that if they are sold you'll get a larger share of the income.

An agent cannot guarantee a sale for you and, in my experience, cannot guarantee you a better or closer reading, except for those times that the agent and the editor have an excellent working relationship. There are some agents I believe implicitly and whose taste is close enough to mine that if they say something is great, I will probably look at the manuscript a bit more quickly. But they are few and far between.

There are some agents whose submissions are treated as jokes; people from whom no one in the company has bought a manuscript in ten years; they are poorly presented, badly written, and inappropriate in terms of the editor's needs. There are agents who sign everyone who comes to them and then sends everything to everyone, with no thought at all as to what's going on on the receiving end. I'll put it this way: There are some agents whose submission I read after all the unsolicited manuscripts are considered (if I read them at all).

Finding an agent—not to raise the issue of finding the *right* agent—is as time-consuming and frustrating an experience as getting the manuscript published at all. But it can be done; the evidence is all around you. So, how do you go about it?

Ideally, given the nature of the relationship, you'll want to meet the agent before you sign up. That's most effectively done by attending writers conferences and workshops. If you can arrange to be introduced by someone, do so. If you can't, don't despair: the agents are attending because they are looking for new clients, and most conferences arrange for appointments.

Next best is being introduced through the mail by one of the agent's clients. If a member of your workshop is happily represented, ask about the agent, ask to have a letter of introduction, assuming that you're writing the same kind of material. If your friend turns you down, look for a new friend. If the agent turns you down, and you've run out of friends . . .

Literary Market Place contains a list of agents, their affiliations (there are two major organizations to which literary representatives may belong, the ILAA—Independent Literary Agents of America—and SAR—Society of Authors Representatives. The two are merging—becoming the Association of Authors' Representatives—even as I type), and some other basic information. Writer's Digest Books publishes a slightly more detailed listing, based on material that they used to include in their annual *Writer's Market*. The best guide I've found, though, is *Literary Agents of North America*, published by Author Aid/Research Associates International (340 East 52nd Street, New York, NY 10022). It is a detailed listing of more than 800 literary agencies in the United States and Canada, and includes responses to a questionnaire the editors sent to the agents, so that you get a good idea of the agency's policies, charges, and needs. One of the most useful aspects of *LANA* is the set of indices: by subject matter, by policy (the agency acts as a packager, does not charge a reading fee, provides editorial services, etc.), by size (number of people in the agency), by region, and by name. This makes it easy for you to pick and choose based on the decisions you've made—like what you're writing, or knowing that only an agent in Hawaii can represent you properly, or wanting to be with an agency that has many (or few) agents peddling work. It doesn't guarantee anything beyond that. But then again, neither can an agent.

Other decisions you'll face are whether or not you want to sign with an agency that charges a 10 percent commission (there are some of them left) or 15 percent; whether you feel like paying a reading/evaluation fee; whether you want to pay some of the "hidden" charges involved at some agencies: there are those that bill you for long-distance phone calls, for duplication, for postage, and in some cases, even for the privilege of signing with them.

As in every business, there are the reputable and the questionable; those who can be trusted. There are agents who don't have contracts with their writers; it's all done on a handshake, and if either party doesn't think the marriage is working, the parting of the way is clean and simple. And there are agents you probably shouldn't turn your back on. Treat the relationship as you would any business arrangement: ask questions, get references, and if anything strikes you as being amiss, walk away. A bad agent can be a disaster.

One of my favorites is a woman who spends time listening to what I have to say, so that when something comes in, it's right. I might not buy it for any number of reasons, but the manuscript fulfills my basic publishing needs. Unlike the agents who don't look at the manuscript as a physical object and send dog-eared pages, still stained with the coffee spilled by the last editor to see the project, this person makes certain that, at the very least, the first chapter is a fresh photostatic copy. The boxes she uses cost about $2.50 each and the manuscript gets a new box each time it goes out. In short, she treats the manuscript with the same respect we'd expect from you as the writer. Unfortunately, those great expectations are more honored in the breach.

In contrast is the agent in Georgia who sends one-page descriptions of the books she has to submit (although the letter says that chapters and synopsis are enclosed), without any thought whatsoever as to the editors' needs. The books I'm working on these days tend to be 72,500 word puzzle mysteries; this agent sends descriptions of three-volume family sagas—and that's after she's sent us a form asking for detailed descriptions of our wants and needs so that they may be entered on her data base.

The day after her last submission to me, I received a letter from a man in Arizona, asking if his novel was under consideration; this agent had told him it was. The manuscript in question was the one page I'd just received. Reading between the lines of this writer's letter, I got the sense that the agency was charging for services, rather than earning commissions. There's an object lesson there, if you care to learn it.

But getting back to getting your work onto my desk, if the agent search fails, the fallback is the unagented submission. As I said, if a house doesn't accept unsolicited manuscripts, query them. If they don't accept unagented submissions, to hell with 'em.

There are two reasons publishers want agents involved in the process. The first is so that someone outside the house is acting as first reader. After all, if the agent liked the book enough to sign the writer and go to the effort of submitting it, it must be good. There's a fallacy in the reasoning; all you need to do is look at all the agented manuscripts that don't get acquired to figure out what it is.

The second reason is because it's easier to negotiate a contract with an agent. We speak the same language, don't have to explain the meaning of each and every clause, and aren't faced (usually) with calls after the negotiation is completed and the contract submitted, in which we learn that some lawyer friend of the author's has decided to make changes without so much as a by-your-leave. It is worth the often minimal increase in advance not to have to deal with people who don't know what they're talking about. There was a lawyer who insisted on changing the word "Work"—which is how the novel is referred to in the contract—to "Book" because that's what we were buying. No, we don't buy the book, we manufacture it, and we don't buy it, actually; we lease it for a specified period of time. But that's a subject for another time.

The basics of choosing a house have already been discussed; beyond the basics, use the same networks you've tapped in the search for an agent. Editors show up at writers conferences and they're all approachable; at the very worst, you'll save postage by not having to submit the manuscript to a given house; at best, well, you may make a deal. Speak to published writers and booksellers and everyone else you can think of in the attempt to get your foot in an editor's door. Call the publishing house and get the name of the editor who worked on a book you particularly enjoyed. Or go out into the cold. The only thing you can be sure of is that if your manuscript does not arrive on an editor's desk in one fashion or another, it will not be published, and while the success stories are fewer than the tales of desperation and failure, there are also fewer publishable writers than there are manuscripts arriving.

And the manuscripts do arrive, along with the queries, partials, synopses, and samples. And the letters that accompany them.

Just about every conference I've attended in the last three years has had a panel devoted to the subject, and the editors and agents up on the dais start squirming. We all have our favorite atrocities, but we can't talk about them in public. They do share certain characteristics, however, and those can be talked about.

When the author begins by telling us our business, we don't read too much further. Don't tell us how well a particular kind of book is selling; we know.

When the author begins by telling us why we *have* to read *this* book, our response is usually, "No, we don't."

When the author begins listing credits that have absolutely no bearing on the work in hand—one writer has told me about being nominated for just about every major award in the world, including the Nobel Prize(!) as well as some minor ones, though there's no mention of ever *winning* one, and brags about being listed in *LMP*—we usually remember that we've got to call the tailor and find out if our party duds are ready.

When the author begins by telling us about all the friends, relatives, and neighbors—as well as three teachers, one bookstore owner, and the freelance editor who has professionally edited the book before submission— and how much they all loved this novel, we usually suggest that the friends, relatives, neighbors, three teachers, one bookstore owner, and the freelance editor should publish it themselves.

When the author begins by telling us about all the awards won by this—or another—manuscript in one of the hundreds of contests sponsored by organizations around the country, we wonder why the manuscript was being sent to contests instead of us. We also know that winning the contest is not always a sign of anything more than being better than everything else that was submitted.

When the author does anything but show us "calm competence," in the words of New York agent, Eileen Fallon, we begin to lose interest in direct proportion to the amount of hype we're seeing.

The bottom line is that neither you nor an agent can "sell" a manuscript. The only thing that sells your work is the work itself. Everything else is stuff and nonsense. All the movie interest you think will exist because of the success of whatever was successful last week is a pipe dream. All the attention that will be paid because of the news story on *20/20* tomorrow night is a figment of your imagination.

Don't bother giving us cover art, blurbs, and the advertising campaign.

Just let us know what you've written, what the approximate length is, and any publication credits you have that relate in some way to the work you want considered: three poems in *Grit,* and an article on caring for the elderly in a magazine—national or not—means nothing if you're submitting a novel about a serial killer stalking Cape Cod. Prior book publication, even if it's in another category, is valid information; it lets us know that you can get to the end of a manuscript and that someone saw something in what you'd written.

Lots of writers have taken to getting a letterhead produced for themselves. That's fine, all businesses do that, and a writer is a business. But some of the cutesy letterheads I've seen lately aren't professional; they're just silly. You don't need caricatures, you don't need quills in ink bottles, I don't think you even need "freelance writer" printed on it. Your name and address, your phone number—that's all the information we need. The sillier your letterhead looks, the sillier I'm going to think you are and the less seriously I'm going to take you. Because, see, your mother was right: you get only one chance to make a first impression, clothes make the person, and whatever else your mother told you still holds.

Your manuscript makes an impression, too. Another of the drawbacks to the new word processing software and laser printers is that it makes you fanciful. For the time being, anyway, manuscripts should still look like manuscripts, not like finished books. Double-spaced (not one and a half spaces, not single-spaced, not triple-spaced), with words to be italicized indicated by underscoring, not printed in true italics, the right margin "ragged," not justified and, believe it or not, not in a proportionally spaced typeface. Serif faces are easier to read and work with than sans serif, even if the latter look nicer. Margins of at least one inch all around, your name, a page number, and the title of the manuscript on each page. Indented paragraphs, not block.

It may all seem desperately basic and arbitrary, but there's a reason for it. While we ask for a word count, most publishers do their estimates based on character counts. We don't count every character, of course, we estimate. But justified margins and proportional faces make it difficult to do that accurately. The spacing is for ease of reading and to allow room for editing. When you use italics, it makes it more difficult for the typesetter; when you start using fancy fonts—bold facing, fussy initial caps, or any of the other things you see in finished books—you make the entire production effort, from estimates to design to setting, more difficult for everyone.

By all means pack your manuscript neatly, put it in a box, put rubber bands around the pages. But don't have it bound, don't punch holes in the pages and place them in a looseleaf folder. It is arguable whether that makes the reading any easier. If I'm reading on a subway or bus or plane, I prefer being able to just put the pages to the end of the manuscript rather than dealing with something as large as a binder; it makes the editing and typesetting processes next to impossible. The expense you've gone to does nothing to help in the presentation and tells the publisher that you're not a professional.

Eventually we are going to be working directly from disk, but that day isn't here yet and pushing it isn't going to help. While some publishers are asking for disks *(along with hard copy, not in lieu of it)*, we are not yet setting the books from them and the disk you submit is in all likelihood only going to be a collateral relative of the finished book. As long as we have copyeditors, and I hope we have them forever, and so should you, fine-tuning is going to take place until the day the presses start rolling.

So, again, use the equipment as a tool, but don't let all its capabilities dictate the way in which you work; use the tool, don't let it use you. Editors are not impressed by anything but your writing.

But we can be turned off by sloppiness. Remember the agent I mentioned, the one who uses a new box for every submission, who makes certain that at least the first chapter of every manuscript is a fresh copy? There's a guideline for you in that procedure. If a manuscript looks messy, why should we have any more respect for your work than you do? I can't think of any house that insists on originals; either print out again or make fresh photostats. Don't reuse envelopes, and do remember to enclose a self-addressed, stamped envelope for a response. You may not want the entire manuscript returned because you think it's less expensive to produce a new one, but if you want to hear from us at all, put that envelope in the package. And do think twice about whether or not it is really less expensive to make a new copy—not just in postage, but in terms of little things like the trees that are coming down—or send anything that's going to let us know how long this manuscript has been making the rounds. It might be right for us, but if we think everyone else in the business has already rejected it, it makes our decision a little easier.

What should you send if you're making an unsolicited submission? Most publishers request the *first* three chapters and an outline or synopsis. It makes no sense whatsoever for you to do otherwise. One writer recently sent an entire manuscript, which is not unusual and which won't necessarily count against you; however, in his covering letter he said that three chapters would not give us any indication of how well he wrote nor of the complexities of plot and character development. That set off all the alarms.

At no point in the process do you—or the publishers— have that much time to catch the reader's attention. Granted, word of mouth, satisfied readers telling their friends that the book is wonderful, surprising, whatever, is the single best selling tool we have in this business. But you still have to get the reader to that point, and if you don't catch them in the beginning, they won't be there for the end.

And the cold reality of the matter is this: most editors will not read the entire manuscript if the first five pages (or twenty-five pages) don't hold our interest. At any point in our reading of the manuscript, if we lose patience, get bored, or are otherwise convinced that the manuscript will not "work," we're going to stop. Period.

If we like what we've read, we'll ask for the rest; if not, well . . .

It is only on the rarest of occasions that editors will contract for a novel based on chapters and an outline of an unsolicited manuscript by a new writer. If we've worked with an author previously, or if you have completed novels to your credit and we know, therefore, that you can get to the end of a story successfully, we are more likely to go from sample to contract. So, it is self-defeating to send a partial and tell us that you expect to have the book completed in six months. Be ready to respond immediately to a request for the balance of the novel and, when you send it, include those first three chapters again . . . just to be safe.

Paper has a way of breeding in a publisher's office; I'm certain that two manuscripts left on the corner of a desk over the weekend will magically become nine manuscripts by Monday morning. We do what we can, but, like in a bookstore, there's only so much space and things do have a way of getting lost. It's not a lack of caring, it's a fact of life. It doesn't happen often, but why take chances, right? And at publishing houses like Walker and the other few that still welcome unsolicited submissions, the problem escalates. Do you have any idea at all of how many people are out there with manuscripts?

And how few make it through the swamps of submission to the fruited plains of published?

The odds at any given house are against you, and it is not only a function of your writing. While it looks as if the books just keep coming out (breeding like the manuscripts), the fact is that each house publishes a fixed number of titles each month or season. The editors know how many titles they need, how many mysteries and how many of each kind, how many romances and how many of each kind; well, it doesn't have to be spelled out for you beyond that, right?

Every manuscript is in competition with every other one for a slot on the list. Inventory and budget and the delivery of already commissioned works and option books and the general economic climate all have their impact on the decision-making process. And that means that we have to reject more than we acquire.

Here's a letter we received recently, addressed to the submissions editor. It looks like a cheap mimeo (I didn't know people mimeographed anymore); it may have been a poor photostat. Nothing's been corrected or altered:

THE AUTHOR

* * *

ANYPLACE, U.S.A.

Dear *The Editors:*

Thank you for taking the time to remove my query from the envelope in which I mailed it, stick it into my SASE, and put it in the mailbox (you didn't strain yourself, did you?)

Your letter said that my manuscript does not sound right for your list "at this time". At what time will it be right for your list?

Furthermore, you forwarded your "best wishes" for my success elsewhere. I somehow doubt the sincerity of your statement, for if you really wished me to succeed, you would have published my work.

Finally, I would like to mention that editors, agents, other writers, and writing instructors are constantly harping on how we would-be authors should always be "professional" in our work, our queries, our submissions, and all dealings with publishers. I am still waiting for some indication of professionalism on the part of the publishers and their editors, though. How professional does an unaddressed, unsigned form letter look to you? How professional is it to respond in this manner to someone who has put months of his life and his best effort into a manuscript, even if the end result isn't worth publication? If you have the time it takes to read the query letter, the outline, and/or the sample chapters, how much more of your valuable time would it take to add just a note to your form letter to let the author know <u>why</u> you rejected his work, and to sign your name so he'll know he's dealing with an actual human being?

Remember, authors who really want to write could write and publish their own work if all publishers and editors vanished from the face of the earth tomorrow, but if all the authors vanished, you'd be out of a job! Try to keep things in prespective. [sic]

Sincerely,
The Author

At some point you, too, are going to receive that unsigned, ambiguous form rejection note. Sometimes you'll get the very same note, but rather than a mass-produced copy, it will be typed and signed. Sometimes you'll get a letter offering some direction. Whatever happens, though, I sincerely hope that you never sink to the depths the writer of that letter has reached.

I guess he thought he was being cute, sending us a form letter (and I'd guess that lots of other publishers have received it, too), but I wonder: why didn't he address it to the editor to whom he sent his manuscript? Could it be that, like the letter, his material was just sent to the submissions editor, that he never bothered trying to find out who the right editor at the house might have been?

The author wants to know when the manuscript might be right for my list: maybe next week, maybe not. Maybe never. But right now, it isn't.

If my best wishes were sincere would I have published the book? Not necessarily: what if his novel were in a category that my house is having difficulty with, one for which we have no sales foundation? Publishing the book, then, would have been a disaster for all concerned. Success is not simply having the book published, it is having the book published *well*. For one reason or another, the editor who rejected this book might not have felt competent to edit it correctly or felt that his taste did not allow for him to make a fair judgment. Success is finding the right editor for your work; editors are not interchangeable word mechanics. They're professionals with areas of expertise.

Being professional means understanding the workings of the industry in which you're involved; in this case, that professionalism calls for an understanding of why we use form letters.

Do you, as a writer, really want me to pen a note telling you that I think you should pawn your typewriter? Do you want me, after the months of work you've put in, after all your friends have encouraged you, after the members of your workshop have praised you to the stars, to tell you that you lack even the most basic skills? And if I do that, won't you expect me to go further and explain what I've said, give you pointers, give you more to work with?

And if I do it for you, I have to do it for the next one and the next one, and suddenly the already unconscionably long wait for a response to your submission increases by a factor of seven.

Who's writing this letter you want? In many publishing houses around the country, editors don't have secretaries or assistants (another function of the economy, though we like to think that the money saved on personnel overhead gets used on the books). We don't have the time to respond to everyone.

And it isn't always safe to let a writer know why they've been rejected. I've done it, I've explained why a 900-page, single-spaced, quarter-inch-margined manuscript will not be read, and received abusive phone calls for a month afterward. I've explained to writers that their stories just weren't interesting, and have had them show up at the office to argue with me, to show me all the other books they think they've at least matched.

Our correspondent here says he's still waiting for some sign of professionalism on the part of the publishers. Reading between the lines, I'd guess that he's been receiving form rejections for a while. It's frustrating, but I'd suggest that the failing is in himself, not in his stars, not in unprofessional editors.

The writer is right about one thing, though: if all the authors vanished, editors would be out of a job. Except for those of us who are also writers, who'd then have the time to do our writing. We also know better than to think that we can successfully self-publish. Publishing the work isn't the end, selling it to the *public* is.

If "The Author" had had the courage to sign his name, to confront us directly, I might have suggested that he try to publish the book himself, that he contract with a vanity press. And as he watched his expenses rise and his sales remain a figment of his imagination, I'd ask him whether he wants to acquire another book from himself . . . and what he'll tell himself when the submission arrives?

In publishing as it exists today, there are—and always will be—more manuscripts looking for a home than there will be slots for them. There will always be more writers awaiting responses than there are editors to give them. Some writers are experimenting with putting their novels "on line" on the computer bulletin boards, and while it remains an interesting experiment, it is not the point of the industry of writing and publishing. And you and I are living and working today; try to create change if that's your desire, but don't expect everyone to applaud. As for tomorrow, those of us around to see it will deal with the problems it brings.

Don't expect anything more than a courteous, if curt, rejection form. If you've done everything else correctly—from the writing itself to choosing the publishers to whom to submit to following the guidelines you've learned here and the ones you've received from the publishers, reality may very well exceed expectation. And if it doesn't, there's always another publisher and the next manuscript.

■ ■ ■

While we're on the subject of letters, there's another one I'd like to share with you, if for no other reason but to prove that even putative professionals can blow it. I still find it difficult to believe that the guy wrote it; it is even more difficult for me to believe that I responded. But I did, so . . .

The letter appears like another example of revision. The reason is that I *did* revise it, as part of my response, which follows it. It should be self-explanatory:

Dear Mr. Seidman:

outlining

I have your kind letter /~~outline~~ the requir^e/ ments Walker/^has~~makes~~ for the submission of a novel.

I thank you but I must decline the offer. I have not time to do an outline, or futz around with your internal guidelines. I'm fully aware that you do not need me. You have an abundance of masochistic writers to swallow up. But the great truth is that as much as you don't need me—I sure don't need you, or any other publisher or editor and /^especially~~especailly~~ any agent.

To ask ~~that of~~ me, a published writer of long

to meet your requirements
standing, /~~to do the requirements you put forth~~, is insulting.

But this feels good, an expression of independence, no longer waiting breathlessly (with pounding heart) for some son of a bitch publisher to decide my fate.

Michael

I don't cry anymore, /~~Mike~~. Isn't that wonderful? The field of writing, which once made
/*me*

suffer and never provide/*d* a living wage is paying me back for all my tears and suffering. I operate a very lucrative ghostwriting business that removes me (and my Ego) from parasitic agents, ten percenters who don't know their asses from a hole in the ground. If they knew, they wouldn't be agents. They'd be living in penthouses. Do I hate agents? No. They do what they have to do, however
clumsily
/~~clumsy~~, in an aggressive way with limited ability.

I am a veteran of the writing wars. I've been through it all and I know the score. I can tell ~~you~~ a good book from a bad book just by reading the first few pages. ~~Because my judgment is based on long experience and exten-~~

sive success. Between my editor and /~~me~~ *I*, we
turn out over 20 books a year, with /~~very~~ *a* very
high percentage of success for my clients.

If you want to see the <u>full script,</u> I'll be
pleased to send it to you. I know you're loaded
with reading material, but I don't aim to let
my work sit in Walker's office for eight
months gathering dust.

So my question to you is: what do you want
to see from me? An outline is out. A brief re-
sume is in. Do you want the full script, half a
script, one third of a script? You got it. Say
what and when.

As I said, I should have ignored the whole thing. But I
didn't like his language, or very much else about the letter. And I didn't like his attitude. So, in addition to his
copyedited letter (and as I read it now there was even
more I could do, but there was only so much time to
waste), here's what he got:

Let's see, where shall I begin? How about suggesting that you take a look at your edited letter; as
"a veteran of the writing wars" you should appreciate that. Quite simply, even your letter doesn't
meet our basic needs.

I don't know why you're so down on agents and,
frankly, couldn't care less. They're important, they
know what they're doing, and they provide several
important services, not the least of which is
preventing an author from so antagonizing an editor that the author's work will not be considered
for publication.

I am not a sonofabitch, but I am one mean mother, and I'd suggest you think twice about calling me—or anyone else—by anything but their proper name. And mine, incidentally, is Michael, not Mike; I am, I think, entitled to my own name, don't you?

My internal guidelines, for which you don't have the time, are what allow me to consider unagented submissions. By following them, the author is offering me a book that meets my needs as an editor and my list's needs as a publisher. But, hey, why should you bother worrying about my internal guidelines, you're a published writer of long standing. (Your listing in *Books in Print* is awe-inspiring. I wish I had written . . .)

So, my answer to your question is this: I don't want to see anything from you, not now, not ever. I'm certain there are hundreds of wiser editors waiting for you to grace them with your presence. I'd suggest you write to them. Perhaps they'll be more understanding of your needs and requirements for submission.

Okay, it was childish. But all the editors I shared it with —each of whom knows the writer's name and the title of the one book he authored that I was able to find in *Books in Print*—understood the reasons for it. And will welcome the writer with open arms, I'm sure.

There are going to be times when you're going to feel as frustrated as this author does; there are days when things don't go well, when the rejections arrive hot and heavy, when the demands of your editor seem outrageous. Whatever the problem is, don't make the mistake this guy did. He's cut himself off from at least three markets. Given his attitude, how amenable do you think he'll be to editorial guidance?

When it happens, do what I should have done: write the letter, then throw it away. Don't mail it . . . especially not to me.

Chapter 19

AN OUTLINE FOR A LIFE IN FICTION

Because an ounce of prevention is easier to carry than pounds of "I shoulda dones," let's take one last look at what you're going to do as you prepare to commit yourself to writing.

You are willing to take risks, knowing that sometimes you will lose.

You've picked a category or have chosen to simply write in the mainstream. The decision was based on what you want to do, not on the comments of friends, relatives, teachers, other writers, or the last market report you read. You've come to it with integrity, as Thomas Chastain, a former president of MWA put it recently, with an understanding of what it is you're writing, of the history and background and foundations of the genre, not because you see a particular writer making a mark and think that you can just do the same thing. You can fool yourself, and you might even fool an editor, but you will not fool the readers.

You've made all the arrangements necessary to allow you to write: you've come to terms with the time you'll have to put into the effort, time not only spent in front of the keyboard, but in research, in rewriting, in keeping up with the literature. Your family knows that you are not to be disturbed (obviously, you're disturbed enough already) when you're writing, even if they should wander by and see you seemingly staring into space.

You are willing to take risks, knowing that sometimes you will lose.

You know your potential markets, the houses that are looking for the kind of work you're planning to do. You've made an effort to discover the names of the editors, have joined the various organizations in which membership will make you part of the network, and subscribed to the magazines that will keep you aware of who is doing what, not only terms of recent releases, but of trends that people see developing within your category.

You've outlined your novel, not only so that you know the storyline, what happens when and to whom, but also in terms of the point you want to make at the core of the story, the reason for it to exist. The storyline may change, but the point rarely does—unless you've taught yourself something very special during the writing.

You've looked at what you want to do in your novel and answered two crucial questions: Do I care? and Will anyone else care? Is there a reason for you to write what you've chosen and as strong a reason for people to read it? Entertainment may be a good enough answer for some, but is what you're planning to do entertaining? Will it allow your readers to escape and come away from the reading experience pleased that they spent the time with your characters?

You are willing to take risks, knowing that sometimes you will lose.

You've looked at your characters closely, given them the traits that mark individuals (and the little contradictions that do the same thing), speech and thought patterns, body language, voices, attitudes, and *a reason for being there*. Don't make your characters ciphers, some abstract "everyman." There is no black and white, only shades of gray; if you choose to forget that, your characters will be cardboard, your story dull. It is in the surprises that the characters take on dimension. It is in your ability to create the contradictions in the character make sense, in your presentation of the facts and the slow building of the personality. Something out of character for which there's no groundwork will not be believed.

You've trained yourself to keep the world you live in and the world you're writing about separate, acknowledging that reality in fiction has little to do with the real world. You are creating an elaborate lie; in order to bring it to life, you have to create all the elements and *show* them to the readers, not tell them about it. You observe the world around you, the physical details and the people and their actions, you notice the play of light as a cloud passes in front of the sun, the silence that strikes a city when the snow falls, that particular moment when all sound seems to stop, no matter where you are or when. You are lying, but you are also reporting, and the readers are counting on you to reveal a truth at the center of your fabrication.

You are willing to take risks, knowing that sometimes you will lose.

You've listened to people speak, to the sloppy habits of speech as well as the fine, and know which people speak in which way. You know the idiom of the time and place you're depicting, the language appropriate to each character in each situation. As you write, you look at each conversation and determine the reason for it: does it advance the story, develop the character, provide a needed break in tension, foreshadow events, recapitulate important discoveries? Or is it there because you like the sound of your voice?

And you have been careful about dialogue tags and said bookisms, giving the definition to the words themselves, so that the reader can hear them and doesn't have to be told that something is ironic, or angry, or an observation. If you choose to use a tag for one reason or another, you are also careful to use the right one, not using "hissed," when there are no esses at all in the sentence, using words that describe physical actions to replace manners of speech: *"Yes," he nodded. "Sorry," he frowned.*

You've blocked out the important scenes and know the reasons for them. You've thought about action and reaction (even if it is inaction), about what follows every meeting of the characters. If there's a fight, you know what the result of it will be—even if you change your mind later, when the characters have taken over some of the storytelling for you. If a couple makes love, it's not simply for the sake of playing out your sexual fantasies on the page, but because it tells us something about them or creates a situation, a conflict, that will have to be resolved.

You've considered what you're going to do so that you can use verbs to carry the story and not have to rely on adjectives; you've "seen" what is in the room and brought your characters into that space in such a way that the reader sees it, too, and isn't simply told about the table against the wall. (If the table has to be there at all. A good lie, even with its embellishments, works best when there aren't too many things thrown into it . . . all that should be there are the things that create and maintain the willing suspension of disbelief.)

You are willing to take risks, knowing that sometimes you will lose.

You've defeated the very natural drive to write "in the style of" so-and-so because you've learned that only so-and-so can write in her "style," and that the readers don't want *you* to do that, they want to read *you.* So you are going to take the risk of being yourself, saying what you want to say in the way you want to say it. You've realized that it may take some time, that there may be some reluctance to whatever it is you want to try, but you also know that if what you're doing is good, it will be noticed. It is worth it to you to put the effort into creating your own bandwagon, rather than simply re-creating the wheel.

You've accepted the fact that writing is not simply the act of putting one word after another, even good words. You've also seen that neither is writing revision but that revision is part of the act and the art. You've committed the time to reading the words you've put on paper, to making sure that you've remained consistent (characters don't change physical descriptions), that nothing happens without cause and for no reason. You are listening to the words you use not only for meaning, but for rhythm, for flow, so that your story is memorable.

You've acknowledged that your words—as much as you love them—are not carved in stone, that for all that you love a phrase, a scene, a character, they can be cut from the work in progress (and all your work is always in progress; like the world, it is always changing) if they do not add to it. And you know that they can be saved, on paper and in memory, for use later.

You reread to make certain that each word and sentence says what you want it to, that little things like parallel structure and pronoun agreement are in place, that the only ambiguities are those of artful design and not poor craftsmanship.

You know that you are one of thousands who are finishing a novel every day and you're willing to fight for your space, on the terms of the game as it is played. Change comes slowly and you will not let frustration at seeing your vision disregarded turn you away from what you've set out to do. More important than knowing how much money a particular first novel received is remembering all the books—like, say, *The Godfather*—that were rejected again and again and then went on to bestsellerdom. (And you've kept in mind that Mario Puzo considered himself, first and foremost, a "literary" writer, and that even with the success of the Corleone saga, when he tried to write something else, his readers did not support him as strongly.) *It is, finally, the readers who will tell you what to do and what part of your creativity and talent and vision they want to see.* And the readers tell us, on the other side of the editorial desk, the same thing. We try to be proactive, to create; in order to do that, we spend most of our time being reactive.

You are willing to take risks, knowing that sometimes you will lose.

Having listened to the readers—not the reviewers and critics—you will do what you want to do, what you must do, knowing that the decision and responsibility are yours. You've decided, through your experiences, whether you are going to seal the envelope of your creativity or expand it. You know that there are writers who've become successful doing one thing or another and who then try new things under pen names, which may or may not become public, and can see the endless possibilities, each attainable in order, and that order begins with doing the first book right.

Filling in the blanks in formulaic writing works, and works well. You can create a career that way, and make money, and be happy. Or you can start that way, and then push for the sake of the inner you. The lovely thing about it is that it is a win/win situation. Whatever you choose to do is the right thing for you to do, and you are the one who counts.

You've learned that the unexamined life is not worth living.

You are a writer, know thyself.

You are a writer, to thine own self be true.

And you are writer, therefore you must keep learning.

Chapter 20

THE RETE WAY: WORKSHOPS, CONFERENCES, AND GROUPS

It took me a minute or two of serious decision making before going ahead here because I ran into a serious problem. Is it a writers conference, writer's conference, or writers' conference? I mean, have you ever just struggled with the question of where the bloody apostrophe goes? I've decided, after giving the matter much thought (or as much as fits in a minute or two) to forget the damned thing. Any complaints can be sent to me in care of the publisher. They will be forwarded to me and I will proceed to ignore them.

But I never ignore requests to speak at conferences, workshops, or groups and, given the opportunity, I recommend them to you, especially if you are out there alone with no contacts in the community. At the very least, they are the places at which you'll meet editors, agents, teachers, and other writers, each of whom will have something to teach you. Whether you accept the lesson is up to you.

At the very most, you may even make a sale.

And in between those results you'll become part of a network of support and information, will learn that you're not alone and not—sorry—particularly unique in what you're facing. It helps, sometimes.

It certainly helps to pick sensibly; there are literally thousands of choices to make and then dozens of things for you to do to get the most out of the choice you've made. We'll start small, the local writers group.

They're in every community, from the heart of Manhattan to the edge of Dubois, Wyoming. Some groups are focused on a particular category: the Romance Writers of America, for instance, has satellite organizations which concentrate on romance writing, but usually not to the exclusion of other categories, while some, like the Rocky Mountain Fiction Writers in Denver and the Southwest Writers in Albuquerque, are wide open and so large that the members have formed their own critique groups within the larger framework. Others have names that might make you think that you don't belong with them, like the Detroit Women Writers, which accepts anyone interested in writing.

Information about the groups in your area is easily enough come by: check at the local library or college; someone there is sure to know something. If you start attending conferences, you'll meet members of groups from around the area, if not the country, and can make contact that way.

Attend a meeting or two of the group most convenient —or interesting—to you before you commit yourself. As in any organization, there will be members with particular agendas, and if you're not comfortable with what you hear, with the way people speak to each other, the comments they make during the critiquing sessions (the most important reason for joining a group), don't join.

How does the critique work? At the meetings I've attended, people with material ready for reading are given a fixed period of time in which to read from portions of their work-in-progress. When they're done, the other members of the group react to what they've heard, making comments and suggestions. And this is where it gets tricky.

At some groups, the DFW Writers Workshop, for instance, the person who has read is not supposed to do anything but listen; you don't respond with explanations or excuses or anything else. The people making the critique, on the other hand, are committed to being supportive, and must give the reasons for what they're saying.

At other groups, it becomes a free-for-all, writers getting defensive about what they've done, the listeners swinging wildly without any spoken logical support for what they're saying. This can be fun, but you've got to have several years membership in a street gang in order to deal with it.

In either instance, the advice offered is just that: advice. If it makes sense to you, use it. If it seems like nonsense, change for the sake of change, ignore it. I think the reader is always best off maintaining a dignified silence in the face of the comments. There is time later, lots of groups take off for a local coffee shop or diner after the meeting in order to talk about "stuff," for discussions about the whys and wherefores of what you've done.

One of the problems I've discovered at groups is that many of the people making comments are speaking from an experiential vacuum; they haven't been there in the sense of having gone through the publishing process. What they're offering is theory, and that is born strictly from what they'd like to see, unsupported by having faced the real world and seen their theories shot down. There'll be someone who wants you to make not only your narrative "formal," but speech patterns as well. Someone else will jump on every scene in which a perceived minority is painted in a less than politically correct light. That guy in the corner, who's taken three dozen writing courses to no particular avail, will tell you that a chapter must consist of "x" paragraphs, each made up of between "y" and "z" sentences, and that the entire novel must be "q" chapters long.

There'll be the person—maybe one or two in the group —who has had a book published and whose words are taken more seriously than perhaps they should. Unfortunately not every published book—or author—should've been. Their critiques begin, "Well, when I wrote. . . ." They may have something to tell you, but it isn't necessarily about writing. Nor necessarily wrong. You be the judge.

The biggest drawback I've found in the groups is the commitment to support. All too often it means that writers who should be told some cold, honest truths are encouraged in directions that may not serve them very well. That's a call of conscience. Not everyone can be a published author; you may be able to write, but not well enough to sell your work. You may also be able to bowl, but not be able to play with the pros. What kind of reaction do you want from the people listening to you? Do you really want a pat on the back or do you want to know the truth? And do you know that what you're hearing from these people *is* the truth? What are they basing their comments on? In today's hot parlance, where's the empowerment coming from?

At a conference several years ago, I was asked to read and critique partial manuscripts. I agreed, with the caveat that I'd read only as an editor, as someone who must judge manuscripts and ability every day. One woman traveled two thousand miles to attend the conference, and brought with her a partial that had been worked and reworked at her local writers group. The manuscript was abysmal, period. There was nothing of value in it: not the story, not the writing, not the underlying idea. It might have been written by a six-year-old. It was a crime story with a prison setting, and it was obvious that the author had never even seen a prison movie.

I pondered and worried and realized that there was nothing I could say to encourage her. (I know, I know, I said I'd read as if the partials were landing on my desk, but still. . . .) Finally, I said that she had captured a certain Jim Thompson *noir* tone, but that the book needed lots of work, beginning with research. She looked at me across the table, hands shaking, and asked whether there was anything good I could say. (I thought a comparison to Thompson, while not true, was pretty good. But she'd never read him.) I had to say "no."

And she complained long and loud that I didn't encourage her, and that's what she was paying for. Silly me, I thought she was paying to learn. Something akin to that happened at another meeting, where I told people the truth about publishing (the kind of truth you'll find in *From Printout to Published: A Guide to the Publishing Process*), and one aspiring writer berated me for not being encouraging. I see it this way, if I discourage you, I've done us both a favor, and if I don't, I've done us both a favor. But I'm not going to lie.

Sometimes, though, in the groups, you hear lies. It's up to you to figure out what it is you want to hear, what it is you need to hear, and what it is you'll listen to.

A group may not be for everyone, but lots of people have been helped and have helped, through membership, and joining does give you the advantage of having people to speak to, people who are sharing your concerns and interests, and it's nice to have folks around who speak the same language.

▪ ▪ ▪

When I spoke at my first major conference (the University of Oklahoma Short Course on Professional Writing) after years of speaking in small group settings, generally as part of publishing or creative writing courses, I looked up at the audience and said, "If you want to be writers, why are you wasting your time here?" I've discarded the arrogance of my relative youth since then; I know why you're there, why I'm there, and I'm thankful that we have the opportunity.

Writers conferences, no matter what you do with the apostrophe, are valuable learning experiences as well as the best way to meet the people who can make a difference in your career. No matter where you are, there's one near you; no matter how much you think you know, there's something for you to learn. And you can meet people.

How to start? Well, every May, *Writer's Digest* runs a guide to the conferences; the 1992 issue highlights more than 400 of them. Begin by checking that list or the local newspaper or library bulletin board to find a conference that's close enough, and is at a time convenient for you to attend. There are people who'll travel from New Mexico to Wisconsin, from Toronto to Denver to attend conferences that interest them; most of us have more mundane budgets.

Having found the conferences that are physically feasible, get in touch with the director and find out who's on the program. If you're specializing in children's books and none of the speakers are addressing that subject, you may not want to attend. Just as possible is that someone will be there who's worth hearing anyway. That's your decision.

What you're looking for is a mix of agents and editors and writers, people who can address most, if not all, of your concerns. It's likely that the organizers won't know what topics are being covered yet, but that is really a secondary concern. If you've written a romance and an editor who does them is at the conference, or if an editor representing a house that does them is there, you've just taken the first step toward overcoming the "unknown" syndrome.

The agent may not be right for you because of specialization or because she doesn't have any room on her list right now, but she'll make time to speak with you, give you advice, and become another contact. Look at that: two paragraphs and you already know an editor and an agent who might help you! And it is almost that easy.

Ask the organizers if individual appointments can be

arranged with the speakers; some groups have a formal system under which you may get ten or fifteen minutes with the speakers of your choice (though time constraints may make this difficult if you register late: there's a first-come, first-served obligation). At other conferences there are round-table meetings, which aren't quite as good as a one-on-one, but are better than nothing. Under that system, the editor or agent is in a room for a given amount of time, and talks with everyone at the same time, answering questions, giving advice, and sometimes making individual appointments if there's time. The beauty of that arrangement is that you learn more by hearing another person's questions even if they strike you as being too basic.

Finally, you can often corner a speaker and wing it.

Another question you might want to ask is if the conference is running a contest in conjunction with the meeting. Then you have to make a heavy-duty decision: Do you want to enter?

I've judged hundreds of these contests and I really don't know what the best advice is. I know that there are writers who seem to do nothing but enter contests, winning prizes for best synopsis or whatever, but never getting beyond that stage: all their effort goes into preparing material for the judges. I guess it's a lot like entering sweepstakes; eventually you have to win one if you put your name in the hat often enough.

Sadly, the winner of a best in category (and sometimes even the best overall) is not necessarily being rewarded for doing anything except not being as bad as everyone else. That's one of the reasons I suggested that you not mention those awards in your submission letter. The contest often includes a critique along with your "grade"; I've already told you about the person who didn't like my critique, and that's also the kind of risk you take.

There's been some debate about the value of the critiques, generally. The judges have a relatively short amount of time in which to read three or five or ten partial manuscripts and then to respond to what they've read.

Some feel that they owe it to you to be positive, uplifting, encouraging. I have a different agenda, obviously.

Then there's the question of just how much of value you can tell someone in one typed page: if I tell you that your characterization is weak, and then explain why and try to instruct you in how to improve it, I'm not going to get to the next manuscript, not to mention on with my life. So, you're paying whatever the registration fee is for . . . what? I've bought two novels that I read in contests and helped someone place another. The odds are long. But who is offering you anything better?

If someone is, go for it. If not, try a contest (the registration fee is minimal) and see what kind of feedback you get. If you're satisfied, try again. If not, forget about them.

How's that for straddling the fence?

There's one other factor you might want to consider before going to the conference: is it residential or commuter? My experience has been that I prefer the conferences at which everyone (or at least many of the people) are staying at the same hotel or meeting center. The reason is simple: it is in the evenings, after the formal panels are done, after the dinner has been eaten, that some of the most exciting discussions take place. People tend to wander into the bar (or the hospitality room, if the conference offers one; in Albuquerque there've been two, one for smokers, the other for the rest of you), and relaxed and comfortable, they exchange ideas freely and easily, not only among themselves, but with the speakers, who are also down in the bar relaxing.

Maybe it's the atmosphere, maybe it's because the classroom barriers we create have been broken down, but I've found that people ask me the kinds of questions during that period that they never do in the sessions. It could be that they're less worried about embarrassing themselves since there isn't as large a group listening in; whatever it is, the people with whom I've shared those moments at a conference remember it and, when I come back the next year or the year after that, the first thing they say is, "See you down there tonight, okay?" Absolutely.

This sort of informal gathering is more difficult at a conference that doesn't offer lodging because everyone goes home in the evening. The speakers, though, are still there (most conferences are at least two days long), and there's nothing preventing you from asking someone you'd like to speak to later if they're going to be around, because you'd like to buy them a drink or whatever. Unless the organizers have co-opted the speakers' time, most will be glad to accommodate you. Don't forget that they may be tired or have some other work to do (or may just be antisocial, not everyone's a party animal) and don't make a pest of yourself.

Having settled all the important matters, then, it's time to go to the conference.

You'll want to bring pads and pencils, a portable typewriter or laptop computer (if it's a residential conference; the energy that exists during good meetings can send you to your room ready to write), a cassette recorder, and two or three copies of your proposal, along with an appropriate number of S.A.S.E.s, just in case.

Most editors and agents do not accept material during the conference. The logistics of travel make it difficult to deal with everything and there isn't always time to read and react during the hectic days that you'll be together. But there's always the one who will look at something, and if you're lucky enough to meet that person, you want to be ready.

Comfortable clothes are a good idea, too. I don't care what type of convention you're attending, the meeting rooms are always too hot or too cold. Some conferences may also call for you to go from one building to another to get to panels, so be prepared for anything.

When you arrive, the first thing to do is register. You get your name tag and a kit that contains the schedule of events. There may also be a sign-up sheet for appointments with the speakers; if there is, arrange your appointments immediately. You may miss part of one of the sessions you want to attend, but there are ways around that, as you'll see.

There are often other giveaways in the packet, the most important of which are the guidelines for the various houses represented. They don't always send them ahead, but when they do, it gives you a chance to check immediately as to whether the project you're working on fits in with the needs of the speaker you were planning to corral.

There will also be an evaluation form of one kind or another; don't lose it.

Check the program, see what panel is when, and figure out your schedule. At larger conferences, there may be as many as eight panels going on at once; others will have as few as one or two. You already know the speakers you want to hear, the sessions that promise to offer you what you need. As you're deciding, keep your ears open: some of the people at the conference may have heard one or another of the speakers over the years and will be commenting on them; you may discover that something you thought would be boring or beside the point is considered a highlight of the conference. It doesn't mean that it will be for you, but if everyone around you is saying that something is very good or very bad, it probably doesn't hurt to pay attention.

As conferences have gotten bigger and started offering more multiple tracking (simultaneous) events, organizers have begun arranging for professional audio people to record sessions and then offer the tapes for sale. That's why you don't have to worry about missing a session if you have an appointment or if you can't choose between two panels. Many participants buy tapes of the sessions they've attended, because they found the information particularly valuable.

So why did you bring your cassette recorder? Because some conferences don't supply tapes and because many of them, whether they're offering the tapes or not, will allow you to make your own recording. You can check with the sponsors when you register, just to be on the safe side, but I've never seen anyone denied permission to record. I do think that you should check with the speaker or moderator before a session begins, though, because some of the speakers may be reluctant to have you tape them. Lots of speakers earn a substantial part of their living through lecturing, and having an unauthorized tape of a speech making the rounds can affect their income. (Speakers have to sign releases for the organizers before the professional tapings are done.) And since we don't know to what use you're going to put the tape (you might even be selling it to friends back home), this little courtesy would be appreciated.

The speakers will make it clear whether they want to be interrupted with questions during the course of a talk or if they'd prefer to have them held for the end; whichever way it goes, don't be afraid to ask a question if something isn't clear. The people addressing you know that the reason you are there is to get information, to learn, to better equip yourself for a writing career. And we've heard everything. The only dumb question is the one you don't ask.

The only *stupid* question is the one that was answered thirty seconds ago. Pay attention to what's going on. There isn't enough time during the course of an hour's talk to repeat something. If something remains unclear, if something seems confusing, then by all means ask. But if you missed a point, wait until the session is over and try to get the speaker's attention. Most stay in the room for a few minutes after the thank-you's are said just so people can do that.

There's a question—or more accurately, a statement—that crops up at every conference: What chance does a first novelist have? No one's interested in us. Editor Peter Rubie has the perfect answer to that, and I'll share it with you now so that when you get to the conference you don't have to ask the question. "When," Peter asks, "did you last buy a hard-cover first novel that you hadn't heard of until you saw it on the shelf?" As the silence deafens us, we'll go on to the next point, remembering always that first novels are published every day.

One thing that is definitely frowned upon is getting into an argument with a speaker. A discussion makes every bit of sense, that's what you're there for. But there are people who come looking for a fight, who want to argue some fine point about a contractual term that they've heard of, and expect the speaker to defend the other side. Good speakers will answer once, politely change the subject the second time, and cut you off rudely the third. There may be time for that kind of thing at the end of a session or later, in the bar, but a little respect for the person behind the lectern and the other people in the room goes a long way toward making the experience more pleasant for everyone.

As the day wears on, you may find yourself taking a break or just wandering from one room to another, and you'll see one of the speakers sitting in the lobby, staring idly. My rule of thumb as a speaker is this: If I want privacy, I go to my room or someplace else where no one can find me. If I'm sitting around, you should feel free to approach me, sit down, and start talking. That's why the speakers are there—to be of use to you. Obviously, if we're talking to someone else, you don't want to interrupt, but if we see you looking over toward us, we'll give you an indication of whether or not it's a good time to join us. Before you know it, an unscheduled panel is taking place, and it's on a topic that is of particular concern, a specific area of what we're there to discuss, because the people who've created the group have also created the questions to be discussed. It's a lot like the scene I described in the bar.

When your opportunity arises to discuss your work with one of the professionals—particularly the editors and agents—listen to what they have to say, answer their questions, and if they tell you that your work doesn't seem right for them (with or without further explication), accept it. Don't try to convince them that they're wrong. They know what they need, what they can do, and whether you want to accept it or not, they also know more about their jobs than you do.

They'll ask about the project you want to discuss, and at that time you can put your proposal or outline on the table; but don't give it to the person. Be prepared to talk about your novel: what it's about generally, the genre, where you think it might fit in the scheme of things ("I'd like it to appeal to Tom Clancy's audience"), and the approximate length, whether it's completed or not . . . and then be ready to answer questions.

The person you're meeting with may ask to see the proposal then or tell you to send it on to her. She may tell you that the book isn't right for her, but will recommend someone else. Or she may just shake her head in dismay and tell you that she wishes she could help, but good luck. No matter what the outcome, say thank you and move on. The appointments are stacked like planes coming into Kennedy Airport at rush hour during a snowstorm, and once things start running late, the whole day gets thrown into disarray.

If you are asked to forward your material, mention the meeting in your covering letter, thank her again for the opportunity, and wait as patiently as you can for a response. There seems to be a definite correlation between attending a conference and the sudden rise in submissions; even people who weren't asked, as well as those who didn't have appointments but liked what the speaker said, will send manuscripts.

There's a story that may or may not be true but that has become part of the lore of the speaker. An editor had given a good talk, really inspiring the listeners. Afterward, one of the writers approached her, carrying a box that could contain nothing but a manuscript. The editor had made it clear that she didn't want to take anything home with her; the writer just wanted a quick glance. The editor excused herself and went to the ladies' room. And the manuscript was shoved under the cubicle door. I'd suggest that this isn't a route for you to follow.

Most conferences—and certainly those that are sponsoring contests—hold a banquet or special luncheon at which awards are given and a keynote speaker addresses the group. The keynoter is a highlight (or should be); it might be a top-name writer like Mary Higgins Clark or a celebrity like Barbara Walters; sometimes it is a member of the sponsoring organization who's made it through the non-sense and onto the lists. I've only regretted attending one banquet: it took three and a half hours, there was a prize awarded for everything from best novel to neatest typing, and I had to sit at the head table smiling encouragingly through the whole thing.

The informal atmosphere of the meal also allows you to meet and talk to lots of other people, all of whom have something to share. They may be a step or two ahead of you and can give advice, or they're a step or two behind and are looking to you for answers. The speakers are usually seated randomly around the room, so you could very well wind up having dinner with someone you wanted to meet but couldn't get to see during the day. The network continues.

But the conference is coming to a close. Fill out the evaluation form, letting the sponsors know exactly what you thought about the experience. Very serious attention is paid to your comments because they want you back next year and they want to know what worked and didn't work. If a speaker was particularly helpful, enlightening, or enjoyable, let that be known. If a speaker was rude and aloof, and those are the nice things you can say, let the organizers know that, too. Conferences work best when everyone involved is there for the same reason. A speaker who throws all the manuscripts in the trash before checking out (it happened, but I won't tell you when or where, or who), makes it bad for everyone.

You should also consider dropping a note to anyone you found helpful. Believe it or not, editors and agents like to be appreciated and they like to know that their time wasn't wasted. And, hey, look at it this way: you invest twenty-nine cents on a letter to an editor and two years later, when you have something that's right for that person, you mention in your covering letter that you met her and really appreciated the time, and the editor may very well remember you because you took the time for a bread-and-butter note.

And to tell the truth, I've developed a number of pen

pals over the years as a result of my conference touring, some of whom have begun as authors on my list, some of whom are at other houses, and some of whom have stopped writing but haven't stopped corresponding. That's pretty nice.

One last thought: I've never bought a manuscript *at* a conference, but I have bought them within weeks afterward. First novels, as a matter of fact.

If you do decide to attend a conference, and I happen to be there, be sure to stop by and say hello. And if I'm not there, say hello to someone else. You'll be a happier writer for it.

Chapter 21

....

THE ROAD TO CREATIVITY

I don't really get my ideas from a pretzel vendor near Central Park. But because of some questions I was asked recently, I've had to give some thought as to where they really do come from. The answer is as simple and as complex as: from within. (Uh-oh, he's getting metaphysical.)

Some sort of proof of that is in the exercises we did when we were dealing with writer's block. Relaxing, knocking off the little editor, and going with the flow seems to release whatever it is that we have hiding within.

The problem for a lot of people is that this entails a certain amount of risk; when we engage in what may be called "automatic writing," we reveal things about ourselves that we may not want to confront. Judging what you're willing to risk for the sake of creativity is your decision.

And what is creativity?

According to the dictionary, to create is to bring into being, to cause to exist, to produce where nothing was before, to form out of nothing. It's what we do, or try to do, every day. For some of us it's frighteningly easy; for others it's depressingly difficult. For the people who don't have problems coming up with ideas, who are not only not afraid of asking "what if?" but then go on to an answer, the question of creativity is rarely considered. Why think about it when it isn't a problem?

For the people who struggle to find the "what if?" they want to answer, the question takes on serious weight. Sometimes the solution can be as easy as those writer's block exercises. At other times the answer is in quitting.

Giving up isn't a very good answer; priming the creative pump is better. And it works. It may make the difference in your writing, raising you above the crowd, it may even make you a better storyteller. Nothing will guarantee your success; if you don't have the ability to be a storyteller in a competitive marketplace, you probably won't make it at that level. It doesn't mean that you can't derive pleasure from the act of writing; it doesn't mean that you should give up altogether. At worst, it means that you can't go head-to-head with someone on the bestseller list. Most runners can't compete in the Olympics, most basketball players will never get out of the playground. It's no different. But there are lots of other kinds of writing you can do, using the talents you have with the written word, using the techniques you've learned in these pages, most of which are applicable to any kind of writing, and those you've developed on your own.

A lack of patience, a lack of effort—quitting—will assure your failure. If you don't explore the other areas, if you think that if you fail as a novelist or short story writer you have no where else to go—if you're not willing to take a couple of risks, don't even start.

And taking risks sometimes means ignoring all the advice you receive. Most editors will tell you not to try crossover stories (works of fiction that attempt to combine genres), and they're absolutely correct. But writers try it every day, and some succeed. Some succeed so well that the end result is not only a great piece of fiction, but an entirely new subcategory. Something where nothing was. Something brought into existence. Creativity.

So how does one prime the pump?

There are a number of schools of thought on the subject of imagination and creativity. For me, based on what has worked (the proof of the pudding being in the tasting), creativity stems from an openness to both receive stimuli and then store them, allowing them to surface when they're ready.

When I'm making notes about a place or a person, I'm not committed to using those notes immediately. When I stand on the fire escape at my office, smoking my pipe (I work in a nonsmoking office, though it has burst into flame on occasion), I watch the rooftop pigeons doing their courtship dance. I watch them walk, heads bobbing like Jews at prayer. I watch them bill and coo and mate and roost. There's something in what I've observed; something that may be a story or a part of a story or a metaphor in a story. Having seen it, I'm consciously filing material away for a rainy day.

The same thing is happening with the lines I've recorded, the bits of overheard conversation, the images that have come to mind: my crossover story, "The Dream That Follows Darkness," developed from two sources. One was the story of David and Bathsheba, reread during a moment of boredom in a synagogue. The other was a line that popped into my head one afternoon: "Then, when the rain stopped, the wind began."

The line stuck with me; every time I sat down to write it started tickling my fingertips, aching to be typed out. Sometimes I'd give in, putting the words on paper, editing them out later. One day, though, after having been scoured by an Oklahoma wind, I put the words down and just kept going.

I didn't worry about the line, or any of the others. They're there, waiting. Like the sentences we've created to defeat block, I'll sometimes pull my lines up and look them over. Something may be there. If it is, great. If it isn't, great.

You can't struggle for ideas—

Well, yes you can, you can struggle all you want. The results aren't always happy, though. I remember something we used to say out on the street corner that was our hangout back during my teenage years: if you went out looking to pick up girls, you'd always wind up sitting by yourself. If you went out to have a good time, the good times would take care of themselves.

We don't pick up girls anymore; we interface with women (or whatever the acceptable phrase is by the time you read this), but the basics are the same: If you go out looking to make contact, you'll usually miss whatever it is you're looking for. If you relax, you've got a better chance of accomplishing your task.

And to keep the metaphor going for just a moment longer, if you are hunting and you do meet someone, the odds are that the relationship is not going to be much more than something to fill in the moment. And if you force the ideas for your fiction, the result is going to be something that you've seen before, a variation on a theme with nothing to make it noteworthy.

If there is any valid complaint about category fiction it is in the fact that far too many writers don't bring anything more to their work than new names for old characters. Too many writers don't take risks, because too few of the risks pay off with contracts. As a professional, you have to make a living, you make a living by providing what is wanted. As a writer, though, don't you want to at least *try* something else?

Enough editorializing: you've registered a stimulus and left it to sit and stay warm, to incubate. Finally, whatever has been cooking is ready to hatch. Bam, and it's there. Another example from my experience.

"What Chelsea Said," a story published in *Stalkers,* an anthology edited by Ed Gorman and Martin Greenburg, was the result of saying "feed the homeless to the hungry" to Charles Grant, a horror writer and anthologist. It was a throwaway line, but a half hour later, Charlie said, "You know, there's a story there." After I figured out what he was talking about, and shrugging the idea off (who wanted a story about cannibalism? Too risky), I walked home and noticed that a couple of the homeless people who were usually in the park on Broadway weren't there. I realized that I hadn't seen them for a while.

A month later the story was done. It was "written" in one long night's work, but the creating of it began at that moment. For a few days I didn't think about it very much; after that, each day brought another scene, something I'd rework and rehash in my mind while walking, still not putting anything down on paper.

Within a week, the key scenes, the beginning and the ending, and all the characters existed almost tangibly. All the things I thought I hadn't thought about were also in place, as I discovered when I sat down to finally commit the story to paper.

I'd say that 90 percent of what I've written, both fiction and nonfiction, has been a result of that process. The rest has come because of a particular stimulus: my boss saying that catalogue copy had to be done, or an editor asking for an article or a story. Most of those were simply a matter of putting the facts down one after another. Sometimes something more was required, something that's part of my regular writing process.

Creative or guided visualization is a technique that has received a lot of attention as part of a number of so-called New Age philosophies. In one form or another, however, it's been around for years; it just wasn't a buzz word. It's probably falling out of favor again these days. When an agent friend asked what I'd be speaking on at an upcoming conference, I told him I was doing my visualization exercises and he shook his head in dismay, refusing to believe that I was "still doing that imagery stuff." Whatever works, works.

Bertrand Russell, Albert Einstein, Mozart, Stephen Spender, Vincent Van Gogh, and dozens of others have described the process: Einstein claims that he discovered the theory of relativity while visualizing himself astride a ray of light, and that images alone—images which can be voluntarily reproduced and combined—were in his thoughts. Words did not play a role in the process of *creating* the theory.

We can do the same thing.

Visualization, at its simplest, is the calling up of images in the mind; writing is translating those images into words so that audiences can share them.

One of the things I do with my darkened computer screen is to play out the scene I'm writing against it; it becomes a television on which I control the programming. It beats looking at the letters form.

There are a number of books available that can teach the process, as well as audio cassettes designed to help get you into the relaxed state that serves as the beginning of the visualization process. We'll discuss some of that here; if you're interested in pursuing the techniques further, check the bookstore or library for a book you're comfortable with; some of them take things further than you need, discussing the processes in terms of spirituality and healing. Many of the techniques are used in hospitals, especially as cancer therapy; I know people who swear by it. And others who swear at it.

We begin by relaxing. There are lots of ways of going about that: having learned Lamaze procedures, I've found it easiest to adapt them. What you're looking to achieve is a relief of muscular tension. Take a couple of deep cleansing breaths, and then begin tensing your muscles for a count of ten, and then slowly relaxing them. I usually start at the feet and work my way up—calfs, thighs, buttocks, back, stomach, arms, shoulders and neck, even my face and head. The whole thing takes about five minutes and I do that every time I sit down to write; it's just more comfortable.

Once you're as relaxed as you're going to be (it gets easier with practice), begin small. Look at some simple object for a couple of minutes: it can be a drawing of a geometric figure or a pencil or a piece of fruit. After studying it, close your eyes and try to see it. This isn't a test, and 100 percent accuracy isn't your goal. What you want to be able to do is call that image up whenever you're of a mind to do so.

Having gotten the image, open your eyes and look at the object again. Was there a bite taken out of the fruit that you didn't see? Was the eraser on the pencil worn down? If the real thing differed from your visualized image, close your eyes again and add the "missing piece"; file it away with the rest of what you've been looking at.

Do this for a couple of days; as you become more secure in your ability to see and remember, start using more complex objects. There's a game in "increase your brainpower" types of books in which you study a picture of a room filled with stuff, then turn the page and write down what you remember seeing. There's also a game called Concentration which calls for you to remember where particular items are hidden on a grid. So far, we're talking about the same thing.

Once you can call up objects you've seen, start experimenting by visualizing something and altering it in your imagination. If the pencil was fresh out of the box, let your imagination sharpen it, put some tooth marks on it. You know what it should look like . . . and what you want it to look like.

Having worked with "real" objects, close your eyes, relax, and start "seeing" things you've decided you want in your story. You've gotten, for instance, the basics of a character down. Now, visualize the person; don't stop with seeing the physical characteristics, let the person move through your imagination, let him or her speak to you. Put one character together with another and let them speak to each other. Give them a scene to play out for you:

their first meeting might be a good one, or the scene in which their conflict is going to be made apparent to the reader.

Imagine the room they're in. You've already got a picture of it, or the notes you've made, based on looking around you and the places you've been. Now, by putting them into the room, the extra chair will either appear or be gotten rid of, depending on the needs you've created. Even as you look at the image, do what you did earlier: frame parts of the scene and see what's in the way of getting your story told right.

You can do that with every aspect of your tale: characters, places, objects: would that red vase have more impact if you took a chip out of the lip? Should Joe have a cowlick that he keeps trying to hold down when he gets nervous? Can the murder weapon be left on the table, à la Poe's "The Purloined Letter"? Don't force the issue, don't ask the questions. Let your subconscious guide you. Trust yourself.

If I have a scene that's giving me trouble because, as I write it, even I can't see clearly enough what's going on, I put it up on an imaginary screen and let it play out by itself. Usually, I do that as I prepare to go to sleep. I also use an autohypnotic technique; there are books, tapes, and teachers around to help you learn those if you want to go in that direction. I know lots of people who like it; I also know thousands who find the whole concept abhorrent. I also do it while I'm walking: but once I've planted the seed, whether I'm awake or drifting off, I don't keep nagging at it like a parent with a recalcitrant child.

One of the points all the people who've come to the answers they're seeking through visualization methods have agreed on is that the imagination works best when left to its own devices. After the solution has presented itself, it can be revised to suit your needs, just as you revise a manuscript after completion.

As I mentioned earlier, I keep a record of lines, ideas, characteristics, whatever elements strike my fancy, that I think I'll use someday. Everything is grist for the mill. (By writing them down, incidentally, I'm also fixing them in memory where my subconscious can work on them at its own pace.) The line I quoted, about the rain stopping and the wind beginning, was one that I'd played with a couple of times, trying to see where it would go.

One evening, I visualized the scene: I had the rain, I had the wind. It began in New York, but the next part of the line—scouring the sky of clouds—called for someplace else; you don't see enough sky in New York City for that to have any impact. But the sky is big on the northern Plains, and the background around the storm changed to the Big Horns. People were camping, protecting themselves from the weather, reacting to it. Why was my character, who didn't really exist yet, up there? Maybe to take some photographs. Slowly, over a period of a few days, the elements fell into place. In the meantime, other parts of the story, the conflicts and themes I wanted to work with, based on a number of free-floating ideas, integrated themselves. The important part of the story of King David, for me, was what was done to Uriah. What did I want to do with that? The country I was in, now, was part of the range of several Indian tribes, their religious beliefs began to fit in.

I don't want to leave you with the impression that "I" had nothing to do with the writing of the story; by letting myself go, by letting impressions tell me something, I was able to bring disparate elements together and bring something into being. If I had just sat down in front of the keyboard and said that I want to write a love story with reincarnation elements, I might still be sitting there doodling. I wrote whatever was written, based on ideas that I had filed away and then called up as I needed them.

It's just another form of research.

Sometimes the things we see when we let control of the story be taken over by our imaginations are not things we want to see; there are lots of parts of ourselves in our imaginations that are there because they've been hidden, not stored. Sometimes the things we see aren't understood or useful. But they may be fascinating, and if you want to write about them, go ahead. Take the chance. Perhaps it will turn out that what you've created is nothing more than a writing exercise, stories that you don't think you can market, though I think that there are markets for anything of value; finding them and deciding whether or not we can afford them is another question. Having written them, though, just like my friend Kara and her colored contact lenses and dyed hair and secret scar, once created, they're always there and you can call on them when the right elements come together.

Nothing you create is wasted. They may not be profitable at a given moment, but just the experience of having done the work has value.

At some point in your life as a writer, you'll have to decide whether you are, in the words of Robert Randisi, who offers a moving and frightening speech at conferences on the subject, writing to eat. If you are, you will follow the path of least resistance; every word you put down on paper will be written because it is the word the easily defined market wants. You will hold your imagination on a tight rein and do what is expected.

Or you will choose to take a chance on something because it says what you want to say; you will have the time and energy to stretch your imagination, to allow your creativity to carry you somewhere else.

There's no right or wrong; there's just the path you have to follow and you're the only one who can choose it. You're the only one who knows if you're right or wrong.

Never let anyone else make that decision for you.

Chapter 22

WHERE DO YOU GO FROM HERE?

Your manuscript is ready, your submission made. While you're waiting for a reaction from the editor(s) to whom it was sent, what do you do? Well, take a break for a week or two, get the finished book out of your mind, and begin the next. Generally, my advice is to keep working in the same genre: if the book you sent out is accepted, the editor is going to want another one like that from you.

One young writer, in rejecting the suggestion, said that she'd work on another fantasy when the first one was accepted; in the meantime, she was going to try a mystery, another category she enjoyed. After all, if the fantasy didn't sell, maybe the mystery would. She's right, maybe it will. And maybe it won't. She wrote the fantasy first because that was the category that meant the most to her, the genre for which she had the greatest feel, the one she thought she could do best. My alternative was to submit the mystery under a pen name, or, if it came to it, choose a name for the first book sold, then a pseudonym for whatever then became out-of-category for her. There aren't enough fans crossing over in category to give any particular value to a name, unless the name itself begins to transcend genre. It would be interesting to see what might happen if Mary Higgins Clark wrote an sf novel under her own name, but I doubt that we'll ever get to experience it. I know, I know, there are writers who use just the one name—Loren Estleman comes immediately to mind, but the sales of his westerns don't begin to compare to the sales of his mysteries; and the sales of some of his suspense novels don't compare to those of his private eye fiction.

At some point, though, whether it is with your first submission or your fifth, with or without an agent, the day will come when an offer arrives and all the effort begins to pay off (though probably not in the amounts you would have hoped for). What happens now?

In the introduction to my previous book, *From Printout to Published: A Guide to the Publishing Process,* I tell the story of its genesis: I was at a party during the course of a writers conference and I became frighteningly aware of something: not even the published writers in the crowd knew what was going on once their manuscripts arrived on an editor's desk. There's no room in this volume to go into all of that in detail—and *From Printout . . .* is available wherever books are sold. (At least I hope it is.) What we'll do, then, is give you a brief survey of what's going on on the other side of the desk, just so that nothing comes as a complete surprise.

Offers are not made arbitrarily: the editor considers several factors after deciding that the writing is up to speed. Do we need the book is the first question that has to be answered. Do I have all the mysteries or romances or whatever that I need for the upcoming lists? If the answer is yes, the editor may have to pass on acquiring your book because the budget won't allow for a deep inventory. Another factor here: some contracts have publication "windows," defining the outside date by which the book has to be released or the rights revert to the author. Generally, this is between twelve and twenty-four months of acceptance of the final manuscript. Will I be able to publish the book within that time frame?

The editor has to decide how the book fits within a particular publishing program: if p.i. novels are weak, and I have two or three under contract, do I want to take on another one right now? Can my marketing department sell a time-travel romance? Do we want to challenge someone else's strength in the western field? Do we have credibility in the marketplace with this type of novel, will the booksellers trust our judgment or decide that only Publisher X knows a particular category?

The editor also has to think about packaging: having decided what the book is in marketing terms, can we package it successfully, can we come up with the kind of art and copy that will be both eye-catching and competitive?

And then there's the question of money. You may not be happy with the amount offered, but the editor hasn't picked the figure out of a hat. Projected sales figures are arrived at—either through an intimate knowledge of how the house sells a particular kind of book or through discussion with the marketing department. Based on that figure, the editor gets production costs (typesetting, cover art, manufacturing costs), factors in such esoterica as cost of sale, net cost per copy, royalties, subsidiary rights income, and in some cases, overhead, adds some, divides by something else, multiplies this, subtracts that, and comes up with an amount the publisher can live with. If things work out better than expected, you'll earn more in royalties; if they turn out worse, the publisher loses money.

When the offer is made, certain things will be discussed: the *advance*, which can range from as low as $500 to as much as, well, as much as you'd care to imagine, though between $2,500 and $7,500 seems to be as much as an "average" as anyone can come up with, the *royalties* (hardcover royalties are pretty much standard at 10 percent to 5,000 copies sold, 12½ percent for the next 5,000 copies and 15 percent thereafter; mass-market royalties are much more varied, ranging from a straight 4 percent to a straight 10 percent; splits are most usually made at 150,000 copies, with the offer being variously stated as "four and six" or "six and eight"), and what *rights* are being acquired (translation, world English language; reprint, book club, serial, motion picture). Most of the rest of the terms (and there can be a lot of them; publishing contracts can range between four and fourteen pages) are part of the "boilerplate," the form contract. Many of them can be negotiated; some, like the author's warranty and liability clauses are usually out of the editor's hands. There's a section on the contract in *From Printout*, and some of the organizations, including SFWA and the Author's Guild, have model contracts and information for you. Having an agent is usually the easiest way; they know the terms and what can be done. Sometimes, though, they make demands that result in the editor backing away from the deal.

The contract out of the way, the editor begins the process from which the job's title derives.

If you're selling your first, or quite often even a second or third novel, some of the editorial matters may have been discussed with you prior to the negotiation: the editor has to be certain that you understand what the house thinks is needed and that you not only agree, but that you can do it. Even after that work is done, though, the real editing is about to begin.

In most cases, the editor who acquired your book is going to be the editor who does the work on it. Sometimes, though, because of the structure of a particular house, or because of events within the house, you'll wind up in the hands of someone new. Don't panic.

There are hundreds of horror stories about writers suddenly being thrown to the wolves or, in this case, stepeditors. While it is true that a new editor might not have the same feelings for you, or for your book, as the person with whom you started working, one fact remains immutable: a publisher does not buy a book in order to lose money. Everyone is committed to exploiting your work for the most profit. The question of what represents "the most profit" is something best left for another time. Not every book is a "lead" title, not every book is going to get equal promotion. When you've reached the levels at which you should expect that kind of support—or if you've been blessed and produced a very special piece of writing—you'll get it.

Another question that gets asked frequently posits that a book acquired by the editor-in-chief, for instance, will receive better support than a book acquired by a senior editor, that by a senior editor more than an editorial assistant. Again, there's a certain amount of truth in that; by the same token, the manuscripts each of them is reading have arrived at the desks with a certain cachet. Still, when it comes time to present the books to the sales force, no matter who is presenting, the reps also know who has lied to them in the past and, frankly, they will often tell the editors which books they think they can do best with.

All of which is to say that there's enough to worry about (like your next book), so don't waste energy on things that you not only can't do anything useful about, but whose dangers are exaggerated.

So, editing. At its simplest, editing is intensive revision. The editor reads the manuscript looking for plot holes, major missing links, and virtually anything else that causes a pencil to start quivering. Some editors concentrate on concept: they're dealing with the story as a whole. The question they're answering is: Does this story work, and if not, what can I do to bring the elements together.

Other editors are more line-oriented. They look at every word, phrasing, the structure of the story and of each sentence, for characters that need more (or less) development. They will change language with abandon, often rewriting things you thought were pretty good. And that requires a judgment call on your part.

You will have an opportunity to see the edited, and copyedited, manuscript (if that isn't in your contract, insist on it). Look carefully at what was done. Are the changes seemingly arbitrary? Has the novel been improved by the work that was done? Has the book been changed in some intrinsic way that destroys what you were doing? Is it now the editor's book? Just as your original writing was not carved in stone, the editor's changes are not, either. Ask for an explanation. If you are not satisfied, you might be able get the rights to the book back (that is in some contracts); usually, the contract calls for the book to be published in form, content, and manner satisfactory to the publisher.

That's an interesting call. The publisher, of course, is risking money on the publication and trusts the editor to put the book into that form. And while your name is on the book, so is the publisher's. (Have you noticed that in virtually every other art, the various craftsmen who work on the production receive credits: from the costume designer to the gaffer—whoever that is; from the choreographer to the lighting director, from the camera person to the assistant to the director, everyone gets a credit line. Except editorial people in book publishing. Think about that the next time an editor seems to be in a foul mood.)

It is conceivable that publication of a book could be canceled because of a disagreement over editing. But if you go ahead with changes that don't satisfy you, keep the experience in mind when the next book is delivered. You might want to try to negotiate another editor; you might want to break the option, just submit some awful piece of drivel you wrote back in the third grade; that'll work. Of course, if the reviews of the first book were good, maybe the editor knew what had to be done.

Once the editor is finished with the manuscript, you may get a call with questions or requests: add a scene here, get rid of something here, are you sure you want to do this there, do you have the permission to sing that song in this place . . . a final series of adjustments. After that's been discussed, and whatever changes you both decide are necessary have been made, the manuscript continues on its journey toward publication.

The next stop is the managing editor's office; a place difficult to define because the job seems to differ from house to house. Generally, though, this is where a copyeditor will be assigned and where the design process of the interior of the book begins.

The copyeditor further refines the revisions that have been done, looking for continuity problems (changing descriptions, people being in rooms in which they cannot be at the time), spelling and grammatical errors, and maintaining house style insofar as it doesn't interfere with your style, errors of fact (can you drive from here to there that quickly?), and anything else that might possibly cause embarrassment for the author or editor. Good authors, when they receive the copyedited manuscript and come across things like that, usually add a little note to the Post-It flag that's been placed on the spot, saying something like "thanks," or "good catch."

Good copyeditors don't make changes, except for spelling or grammar, unless they've been given a go-ahead beforehand by the editor. They do flag things they perceive as problems, suggesting alternatives or requesting the author consider a change. With the manuscript in your hands, if there's anything you don't agree with, anything that seems to be a problem to you, call your editor and discuss it. You'll be receiving a letter with the manuscript explaining what you are expected to do; again, this may change from house to house. As always, when in doubt, shout. Your editor will hear you.

The designer is choosing typefaces and sizes. Sometimes you want to make a book longer, so you use a larger typeface, add extra leading between lines, and decide to start every chapter on a "new right": i.e., a right-hand page. (You can also use thicker paper to give the book bulk.)

The use of running heads (book title, chapter title, author's name) is decided upon, whether page numbers will appear on the top or bottom of the page, centered or at the edges; everything that affects the look of the text pages.

While all of that is going on, your editor is both looking at new manuscripts for acquisition and priming the pump for you. Presentations for sales conferences have to be prepared, cover art designed and commissioned, cover copy written, and the publicity and promotion people given whatever information they may need to do whatever will be done.

Publicity and promotion—and advertising—seem to be the areas most writers grumble about and, I suppose, a case can be made for most of the complaints in that enough is never done. However, how much can be done?

There are several factors to consider: your book is not the only one on the list, and, if it is a first novel with nothing special to hook it to, it is going to get less attention than the new release from Big Name Author that's scheduled for the same month. The talk shows that every writer dreams of being on aren't particularly interested in you. While advertising will be discussed, that can't be sensibly set until we know the print order, and the print order usually isn't set these days until after the initial sales calls are made. (When you see the announced first printing figures in *Publishers Weekly* for a book that isn't being released for seven or eight months, you can safely assume that the figure is a target, not a reality.)

If you're being published in hardcover, there's a better than equal chance that galleys will be prepared of the book. The cost of the galleys, used for reviewers and in the attempt to get early quotes from other authors, is part of the promotion effort. So is your page in the catalogue, any poster or flyer or other sell piece used to get your book into the store, and any other piece of paper on which the title of your book appears.

The harsh reality is that there are too many books vying for attention, both in-house and in the nation, and unless there's something particularly noteworthy about the book —especially fiction—promotion (for which, like advertising, the publisher has to pay) and publicity (which is, blessedly, free) are hard to get. Because of that, there's a booming market for personal publicists, who can work a local area. Sisters in Crime, the powerhouse organization begun by some women who felt they could do more for themselves than was being done for them, have even prepared a booklet loaded with tips on self-promotion and obtaining publicity.

If your publisher has obtained any of the subsidiary rights from you, the people in that department are beginning their efforts: getting ready to sell your book to a paperback reprint house if that's applicable, letting the international reps know about the availability of the book, getting in touch with book clubs, movie studios (an increasingly rare situation), magazine (if a first serial—before publication—sale seems like a possibility for some portion of the book), and looking for any way in which they can make money with your book. You'll be receiving a share of that income (generally at least 50 percent), and additional royalties.

As everything comes together, and publication day (rarely a particular day these days, except for special items) approaches, your editor will probably send you copies of the cover art, may call with questions that have come down the pipeline from the marketing or promotion people, and will be available to keep you reasonably calm.

And then, one day, the book arrives in your home, the copies you're entitled to by contract. Don't, I repeat, *don't* run down to the bookstore looking for a stack on the shelves; it probably won't be there for at least another month. And it may not be there at all.

Publishers cannot force distribution, cannot make a retailer carry a title that they don't want to order. If you go into a store and they don't have copies, you can ask if they have it or expect it in. If they say "no," and offer some excuse ("We never heard of it" is popular; another one is, "We ordered it, but couldn't get it from your publisher"), get the name of the store and, if possible, even the name of the person you spoke to, and let your editor know. Just saying that you couldn't find the book at that store in Ft.

Lauderdale isn't sufficient. It's possible that there was a foul-up; it's also possible that the retailer was mistaken, or that the store is "on hold"; in other words, has a poor record of payment and is no longer considered a viable customer.

The store might not buy directly from the publisher, choosing to get titles from a jobber or wholesaler who offers a better discount or pays freight costs.

Or the publisher may have blown it. Whatever the case, if you call your editor and offer enough information, you'll get an answer and, if the bookstore really wants copies, they'll get there.

In the meantime, you've gotten your next book ready, at least to the point where you have a decent outline/synopsis and three chapters completed, and sent them in to your editor or to the agent you've acquired, and you're ready to begin the process again.

Simple, isn't it?

It would be nice if it always worked this well, but it doesn't. Your publisher may only get a couple of thousand copies of your novel into the marketplace (or fifteen thousand of a paperback), reviews may have been devastating, your editor left for a higher paying position at another house that "just isn't doing that kind of book right now": you're a writer, use your imagination. You can give up. Or you can keep going, looking for another editor at another house, giving your first publisher a chance to try and build you, rather than looking for someone else to start you again. You might consider switching categories using a pseudonym, especially if your reviews were bad.

Or it could be better: another house could start romancing you, one of the editors tracking you down and making all kinds of promises, promises that are well-meant and that might even be kept. Your own editor might call early on and offer you a two- or three-book contract *right now*, because the house doesn't want to take a chance on losing you. Especially if the reviews were great and advance orders and support from booksellers indicative of the fact that you just might have a career at this, and won't have to work anymore because you can just sit home and . . . write.

Right? Right!

Chapter 23

AVOIDING THE
POTHOLES

The farther you go down the road toward a career in fiction, the more things there are that can trip you up. Some of them are avoidable; all of them can be dealt with. All you have to do is be prepared.

Be prepared to be upset by the reviews . . . or the lack of them. Most of the books released each month don't get reviewed at all. For the major review media, the guiding philosophy in choosing the books to be reviewed is, "What will our advertisers think?" The companies advertising in *The New York Times,* for example, like to think of their customers as upscale, both financially and intellectually; that impacts on the choice of books to be reviewed. There may very well be other factors, but I think we're better off keeping it basic and simple.

Because category fiction—except the western—is blessed with so many "fanzines," however, your genre novel stands a very good chance of being reviewed, or at least noticed, in one or another of them.

The local press is pretty good about reviewing hometown authors, and the publishers do try to get word to your newspaper about your book. Whether the review will appear in time to do any good is in the hands of the gods.

Publishers Weekly, The Kirkus Reviews, Booklist, and other review media try to review as much as they can for the benefit of their various readerships—booksellers, librarians, and other book people—but the number of titles is overwhelming.

And when the reviews do appear, they can go either way. Raves are very nice (a good *Kirkus* or *PW* can bring dozens of calls from reprinters and movie people; every once in a blue moon, those calls amount to something), and they may help sales—sometimes substantially. You're rarely going to learn anything from a good review, unless it is written by someone with an expertise in the area you've written about, who goes beyond saying, "This is wonderful," and explains what you've done that's so good. Don't be surprised if you weren't aware of it; the things critics find to praise often have little to do with what you thought you did. Accept the ego stroke and hope that the readers of the review will flock to the bookstores, and that the bookstore owners have read the review and have the book in stock.

Bad reviews can have a negative effect on sales, and a weak prepublication review may result in slightly lowered sales into the bookstores. As often as not, the bookstores have ordered the book well before the *PW* review appears, so there's still hope, even if they pan you. The worst thing about bad reviews is what they can do to *you*. And that's something you have to fight.

There are writers who claim not to read their negative notices. I think you should read them, then consider how seriously you want to take what you've read. There may be information of value, suggestions that will help you. Reviews may be inchoate attacks, reflections of animosity, jealousy, or some other bitterness. You can talk about them with your editor (editors read the reviews, too, both good and bad, looking for information that may guide them in their work), discuss them with friends, who'll probably tell you to ignore them; the best advice is take what seems to be of value in the reviews and ignore the rest. It is not *you* who is being reviewed; it is one book, and that is all.

You will be receiving mail and comments from readers and fans. Some will simply and most eloquently say, "Thank you for the good read"; some will offer the opportunity for discussion with the correspondent about some aspect of your work. Some will be gushing approval of what you've done, and some will drip acid, complaining about everything you've done, from your use of language to your portrayal of a particular character.

As with reviews, be aware of what people are saying (if they take the trouble to say it), and then impose your values on the comments. If your editor didn't have a problem with your language, and if your editor is requesting a new manuscript, take that as the approval you need to continue.

Whether you want to respond to any of these letters is up to you. Some writers do, entering into an exchange that can go on for years. Some answer, but don't put their return address on the letter, requesting that all correspondence come through the publisher. A few ignore it; that's the worst choice. If a reader—and thus a once and future book buyer—is taking the time to tell you something, a reply is deserved.

If the letter is negative, you may want to take a moment to explain why you made a particular literary decision, especially if the person who wrote to you has a good or interesting point. Negativity has a way of being nasty; some readers think they have the right to say anything. As great as the temptation may be, don't respond to that; it's best just to ignore it.

You are the first one who has to be satisfied with your work; your editor is second. Don't let anything interfere with that order.

Be prepared to get more advice than you can possibly use. Everyone is going to tell you what you should do now. Someone will tell you to change categories, that you'll have more success writing romantic suspense than you can possibly have writing hard-boiled p.i. fiction. Someone else will tell you to shift from first-person to third-person narrative. One person will say write longer books, another will tell you to edit down to the bare bones.

Advice is only worth what you want it to be. As you start a career in fiction, you'll discover that things change almost overnight. Tastes and styles and interests that were popular when you sat down to begin writing may have disappeared by the time you're in the middle of your second book. If something works for you, if you're comfortable with something, stick with it, at least until the evidence makes it clear that principle is getting in the way of sales. Then you can start thinking about whether the changes in your philosophy that would be required are changes with which you can live.

As you begin submitting your work for consideration, and as you get to know more editors either through the network or through contact, you'll discover that every editor has a system of beliefs that affect decisions. There are those who don't worry about some aspects of storytelling, for instance, dialogue tags don't bother them at all, those who have a predisposition toward one or another of the subcategories (they may like gothics and hate Regencies), some who think that four-letter words have their place and others who stick a finger in every "damn." Guidelines help a little, but the best indicator is a previous book edited by that person.

Of course, when you contact an editor for the first time, you may not know anything about her biases or prejudices; if the response you receive is anything other than a form rejection, you will, again, have to make the decision as to whether to make requested changes. Is it more important to you to be published than to retain your own vision? No one can answer that question for you.

There is one thing I can say with great confidence after thirty years in this business: any well-written piece of fiction eventually finds a home. It may not always be the home we originally dreamed of, but it *is* a home, a publishing credit, a beginning. Remember, too, that even if every publisher in the country rejects your novel, it is the particular work that is being rejected at a particular time; send your next book out and let the first one wait. Tomorrow will bring a change in the tastes of readers and editors; tomorrow will bring you more knowledge and understanding and strength and you'll see the little changes that you can make that will make the difference, that will result in the book in the drawer making it to the shelves. And it's always possible that you can use it as an "option buster," a book to offer when you need to escape from a publisher's clutches. Nothing we write is ever wasted.

Whatever advice you receive is only someone's opinion; it is your opinion that carries the most weight; it is rarely offered with malice aforethought. When you get right down to it, even the suggestions and instructions offered in the preceding pages are only one person's interpretation of what makes good fiction. If it isn't right for you, don't do it.

You are the first one who has to be satisfied with your work; your editor is second. Don't let anything interfere with that order.

Be prepared for rejection. Even established writers come up with book ideas that just don't fly. The competition for space on a publisher's list and on the retailer's shelves is fierce, and you have to be able to stay in there in the face of adversity, in the face of overwhelming silence and reactions that seem to make no sense, that might even indicate that the editor who read your manuscript doesn't have the vaguest idea at all of what you tried to accomplish.

It's easy to give up, to convince yourself that you either don't have what it takes or that those commerce-driven idiots in New York just don't understand your brilliance. The truth is that there are writers who just don't have the ability to be professional novelists, whose fiction is flat, uninteresting, derivative, or otherwise not commercially viable from a publisher's point of view. The publisher may be wrong (we've all rejected books that have gone on to launch careers; far more of them—and their authors— have disappeared without a trace), but I think we err more often on the other side, accepting manuscripts because we sense a spark we think we can tend into a flame. And we're wrong about some of those, too.

There are no guarantees for any of us. The publication process doesn't always work the way we'd like it to; books don't receive the kind of acceptance and support everyone was counting on, while some other book rockets to the top of a bestseller list somewhere, and we shake our heads, wondering, "Why?" It is because sometimes God smiles.

Should you give up in the face of rejection after rejection? It depends on your strength, on how much writing means to you. You can write and share your stories with your friends even if you aren't published. It's said that only a fool writes for anything but money; I find a certain satisfaction in honing something to my desires, a sense of accomplishment that is fulfilling even if it isn't making me rich. And I don't expect to get rich from my writing. It would be nice, though. Very nice.

What's important—and impossible for lots of people—is to resist bitterness in a situation like that. A more useful reaction would be to find what it is that's working against you. You may be writing in a category simply because you think it is the most lucrative but don't have the feeling and sense of the genre to understand what's necessary. For all that formula may play a role in the creation of a mystery or a romance or a fantasy, it isn't enough—usually—to write it successfully. Just as good cooks adjust recipes to put their own stamp on a dish, good writers do the same thing to fiction.

If you can't write fiction successfully, it doesn't mean that you're a failure; if everyone could do it, if everyone could do anything, it wouldn't be as valuable. Try other forms of writing; articles, essays, how-to, book reviews. All writing requires creativity, all the forms allow you to express opinions about the world around you, all of them allow you to teach and make a difference in your readers' lives. It is the writing that's important, not the form.

You are the first one who has to be satisfied with your work; your editor is second. Don't let anything interfere with that order.

Be prepared for people to tell you that "you can't say that." Especially today, when young editors are driven by a sense of so-called political correctness, writers are being told that certain philosophies or feelings are not acceptable and, even worse, that they must say particular things in order to be accepted.

You have enough to worry about when you're writing; adding concerns about what a group of people might think of you because you don't adhere to a party line is not going to make your writing any easier, or any better, just more homogenized.

You do not have to present any group in any predetermined light. No group is all good or all bad; to depict them in an "acceptable" way may gain you some points with that group, but it won't make your writing any better. Your interpretation of what life is about should be more important to you than offering a picture that you don't believe in. The readers will know if you're paying lip service to a belief, and if they sense that you're lying, they're not going to come back for your second serving.

Back in the early eighties, the late Stanley Ellin wrote a novel titled *The Dark Fantastic*. It is a dark and brilliant novel about a man named Charles Witter Kirwan, now terminally ill and terminally embittered, who lives in a crumbling mansion in Brooklyn. In addition to his house, he owns an apartment building next door, a building whose tenants are black. Kirwan hates them, and expresses that hatred intelligently, rationally, and clearly. He has also decided to blow the building to hell and gone, taking his tenants and himself with the structure. (There's a parallel plot line about a white detective and a black woman who lives in the building; that's something to keep in mind.)

Ellin's publisher at the time refused to publish the book, because it was felt that readers would confuse the character and the author, thus having a negative effect on the rest of Ellin's novels. The biggest problem, I think, is in the fact that Kirwan was depicted with respect. The narrative did not go out of its way to paint an ugly picture of the man. He was obviously intelligent, his feelings and reactions well reasoned. He was not a caricature of a racist; he was a human being whose thoughts were not acceptable, but we were forced to understand those thoughts in a rational context.

Fortunately for Stanley Ellin, and for books and publishing and, I think, the country, Otto Penzler of Mysterious Press believes more in the First Amendment than in protecting readers from unpopular points of view, and he published the book to excellent reviews. There were no bombings, no threats, and the author continued to sell. Those of us who knew Stanley Ellin also knew that he was one of the kindest, most gentle, and accepting of people, a man who lived his life guided by principles with which no one could find fault. The story could not have been told in any other way and that was another principle Ellin didn't sacrifice for the sake of expediency. Or publication.

Every convention and conference these days seems to have a panel devoted to this subject. Invariably, the organizers are hoping that they can get something heated happening; usually, the writers on the panel discuss the subject dispassionately. There are those who do feel that one group or lifestyle is always being depicted negatively, and though they voice that opinion, they still recognize the rights of the storyteller to tell the story. Obviously, making a murderer (or the victim) gay, or black, or female is fine if there's a reason for it other than controversy or shock. Does that mean that you have to have a hero from the same group? I don't think so. I don't think a straight white male can necessarily create a believable black lesbian, and if the central character is going to be stage center for most of the book, that's an important consideration. By the same token, if you're using a character at all, you'd better know enough about the person to be able to make it more than a cartoon, a cardboard pawn being moved across the board of your story.

Intent is crucial. At one conference, during the open discussion after the panel addressed the issues of political correctness, one writer, a white woman, stood up and talked about her new book, in which her character, also a white woman, meets a man in a bar. The man "is black, because I just thought it was right." The audience applauded. No one asked why it was right; no one mentioned that there are both blacks and whites who don't think it's right (maybe their thoughts don't count). I'm certain that she made the decision because she's counting on getting a reaction. As an editor, unless the characters talk about their decision at some point, I don't think I'd have a positive reaction. That doesn't mean I'd reject it or even suggest changing it; I'd just wonder about the writer's agenda.

The temptation to write what you perceive as being of interest because you think it'll be easier to sell is a strong and easily understood one. Your own integrity as a writer should help defend against it. My feeling, oft expressed, is that if you want to send a message, use Western Union; polemic has its place, but it isn't in the fiction that I'm reading for entertainment or escape.

You are the first one who has to be satisfied with your work; your editor is second. Don't let anything interfere with that order.

Be prepared for disappointments with the process, with everything from the contract that's being offered to what happens from the moment the manuscript is delivered.

When the offer comes, whether it is from the first house to see the manuscript or after a year of rejections, don't just rush in and take it because someone is offering you money; don't simply turn up your nose because you think the amount isn't enough. A manuscript, in and of itself, doesn't have any value; it isn't even worth the cost of the paper it's printed on. The value is determined by the marketplace, by the needs of the publishers, by the figures on the P&L that are based on the publisher's insights into its business. Your novel may be every bit as good as the novel at the top of the bestseller list; that doesn't mean you're going to get the same advance as that received by an established, bestselling author.

Yes, you've done the work necessary to write a good, publishable, interesting novel. But no one is going to know if it will sell until it is released. If it does, you'll continue earning royalties. If it doesn't sell as well as our fantasies would have it, you're not in the position of having an editor who can't make a case for acquiring your next book, allowing for the all-important building process.

Your friends will fill your head with stories—not the kind you'll exploit in your fiction, but of horrible experiences someone else has had, or of how you're being cheated because someone else got this, that, and the other thing—but you have to make the decision, you're the one who is finally responsible for what you do. You can turn down an offer and suddenly discover that no one else is there to talk to you; you can accept, and receive another letter the next day, offering you five times as much. There are no guarantees, no certainties, nothing but your own faith in your ability to make decisions; that same faith that allowed you to devote the time to the writing of the book in the first place.

Publishers aren't in business to lose money; they may not do everything you want to see done, but they are going to do what has to be done in order to see the book earn out, in order to maintain their standing with the wholesalers, jobbers, chains, retailers, and readers. If your work has legs, they'll find a way to make it run. You must understand the needs of the publisher as well as your own. Just as there are other publishers available to you, there are other writers available to the publisher; entering the process with an adversarial relationship doesn't serve either you or the house well.

Don't be afraid to ask questions, don't be afraid to request help; your publisher may not be giving you everything you want, but your editor will do everything that can be done to keep things on an even keel. As long as the relationship remains satisfactory and fulfilling for all parties, it will continue; when it becomes clear that continuing the relationship is going to create only bitterness, it is time to discuss divorce. It's sad when it happens, but it does happen. Both parties in the effort have to be satisfied that the effort is worth it.

You are the first one who has to be satisfied with your work; your editor is second. Don't let anything interfere with that order.

Be prepared for the future. If you don't understand by now that writing is hard work, and only part of the process, even for the facile, you're going to be in trouble. As a writer, you're supplying raw goods to an industry; the quality of what you supply is important because it affects every aspect of the business: lousy steel will make bad cars, lousy books will kill publishing. (That's something publishers should be more aware of, too; too many have less respect for the readers than they should. I worked briefly at one house where the publisher told us regularly that "You don't work at Knopf, you don't have to spend so much time working on the books." She didn't understand why we weren't just buying books, instead of spending time on the phone, talking to writers, helping them shape their ideas so that they would fulfill whatever guideline we were being driven by at the time.)

There are thousands of people who dream of being writers, of living a life in fiction. For most, it never gets beyond being a dream.

But when you get the first book (or story or article) written and sold, the dream isn't fulfilled; it's only just begun.

You are the only one who can stop yourself, you are the major block on the road to your success. The editors to whom you are submitting your work—the first one and the second and on to the last—all want you to succeed. Every time we open an envelope, we hope the material will be good, will be publishable, will be something we can work with.

We hope that you've done everything you can to make the manuscript as good as it can be.

We hope that you aren't deceiving yourself.

We hope that you've paid attention to everything you've ever heard and been able to discern the difference between sage advice and unproven theory, between those who want to help you and those who are in love with the sound of their own voice.

We hope that you've written from your heart, with integrity and understanding of the needs of fiction and your readers.

We hope that you are the shaman we're seeking, explaining the world to us.

We hope that you remember:

You cannot please everybody; you are your first audience.

You cannot be afraid to be wrong.

You cannot be afraid to be right.

You are a writer, know thyself.

You are a writer, to thine own self be true.

If you do, if you are, the future is yours.

MICHAEL SEIDMAN, a thirty-year veteran of the publishing industry, is the Mystery Editor at Walker and Company. In 1987 he was the recipient of the first American Mystery Award as Best Book Editor, and was a nominee for the Award as Best Horror Editor in 1991. From 1980 to 1989, he was also the Editor of *The Armchair Detective*, the Edgar Award-winning journal of comment, review, and criticism of criminous fiction.

Mr. Seidman is a correspondent for *Writer's Digest* magazine and a columnist for *Mystery Scene*. His short story, "The Dream That Follows Darkness," was a nominee for the Spur Award, presented by the Western Writers of America, in 1988.

In addition to his editing and writing chores, Mr. Seidman is a popular guest speaker at conferences and workshops where he lectures on publishing and writing matters.